SCULPTURE, FORM, AND PHILOSOPHY

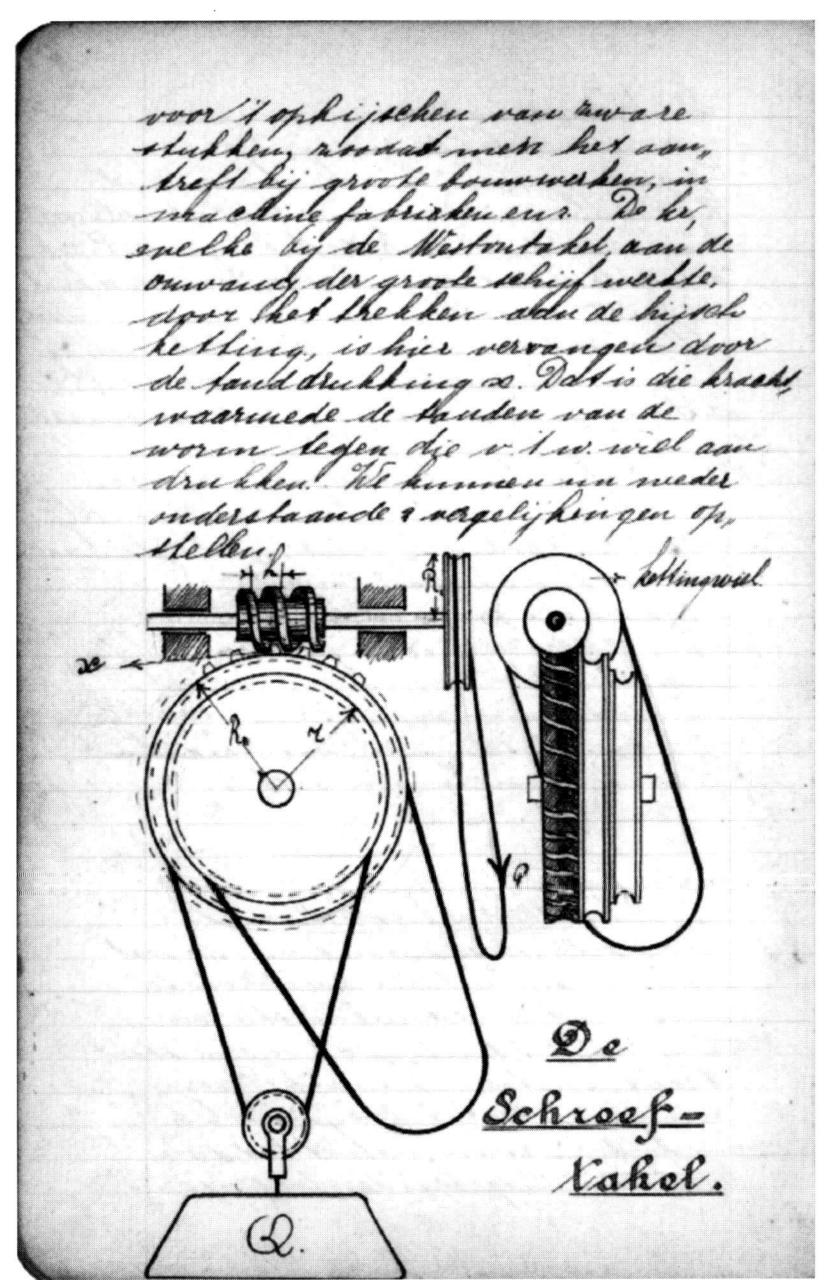

A page from Alex Weygers's high school journal, which consists of 246 pages of engineering drawings and notes written in perfect copperplate script. The work of a determined and disciplined seventeen-year-old scholar.

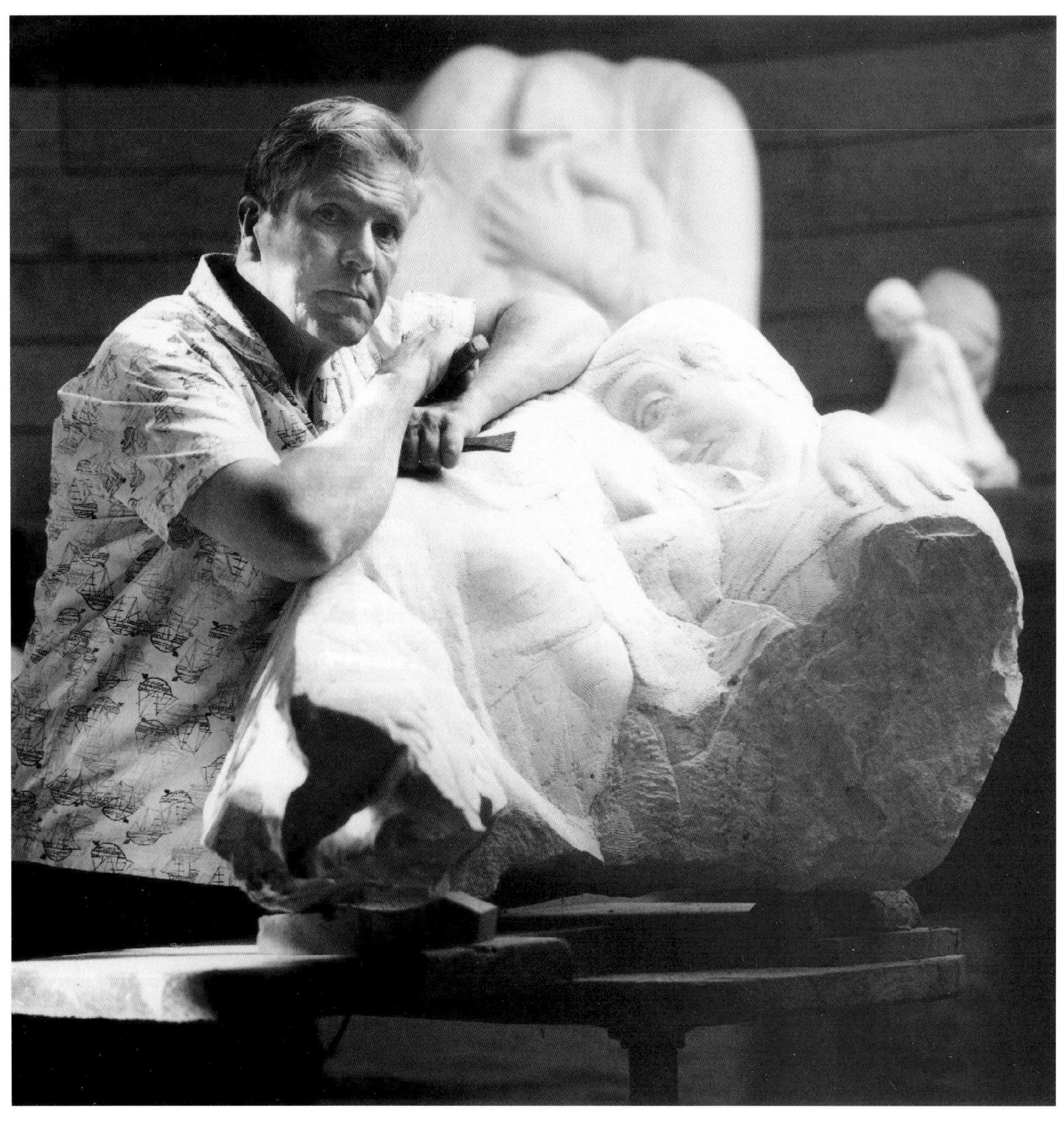

Portrait by Roger Fremier, 1969

Alexander G. Weygers
Born October 12, 1901 - Java, Indonesia
Died July 23, 1989 - Carmel Valley, California

SCULPTURE, FORM, AND PHILOSOPHY

THE NOTEBOOKS OF ALEXANDER G. WEYGERS

ALEXANDER G. WEYGERS

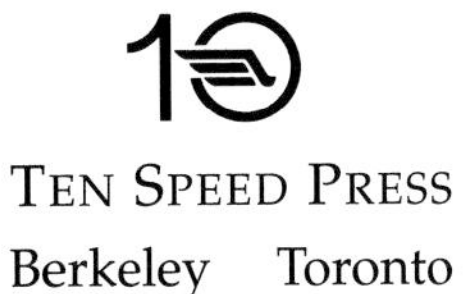

Ten Speed Press
Berkeley   Toronto

First published in 2001 by Cypress Press, Monterey, California

Ten Speed Press
PO Box 7123
Berkeley, California 94707
www.tenspeed.com

Distributed in Australia by Simon and Schuster Australia, in Canada by Ten Speed Press Canada, in New Zealand by Southern Publishers Group, in South Africa by Real Books, in Southeast Asia by Berkeley Books, and in the United Kingdom and Europe by Airlift Book Company.

NOTE ON SAFETY
Before attempting any of the procedures described in this book, please be sure to familiarize yourself thoroughly with every aspect of the tools you will be using. When working with tools, always observe shop safety practices: the safe toolmaker and sculptor is always careful, systematic, and in control of his or her tools and materials, avoiding injury to self, other people, and the tools.

The publisher, copyright holder, and estate of Alexander G. Weygers are not liable for accidents or injury caused by unsafe use of the tools and techniques described in *Sculpture, Form, and Philosophy.*

Cover design by Catherine Jacobes
Interior design by Dave Christensen, Cypress Press

Library of Congress Cataloging-in-Publication Data
Weygers, Alexander G.
    Sculpture, form, and philosophy : the notebooks of Alexander G.
    Weygers / Alexander G. Weygers.
        p. cm.
    Originally published: Monterey, Calif.: Cypress Press, 2001.
    Includes index.
    ISBN 1-58008-458-3 (pbk.)
    1. Weygers, Alexander G.—Aesthetics. 2. Sculpture—
Philosophy. I. Title.
NB 237.W442 A35   2002
730'.1—dc21   2002028498

First printing, 2002

Printed in the United States of America

1 2 3 4 5 6 7 8 9 10 — 06 05 04 03 02

Contents

My husband, Alexander Weygers, passed away on July 23, 1989, before the nearly complete manuscript covering his life's work could go to press. Much of his time in his later years was spent compiling the material, drawing the illustrations, selecting the many photographs, and preparing the written text, which he titled *Sculpture, Form, and Philosophy.* I have therefore taken over the task and, along with many dedicated friends and professionals, done my best to complete this work as he would have intended it.

My marriage with this dynamic Dutchman covered nearly fifty years of art and a uniquely personal way of life that drew hundreds of students as well as enthusiastic visitors... literally the world to our door. With his zest, creative spirit, humor, and absolute sincerity, he made my life full, and rich in memories.

I am sincerely grateful for the expert assistance and support of the following: Peter Partch, sculptor and longtime disciple of Alex Weygers, who spent many hours reviewing the text for technical accuracy; Melodie Bahou, editor and writer; and Dave Christensen, Cypress Press, for typography and graphics.

—Marian Weygers

Foreword

This book is intended to help the earnest student aim
for that highest attainment: becoming a complete
sculptor and free thinker in the arts. At the same time
I hereby aim to encourage a resurgence of sculptors as
hewers and carvers

Since the Renaissance, sculptors have come a long way
in our concepts of FORM. Our ability to solve our
problems in a scientific manner has expanded. Methods
of handling various materials also have improved.
This allows the reader to extend his own awareness of
what true form means. How this greater knowledge
may apply to his sculpture training has been precisely
plotted out in these pages.

Once the sculptor has mastered his hand skills, he
must study and thoroughly understand the intrinsic
nature of *FORM* per se: the basis of three-dimensional
artwork upon which he builds his sculpture. It is
toward this end that this book offers precise guidelines
for self-teaching, with text and illustrations that
resemble, as nearly as possible, the live teacher's
instructions and demonstrations. Each student then
can grow in his own personal way while applying the
attained working knowledge shared between teacher
and student.

The ancients were as perplexed as modern man in
defining the word FORM. Other elusive words, such
as *infinite, forever, remain,* and *never,* continue to rely on
contestable definitions (witness, dictionary definitions).
A definition is not effective if words are used which in
themselves cannot be defined. Thus, the meaning of
the word FORM remains an eternal question mark:
an enigma that cannot be dispelled. The student
consulting dictionaries today is still left without a
clear-cut and final answer.

In my own cautious attempt at defining the word
FORM during my years of studying sculpture, I had
an advantage over the ancients in that we live in an
age in which the field of mechanics has reached peaks
of perfection. We can invent and resort to needed
instruments that can make abstract things, which
might be too difficult to understand without
instrumentation, visible.

I have provided ample illustrations to help translate
abstractions into realities. After a student acquires the
needed hand skills, he shall be able to form sculpture
directly and fluently be it by modeling in clay or
carving in wood or stone without the aid of crutches
(anatomy books, pre-studies, live models, drawings,
measuring devices). He thus shall come closest to
what he wishes to portray, without accidental results.

This book offers the means to overcome the friction
that may exist between ourselves and the carrying out
of the assignments. I hope these words and illustrations

will open the gates wide for the gifted student to
explore beyond what has been presented, through
self-teaching and practice.

Assuming that every artist hopes to minimize
frustration and compromise in his desire for
self-expression (in whatever medium he chooses),
I recommend that the beginner discipline himself to
study for the sake of study until his understanding
of form for the sake of form has been perfected and
his hands have been taught to obey his minds-eye
with facility. Only then will he be truly free and able
to register what he has to say. Using his inborn
talents, he should thus strive toward producing his
best work.

About the Author

by Marian Weygers

Alexander G. Weygers was born in Java, Indonesia at the turn of the century, October 12, 1901, the son of colonial Dutch parents in a family of seven children. His father was a sugar planter overseer, his mother a teacher of languages. The early years of growing up in this beautiful, exotic, tropical world exerted much influence on his life and art.

At the age of 14 he was sent to Holland for advanced education, as was the custom with colonial families: first, to preparatory school (high school), leading to advanced studies in the field of engineering. Here, part of his time was spent in machine-shop training. Blacksmithing was one of the skills he learned there, especially useful later in the forging of fine carving tools for sculpture. (Subsequently, his three popular books on blacksmithing and toolmaking were published by Van Nostrand Reinhold for 17 years.)

Weygers entered the College of Mechanical Engineering in Groningen, graduating after three years. This was followed by extended studies in naval architecture at the Dordrecht Technological Institute for two years.

In 1923 he returned to Java, where he practiced general engineering. In 1924 his Dutch fiancee, Jacoba Hutter, came from Holland to join him. They married and planned to establish their home there. However, she could not become acclimated to the tropics and, therefore, in 1926 the young couple emigrated to the United States. Their intent was to become U. S. citizens and make this country their permanent home. For the next two years, Weygers was employed as an engineer in Seattle, Washington.

Then tragedy struck. Alex's young wife and infant died during childbirth. This terrible event precipitated a re-examination of his life. He abandoned his engineering career to devote the future to his other talent: the study and practice of the fine arts. He caught the attention of the noted sculptor, Lorado Taft, who, so impressed by Weygers' memorial sculpture in memory of his wife, wrote "It appears to me to be the most admirable sculpture that I have ever seen by an untrained hand." He took Weygers as an apprentice for one and a half years at his Midway studios in Chicago, focusing on monumental sculpture.

Weygers was now prepared for extended studies in European art centers. First, he spent a year at the Academy of Fine Arts in The Hague, Holland, specializing in studies of human anatomy, life drawing and modeling. He studied endgrain wood engraving in Paris at L'Ecole Esthetique Contemporaine. He chose one of the last of the old French masters, Paul Bournet, as his teacher, and there began his collection of several thousand original prints by Gustave Dore and other French wood engravers. Weygers always advised his

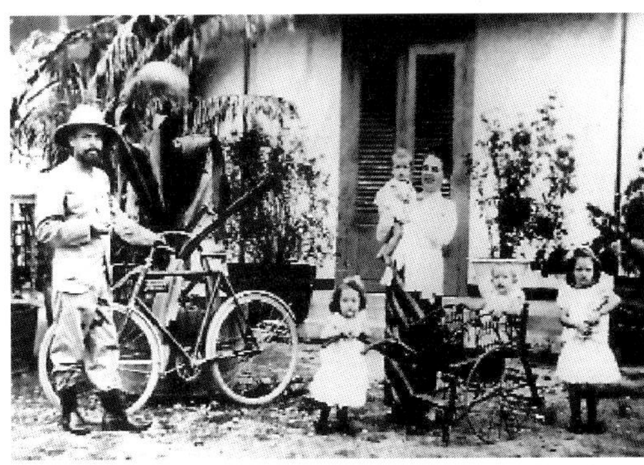

The Weygers family in Java, Indonesia. Alex is in his mother's arms.

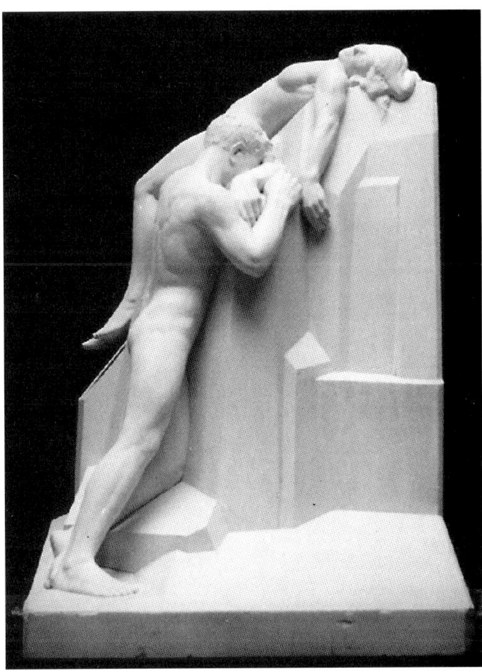

Mourning, 1927. A grief-inspired work in tribute to Alexander Weyger's young wife and infant son who both died during childbirth.

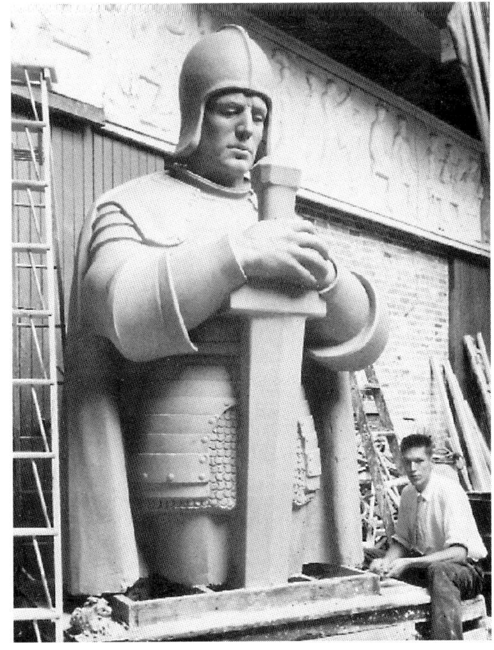

Young Alex during his apprenticeship year with Lorado Taft, Chicago. The statue, here still in clay, was destined to guard Huey Long's Louisiana state house.

students to seek out the best teachers for private lessons, since too much time is wasted in schools and students are often diverted from concentration on their studies.

Already a professional sculptor, Weygers next went to Florence, Italy to work with craftsmen who specialized in commercial marble carving; specifically to learn from them the *techniques* of carving stone as well as bronze casting.

Weygers subsequently taught art in his own studios in Seattle and Berkeley. For a time, he served in Army Intelligence, hoping in some way to work toward the freedom of his family members held in Japanese prison camps in Java and Vietnam during the fours years of the war. His brother Wyk spent those years as slave labor in Vietnam. His elderly mother died in a concentration camp in Java a few months before the war ended.

In 1943, in Carmel Valley, California, Weygers began the second half of his life. A longtime friend, Col. Arthur V. Jones, who greatly admired Weygers' vast and varied talents, granted him half interest in three acres of undeveloped rural land, studded with oaks, surrounded by mountain vistas and not far from the sea.

Weygers and his artist wife, Marian, arrived in the valley driving a 1928 Chevrolet purchased for $45 in Los Angeles. He had converted it to run on kerosene, since gasoline was limited by wartime rationing.

Here in the Carmel Valley he settled for the remainder of his life, over 50 years. His wide-ranging and diverse talents now had a base from which to expand with a driving creative force: sculpting, building home, studio and shops, engraving, printing, photographing, lecturing, blacksmithing, inventing and teaching the hundreds of students who sought him out.

Sculpture

Weygers carved directly in stone and wood, without reliance on sketches, models or measuring devices. He based his work and his teaching on his clearly defined **Form Theory**. This enabled him to control every phase of the creative process. Thus he produced, purposefully and not accidentally, the most subtle of expression in his preferred subject: the *human figure*. He believed that "The final piece is essentially complete when it leaves my hands." He was never particularly concerned about exhibiting or selling his work.

Generically speaking, "to sculpt" means to carve. This term applies most aptly to Weygers' sculptures since they were hewn from the solid material with the artist's own   hand-forged tools. The major characteristic of his carvings is a blending of full, round forms with low relief. All forms seem to interweave and gradually fall into place as an overall composition. Most of his

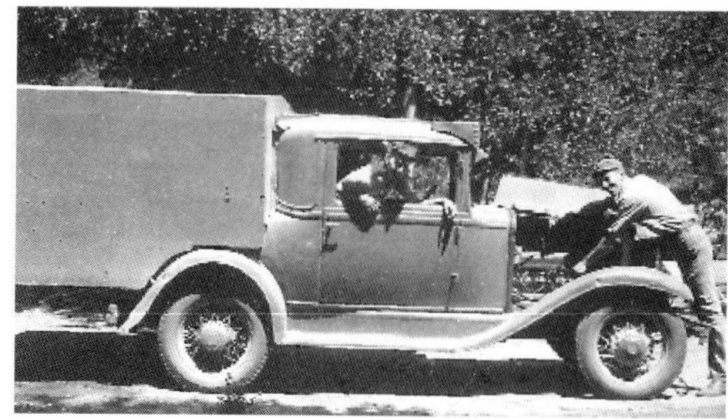

Boxie, a converted 1928 Chevy coupe brings the Weygers to Carmel Valley in 1943.

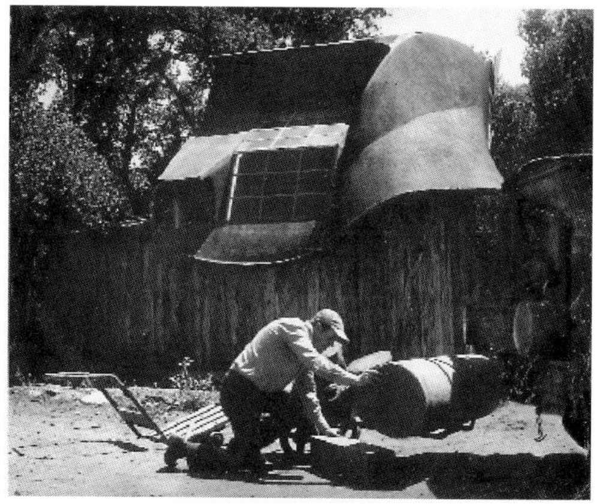

The Weyger's renowned studio/home built with Monterey pine slabs. Above, Weygers unloads teak logs shipped in from Java.

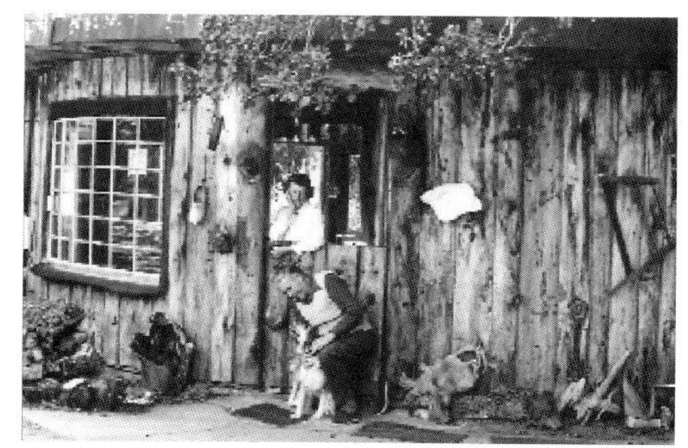

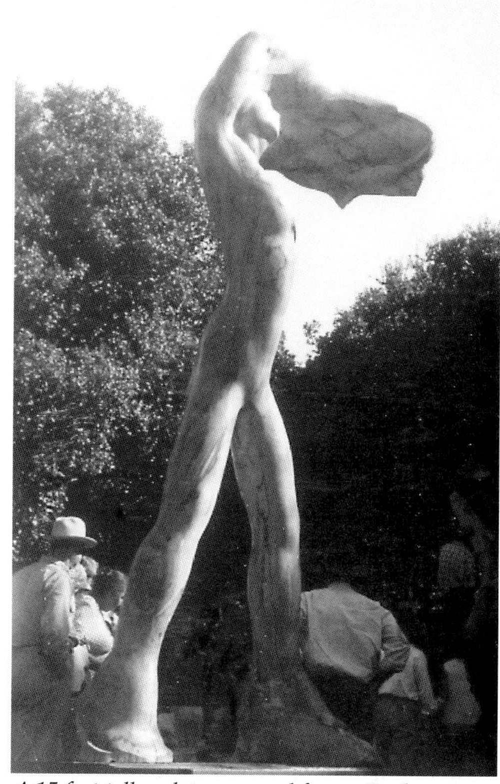

A 15 foot tall sculpture carved from a Buckeye tree.

sculptures are without undercuts, holes or pockets. He admonished his students not to "gouge" or use the chisels for "line drawing" but to adhere to and maintain the quality of *form*.

Wood Engraving

Endgrain wood engraving requires a meticulous artist. Working under a magnifying glass, the engraver uses as many as 40 calibrated burins. Traditionally, the blocks used are of Turkish boxwood, but Weygers also made his own from fine-grained fruit wood and local manzanita, seasoned, cut type-high and highly polished for a fine surface. He made his own burins (for cutting the blocks), as needed.

Weygers used an Acorn Crown Royal hand press. He converted it to print his larger blocks. In the press, the blocks can withstand a pressure of as much as 2,000 pounds. Since they are engraved on the endgrain, the fine lines are not crushed in printing.

Throughout history, sculptors have also been engravers. The major concern of these master engravers is *form*. In sculpture, the form is actual; in wood engraving, the form is an illusion, produced by a series of fine curved line gradations.

Photography

In the early 1950s Weygers traded a piece of sculpture for a Exacta single-lens reflex camera. This spurred his enthusiastic pursuit of nature subjects in macro-photography. But Weygers claimed that "Among professional photographers I would make a fool of myself. My stress is on *art*, rather than the *technique* of photography." Thus, he titled his work "Artography," simply, art-in-photography.

From explorations and experiments with his camera he discovered that, with the lens out of focus, he could capture beautiful abstractions of form and color in close-ups of water drops hanging in the sunlight; he called these "Space Convolutions."

Studio and Home

Writer Jack Arnold described the studio as "a blend of architecture, engineering and artistic originality: a structure that symbolized non-conformist creativity in a world of overrun replication."

The adjoining dwelling followed in the same character, with curving walls of vertical wood slabs. All hinges, framing and fine, decorative iron work were forged in the blacksmith shop.

The studio and home of unique design were built almost entirely with Weygers' own hands. The studio roof was adobe. The great doors, with hand-forged hinges, allowed trucks to drive in with loads of wood and stone to deposit them under the chain hoists.

Weygers never bought steel for his fine, hand-forged

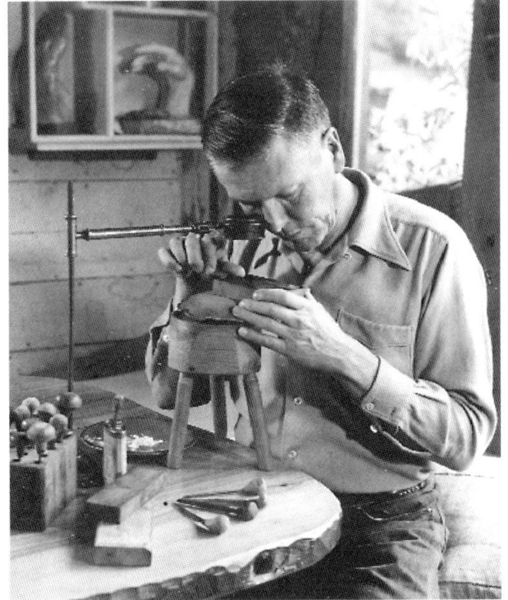

Weygers at work engraving an end-grain block of pear wood. His engravings produced fine wood block prints like these illustrated below.

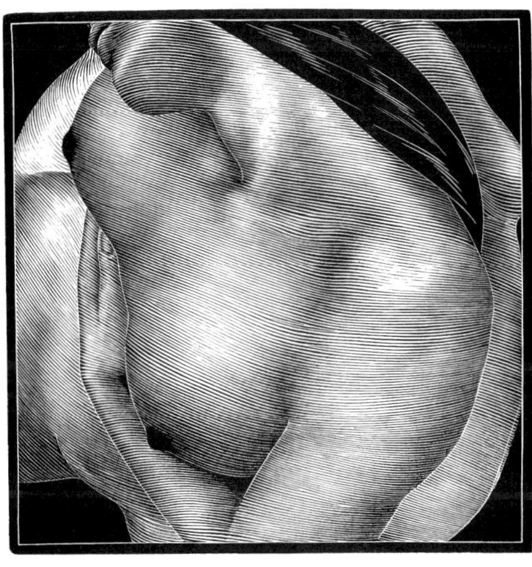

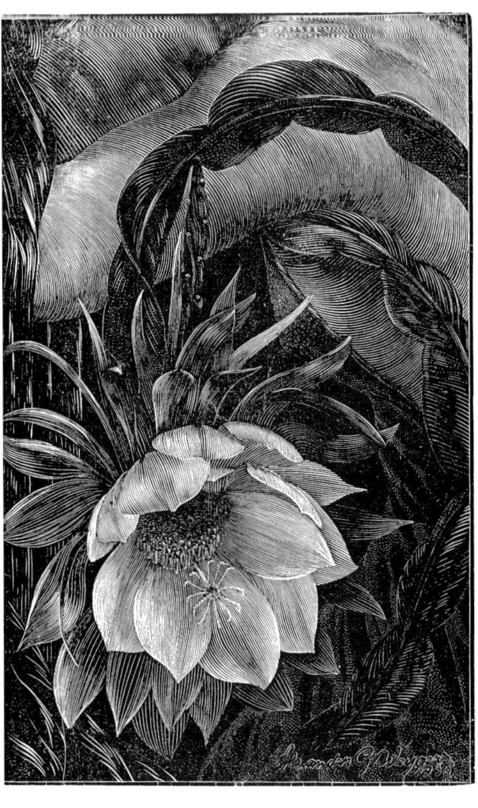

carving tools. All were made from salvaged material, as were the structures of his buildings, including hinges, window frames, even some nuts and bolts and kitchen utensils.

In his studio was the historic Acorn Crown Royal printing press. On another level was the small hand press (clam). Below ground was Weygers' darkroom, where he made prints of his sculpture. He claimed that "Only the artist himself can satisfy his own requirements, showing the refinements of detail and form of his work."

Weygers' hope was "to leave my studio, home and shops, and the land they are on, as a trust for the use of artists, thus passing on the gift. Each year a different artist would be required to leave behind the best piece of his work: a nucleus for a museum. True, my estate is not in dollars, but it is the production of my entire life."

Critical Reviews

A passage from *The Smithsonian Magazine July 1976 Special Issue: A Look into Our Third Century:* (Note: The article begins with a double-page photo of a super oil tanker and ends with a full-page picture of Weygers with one of his hand-forged and temper-colored carving tools.)

The writer states: "I recently visited the author of a popular book called *The Modern Blacksmith* by Alexander Weygers. I found him a fascinating and engaging man whose values and education represent much that is admired, although very little that is understood by modern folk."

"Weygers, who handcrafts all his own tools, is an accomplished artist and sculptor. His initial education was in mechanical engineering and shipbuilding in Holland in the 1920s. In the first year of his engineering studies, he says, 'Half of the time spent in school was in the shops, half in the classroom . . . This is what I have cashed in on all my life: the excellence of handwork.' Today, he passes this knowledge along to his students and apprentices, and is booked years in advance for his classes. 'I believe that in the diversity of knowing as much as possible about as many things as possible is the source of strength. Our society's specification is a product of man's fragility.'

"As I peer at the future course of technology and its effect on our lives, I would prefer the vision of Weygers, the ship's engineer-cum-artist and blacksmith, to the image of the super-tanker."

The well-known writer, Colin Fletcher, author of *River* and *The Man Who Walked Through Time* said, "Last year an engineer-blacksmith-sculptor-photographer and general Renaissance man, Alexander Weygers, died at the age of 88. He was remarkable not merely for his inventions (including a flying saucer-like machine, patented in 1944) and for his widely-hailed toolmaking and sculptures, but for his lifelong fight to avoid the Greed and Growth tentacles of our society. He determined

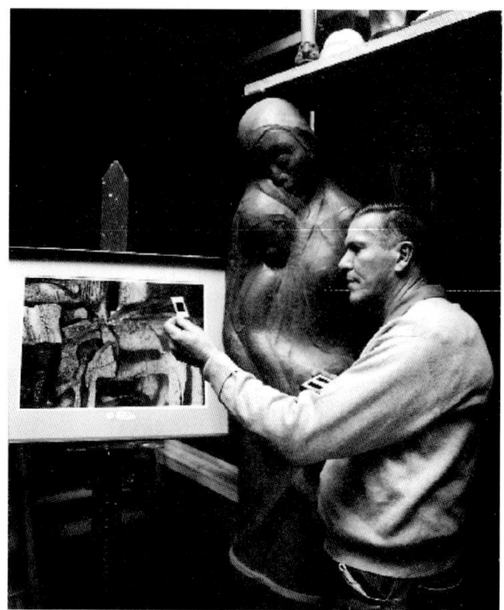

Photography was one of Weygers' most important tools: for records of work, for study as well as a true art form. Pictured here are a macro slide and print of carpenter ant tunnels.

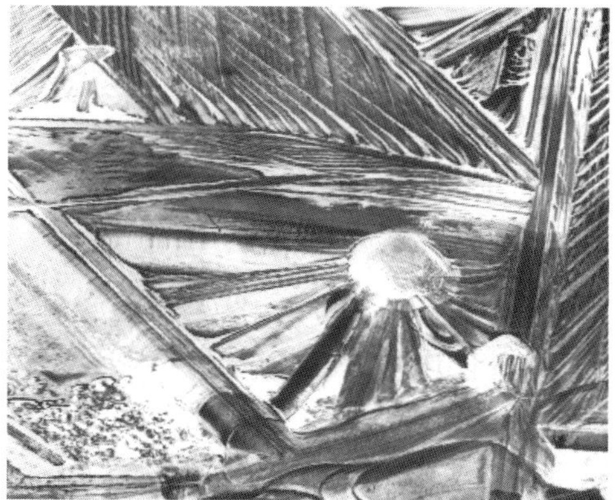

Beauty is where you find it. Weygers found it everywhere, even in a frozen-over chuckhole.

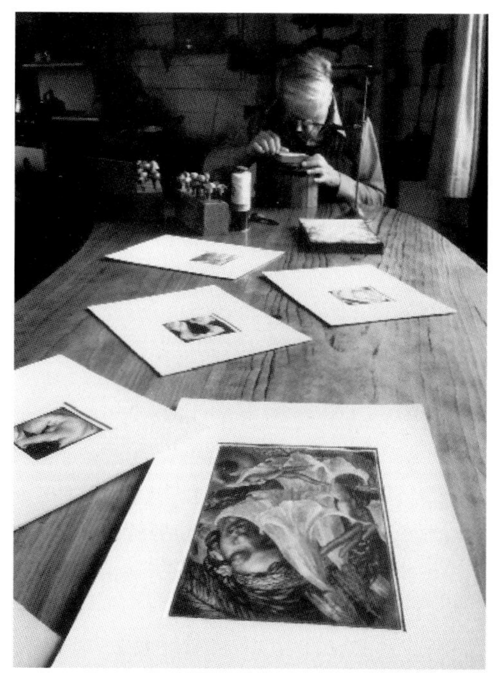

Alex Weygers at work on a woodblock engraving. On the table lies an assortment of wood engragings printed on the Weygers' own Acorn Crown Royal hand-lever letterpress.

to devote himself to his chosen work, untainted by all the compromises that the marketplace imposes. And he succeeded."

The following is taken from *Pageant Magazine*, a national publication, and written by Jerry Root, author and staff writer of the *San Francisco Chronicle*. "It was only after the *Chronicle*, a very colorful paper never given to idle flattery, described Alexander Weygers as a modern Leonardo da Vinci that people began to understand what he was all about."

Mr. Root continues, describing Weygers: ". . . ruggedly nonconforming, versatile genius of the arts and sciences. . . . He commands attention because he is a success by any standard of excellence in half a dozen professions . . . a sculptor of heroic dimensions, an inventor, a marine, mechanical and aeronautic engineer, an artist with a camera, a designer and illustrator, and a virtuoso practitioner of endgrain half-tone wood engraving. He is also blacksmith, machinist, carpenter, electrician, plumber, toolmaker and beekeeper. He is further a teacher and a reluctant prophet upon whom the admiring descend as a pilgrimage . . . 'People seem to think I possess some divine secret, and they want me to start a colony or something.'

"Weygers' way of life is, of course, uniquely his. And people envy it because they know he has conquered the inner agony of deciding what is really important in life and discarding everything else."

Teacher and Philosopher

Several hundreds of students sought Weygers out to be taught the arts of sculpture and wood engraving, as well as toolmaking in his blacksmith shops. His students were inevitably exposed to his philosophy, his "way of life." He thoroughly enjoyed the challenge of surviving by his own wits and skills.

"Nature governs itself, you know; man creates the disturbance. The forces of nature were meant to create a perfect balance. When man harmonizes with these forces, he can live in peace with nature, other people, and himself."

His students absorbed his example, which brought with it freedom and independence. But this did not come easy. Weygers always stressed the importance of a wide-ranging education and training oneself to be self-disciplined. He urged his students to "study, study, study, and practice, until you can throw all the books away. Then you will be able to make your hands the obedient servants of your mind."

"You do not see in the schools enough thorough, basic training, practice and study to teach a student how to be *self-employed*. With a variety of skills mastered, you can make your own jobs, and thereby derive independence and freedom. For instance, not to have to depend on employment with one of the large corporations is a kind of freedom."

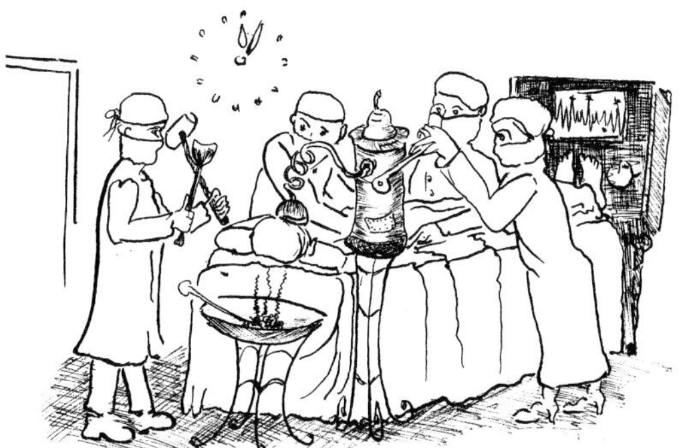

A cartoon drawn by Stuart O'Brien for friend Aex Weygers after bypass surgery.

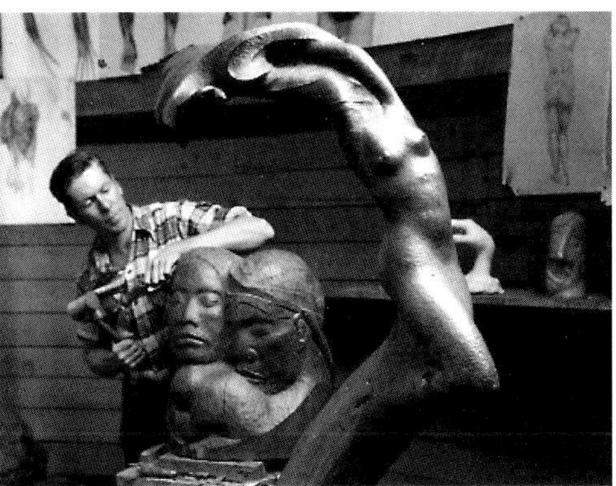
Balinese Family, *now in the Monterey Institute of Foreign Studies. Foreground: Cypress sculpture.*

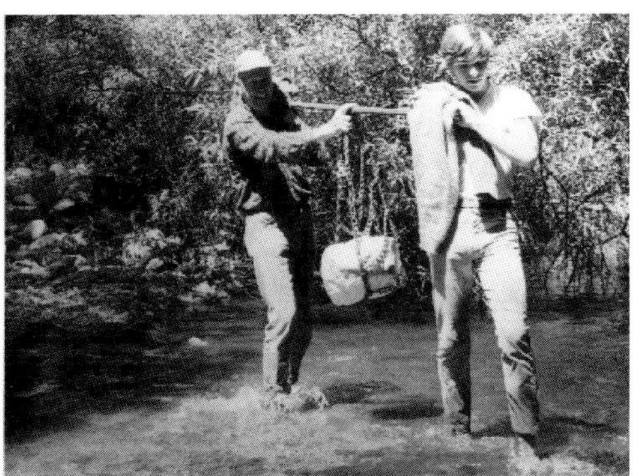
Alex and 16 year old Peter Partch who was destined to become one of Weyger's most accomplished protégés.

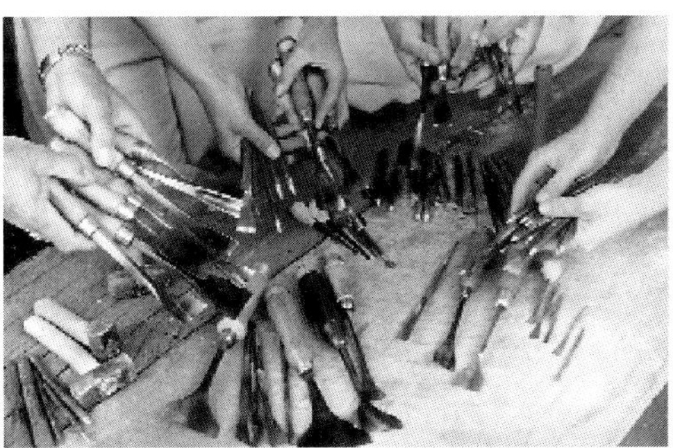
Student-crafted tools, held in the hands of their proud makers.

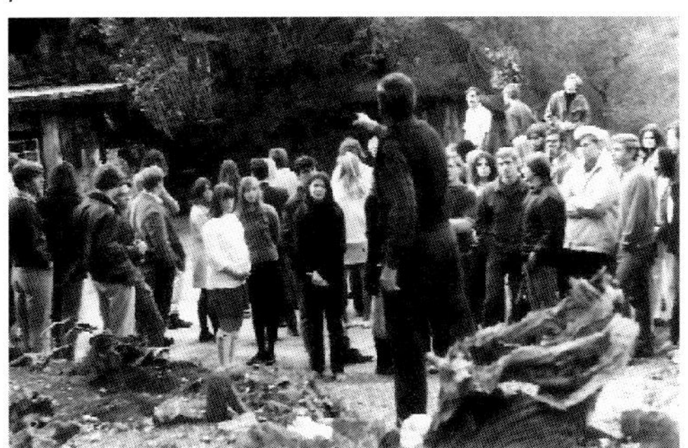
Field Marshal Weygers giving direction to a bus load of students from Carmel High on a field trip to his studio.

The Discopter

In 1944 Weygers obtained the first U.S. patent (No. 2,377,835) for his long envisioned take-off-and-lift, circular-shaped aircraft. He called it the **Discopter**. He believed that the exposed "windmill" blades of the existing helicopters were vulnerable; his design enclosed two counter-rotating blades, using the resultant energy for lift and propulsion. He offered this design to the Army Air Force during World War II but was told that the concept was too advanced to be practical. Though it was never built, the Discopter stirred excitement when, some years later, "flying saucers" were in the news.

Visitors — Sundays at Home

Over the years, a great diversity of people came to the Weygers studio/home to enjoy the Sunday open house.

The guests gathered around his hand-built, 9-foot long, cantilevered table on its steel post. So many hands, arms and elbows rested on it that Alex claimed it had absorbed the spirit of *Sakti*, the Javanese (Indonesian) word meaning *good will* or *blessed*. A variety of interesting people, including writers, actors, artists, musicians, scientists and foreign visitors, enjoyed Weygers' zest, his dynamic, spirited anecdotes, and the mutually stimulating exchange of ideas. At one time, a Japanese Zen master, taking his leave, approached Weygers, tapped him on the chest, and offered the compliment: "*You* Zen!"

Independence

The Weygers together found enjoyment and satisfaction living by their own wits, while at the same time requiring little money to survive. Everything was secondhand: stoves, washing machines, refrigerators, cars . . . An old out-of-date dental chair with hydraulic foot pump could lift many pounds of stone or wood to sculpt; a piece of high carbon steel railroad track made a good anvil; salvaged liquor bottles were turned into tuneful bells, adobe mud into building bricks; with mechanics' skills he maintained the secondhand trucks and cars. Gallons of sauerkraut from farmers' surplus cabbages, prize-winning honey from bees caught in the wild, and industrial illustrations were all part of the mix.

"My wife and I shared the view that we required a certain amount of money to take care of basic needs and keep out of debt. Beyond that it would have been a complication. I have nothing against money, and have certainly have not repudiated it. But when I've considered something that would make money, I've thought . . . Will it simplify my life or will it complicate it? Money may be the measure of a person's achievement in today's world, but I am unwilling to pay the price — to trade my life for it." Weygers' art was not done for making money, thus avoiding catering to the merchants "because if you play their game, they set the rules."

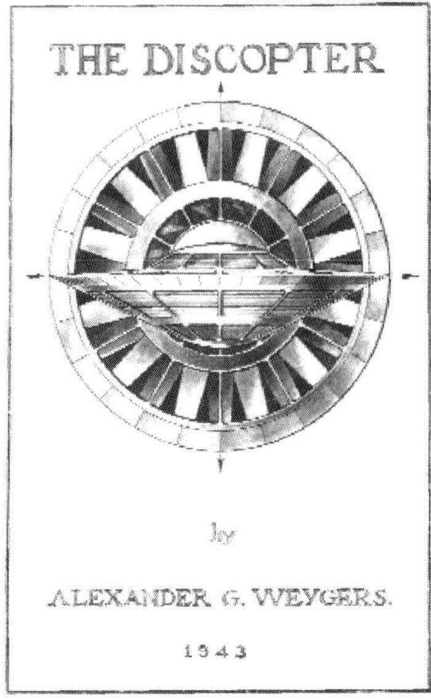

Alex Weygers' conceptual "Discopter," though never commercially developed, the design created a a good deal of interest in the 40's and 50's. Perhaps it's time is yet to come. Weygers was granted U.S. patent #2,3777,835 for the Discopter in 1944.

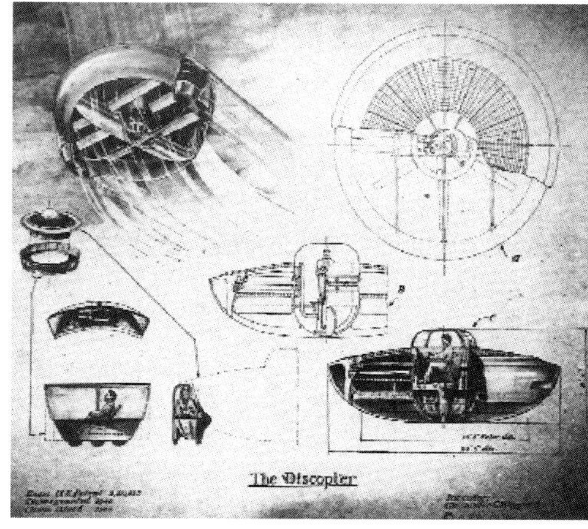

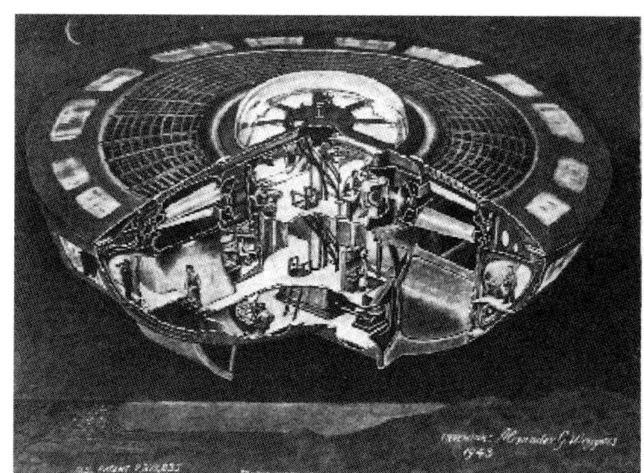

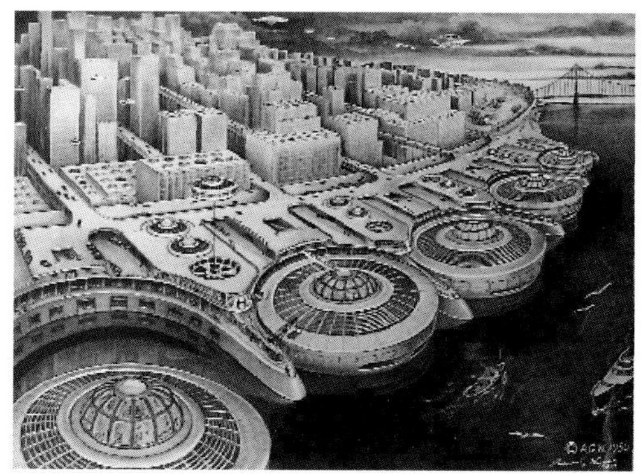

Books

Weygers wrote and illustrated three books on blacksmithing and toolmaking, which were commissioned by Van Nostrand Reinhold. They have become classics of their kind and were available for 17 years. Now the three books have been combined into one, titled **The Complete Modern Blacksmith**, published by Ten Speed Press, Berkeley, CA.

Conclusion

The obituary of a highly respected and loved university professor (a bachelor with no next of kin) concluded with the words: "He left no survivors." But his many students pointed out he left hundreds of survivors throughout the country who practice his teachings. Such is also the case for Weygers . . . as his former students attest. In many ways, the power of a teacher's *personality* is even more decisive and permanent that the knowledge and skills he instills in his pupils. He left hundreds of "survivors" across the globe, who practice his skills, arts and philosophy.

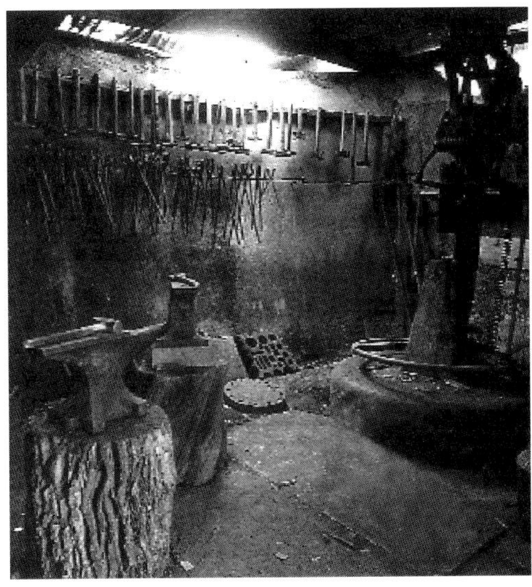

The anvil's ring has fallen silent. . . still it reverberates into the ages through the many lives influenced by

Alexander G. Weygers

October 12, 1901 - July 23, 1989

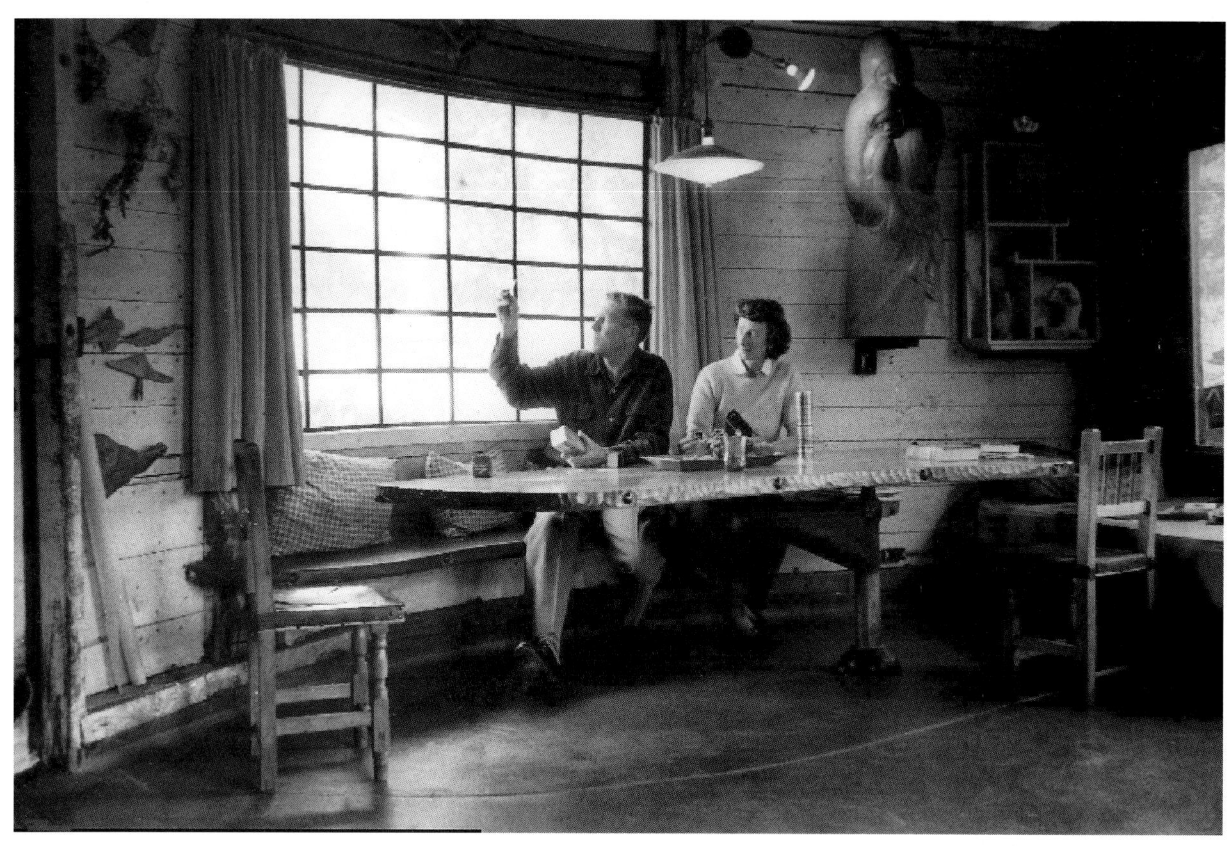

Alex and Marian Weygers sit at the cantilevered dining table selecting
35mm slides for one of his Artography lectures.

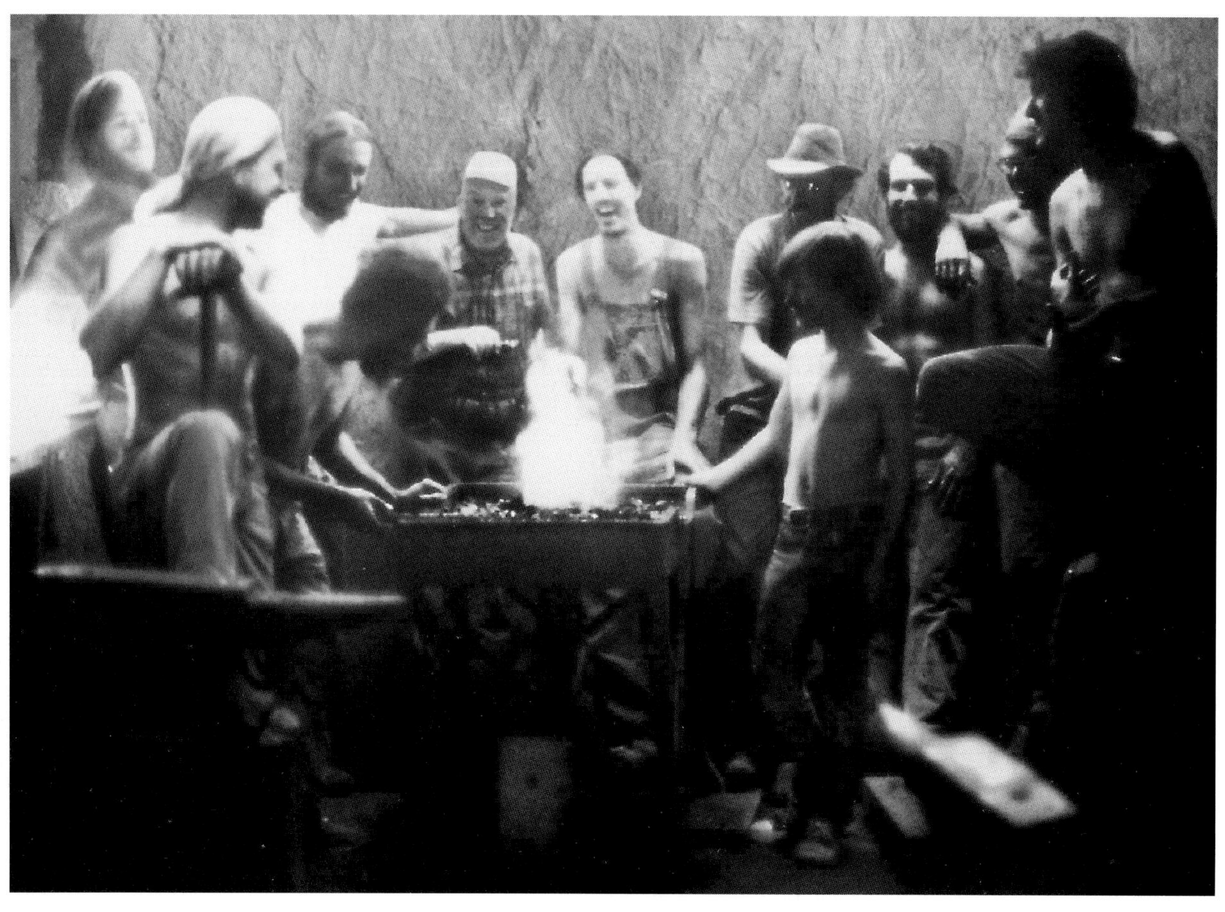

Alex and "The Disciples," Publishers of the Whole Earth Catalog
came to the studio for a few lessons in Tool Making

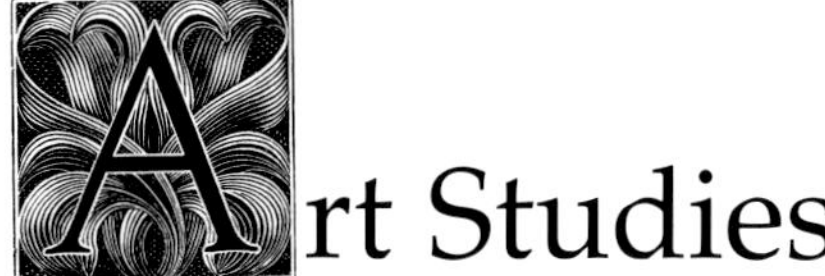rt Studies

The dilemma for many a beginning art student is, "How shall I begin? Should I begin in a school under a *chance* teacher, or should I *choose* a teacher whose work I admire and arrange to be taught by him privately?"

Experience has shown me that even good schools are the slow way, in contrast with the direct way of private instruction and apprenticeship. In my own case, I combined school, private instruction and subsequent apprenticeship as the most effective and rapid means of learning. All the student should require from his teacher is that he can *demonstrate* his knowledge in actual art products.

Art schools, being financed by students' tuition, often prolong teaching as much as the traffic will bear. Giving all schools and their teachers the benefit of the doubt that worthwhile things are being taught, it still remains a reality that the student receives what he needs only by the drop, slowly, instead of by the bucket-full over a shorter time. Either way, for a few years, the talented student faces a series of hurdles in training, but hopefully ends up with an ultimate *breakthrough* which, if persistence and self-discipline are his, will come as "his moment of truth." At last he will work directly as a seasoned artist.

The Essence of Teaching

First the teacher helps the student understand that learning to master the hand craft is one thing, but learning how to use the *mind* that guides the hand to make things is another. Three-dimensional thinking during sculpting calls for abstract thought and the ability to harness it successfully within one's form studies. *Form Theory* offers the key to learning to visualize three-dimensionally in one's imagination. In time, hit or miss results disappear.

After finishing his studies, the art student himself, and no one else, will know whether he fell short of gaining the know-how he sought. If his preparatory training has left him wanting, he ought to prolong his studies. If a good teacher advises him to keep at it until he can work under full control and free of all aids, he owes it to himself to do so. After that, the teacher's job is finished; it is not a teacher's business to tell a student *what* he must say, or *how* he must say it, in matters of expression.

When at last a student has come shoulder to shoulder with his teacher, and can find no follow-up, he automatically becomes his own teacher. For the remainder of his life, he will be responsible for all further exploration that carries him closer to his desired state of competence.

Unexpected Results after a "Breakthrough"

For some artists, a puzzling relaxed feeling may set in at this stage. As in a revelation, the artist begins to review his field with clarity and ease; a relaxed peace of mind replaces the earlier feverish drive and urge to do creative work. He now seems to await a revival of those urges.

In one situation, should this come about, he then simply gets it off his chest easily, working *directly* in the material that best suits him. Work will then flow from his hands as he hoped it would, without guessing or groping. At last the artistic fulfillment he sought as a beginner has come about. He feels in his bones a confidence that each last piece of work reflects his growth of mind and skill. His last piece is bound to be his best.

In another situation, an artist may plan to *hold back* the urge to undertake major pieces until he feels completely *ready* for it. At that moment his pent-up restraint results in a magical bursting open of the floodgates, as his feelings are given free reign. In a veritable surge of self-regeneration, art products keep flowing from his hand.

In rare cases, he may be so rich in spirit and wisdom that all things he has to say are worth saying and are said at their best. Then art will shine through all his work. Some philosophers compare such rare outpouring of divine sparks in artistry with a meteor that dazzles the eye with its light path in the sky. Unfortunately, such intensity in an artist's creative life threatens to burn itself out prematurely.

Those artists who are endowed with *several* outstanding natural talents find each one nourishes the other. All bear the mark of truth that links them together.

Warning: A student could find himself sidetracked by the temptations of financial gain well *before* an artistic breakthrough. Mundane forces may lead him to cater to profit-seeking middlemen who encourage him to keep producing the things that have sold well. Time will prove that his original creative work, once esteemed, becomes vulgarized through quantity and repetition. He loses more and more the quality of his past work, thus bearing witness that art suffers when diluted.

This realistic appraisal of what happens to many promising artists may well raise these questions in the beginner's mind: "Why am I doing what I'm doing? How badly do I want to do it? Do I do this purely for the love of it or to become famous and wealthy, to satisfy the ego or to do other artists one better?" Whatever the goal, pitfalls can set him back or even finish him as an artist.

A typical pitfall can arise when a friend watches a promising student at work. He watches over his shoulder with admiration and pleads urgently, "Stop! Don't touch it any more. It is perfect as it is." That well-meaning friend cannot know that the student, at that very moment, is exasperated with not being able to come closer to his mark.

All the works surrounding him in his studio are in this category: just study pieces, which are simply stepping stones to learning. Should he now believe his friend, or should he trust himself?

If he succumbs to his friend's praises and lets flattery arouse his vanity, he might rationalize thus: "I had no idea I was that good." From then on, a nagging feeling begins to haunt him. Did his friend kid him, or did he, the budding artist, kid himself?

Next the friend talks him into exhibiting all his "studies" in sales galleries. When some sales result, he will talk himself into a state of congratulation: "My friend must have been right. People are paying money for my stuff. It can only mean that society has placed its stamp of approval on me, just as a meat inspector stamps a side of beef. It must mean that I have arrived; I am *in*."

He could have missed the fact that the art *market* is no more than a game devised and played *by merchants for merchants*, whose rules must be followed by the artist. Too often the *arrested* artist becomes a willing caterer to what has been *selling*. Forgotten is his earlier intention: to study for the sake of study until he has mastered his art needs and becomes free of all shortcomings. Doing art for the love of it only, remains many an artist's hope.

Every beginning art student would be wise to contemplate these risks at the outset. All of us have to pay a price one way or the other. Often the price involves a choice between spiritual riches and financial poverty or spiritual poverty and financial riches, although a blend between the two is in general the result.

The only admonition anyone can offer the student is a philosophical one: the artist's safety lies in the self-discipline to **never yield to the seemingly obvious**, in order that self-improvement shall remain most important at all times.

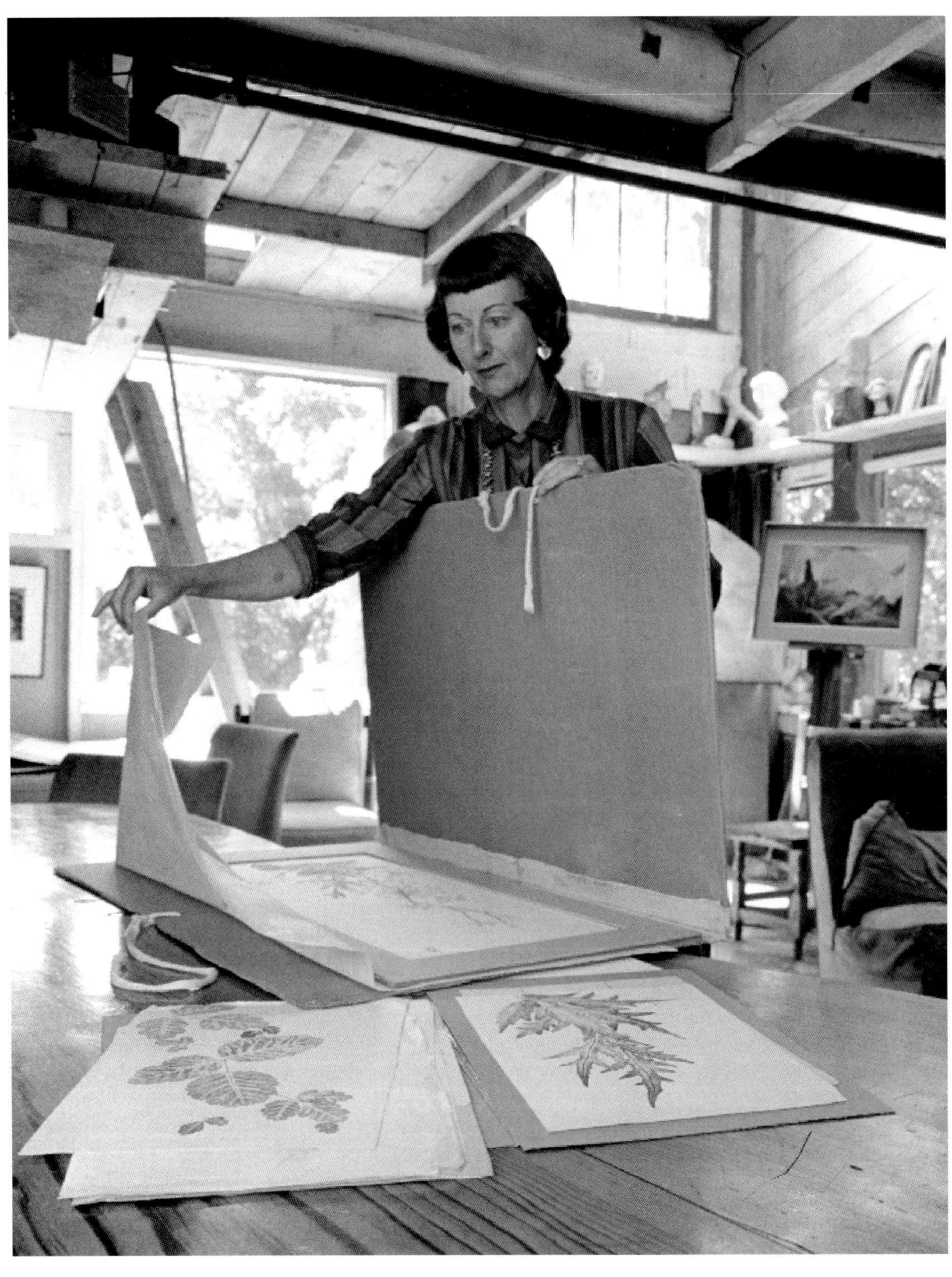

Marian Weygers with a portfolio of her art prints produced by utilizing elements she found in nature, an artist by her own right.

Chapter 2

The Theory of Form

The study of sculpture is in the realm of instinctive emotional reaction to seeing *form shapes*. I found it helpful to invent a way to demonstrate and measure these reactions: a mathematical approach in a world of abstractions through the process of reasoning combined with *visualization* and *instrumentation*. The resulting Theory of Form can act as a guide in art studies and help the student acquire a working knowledge of how best to create form in sculpture.

An understanding of form in sculpture also provides a key to the study of esthetics and philosophy. To this end we will test *the character and degree of emotional reactions* that the viewer experiences when looking at various basic forms.

I have designed a simple mechanical device, shown in the illustrations, with which to carry out these experiments in a series of demonstrations.

To begin with, I have chosen the *cube* as a pure form.

The device is constructed with a thin, opaque, white spherical membrane stretched over a cubical wire frame, approximately one foot square. A tube attached to this instrument leads to a pump which can *silently* pump air in or suck it out. The cube is placed on a table behind a suspended screen that can be raised or lowered in front of it. A reostat switch permits the teacher to increase the light from zero, to dim, to bright.

The reader, not witnessing the actual physical demonstration, can follow the proceedings by means of the written text and illustrations. His own powers of visualization are thus relied upon to follow the events.

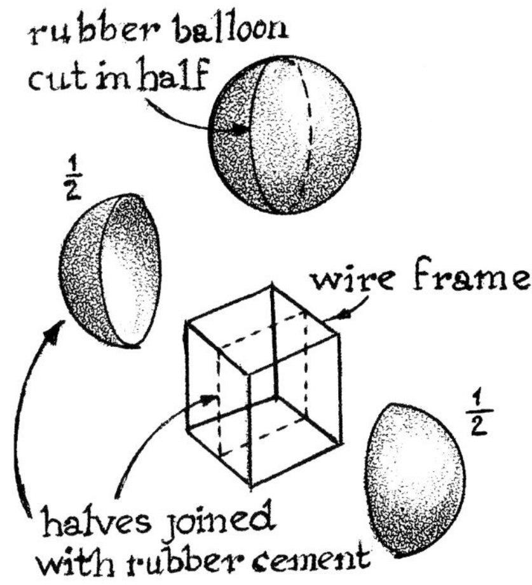

cube frame 12"x12"x12".
opaic white thin flexible
rubber balloon 12"dia.
cut in half, each is
stretched over frame

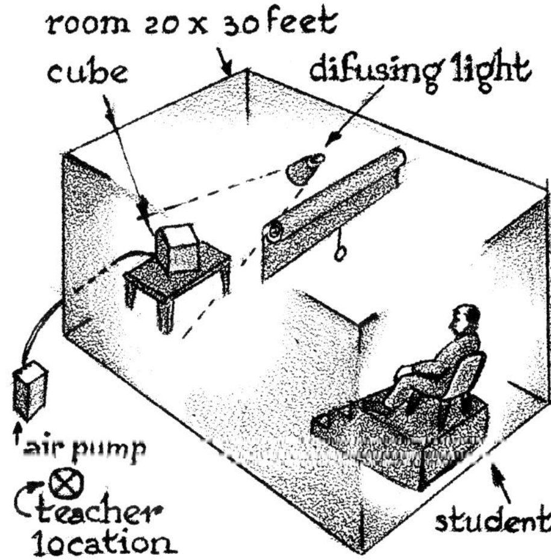

walls, floor, ceiling, screen, table,
painted dull black
cube instrument dull white
eye level of viewer above cube

teacher operates light switch
air pump, screen, microphone
out of view of student

First Series of Demonstrations

At the outset, the student is told to refrain from any comment until the demonstrations have been concluded.

The student is seated facing the screen that conceals the *cube.* The light is switched off and, in darkness, the screen is raised. Next, the light is switched on to *dim* and the *cube* comes into view.

While the student watches, the light is *slowly increased* to bright, thereby his impressions of this form gradually intensify. After a 15-second wait, the light is switched off.

In darkness, the cube is silently blown up until it has become a *sphere.* Again the light is switched on to dim and gradually turned up to bright. After 15 seconds of observation time, the light is switched off.

Next, in total darkness, the air is *sucked out* of the cube until the rubber membrane has collapsed inward. As the light is turned from dim to bright, the viewer sees *a form made up of concave planes* supported by the cubic wire frame. After this image is shown for a few seconds, the room is darkened, the screen dropped, and the light switched on.

This ends the first series of demonstrations.

Second Series of Demonstrations
(to begin one minute later)

In total darkness, the air is let in to restore the *cube,* and the screen is raised.

The light is turned to dim and gradually increased to bright, revealing the *pure cube* once more.

While *the room remains lighted and the student watches,* the air is steadily pumped into the cube. A gradually expanding movement of *form transfiguration* from cube to sphere can thereby be seen.

After a short interval *in full light,* the air is gradually let out and the student sees the flat planes of the cube reappear.

The air is now slowly sucked out, and the flat planes seem to collapse inwardly, as they form the concave-sided structure.

After 15 seconds, air is slowly let in and the student watches the pure cube reappear. The light is left on and the screen dropped, concluding the demonstrations.

Viewer Reactions and Analysis

The student and teacher can now begin to discuss and analyze the reactions to the demonstrations. What did the student *reason* while seeing the simple basic forms in each step? What did he instinctively *feel*?

His first impression of the cube might be a feeling of its *static* quality. Or did it fail to evoke much responsive feeling? Did he reason that it was a form made of seemingly solid material plaster of Paris or marble?

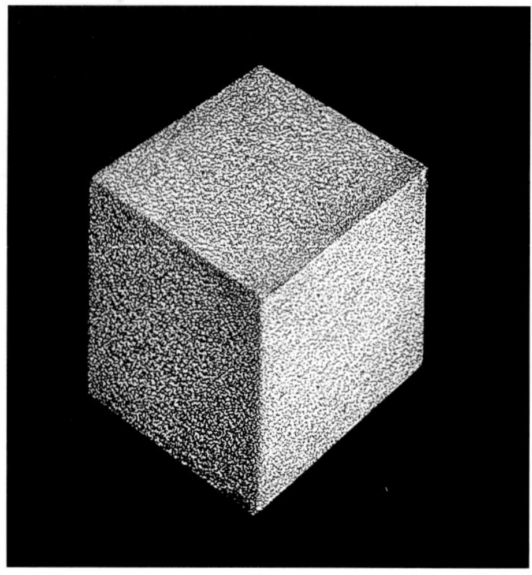

the Cube

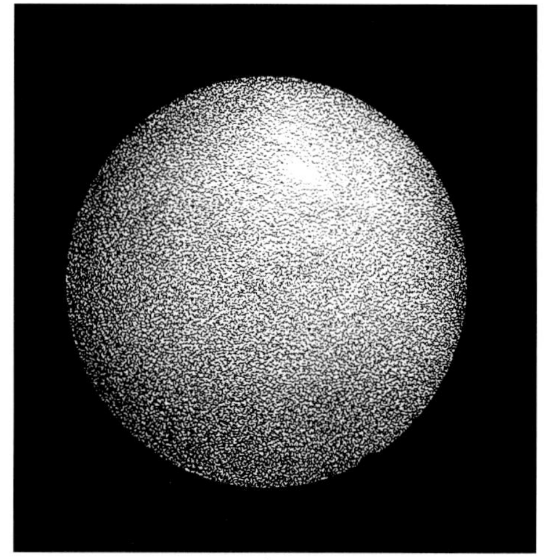

the Sphere

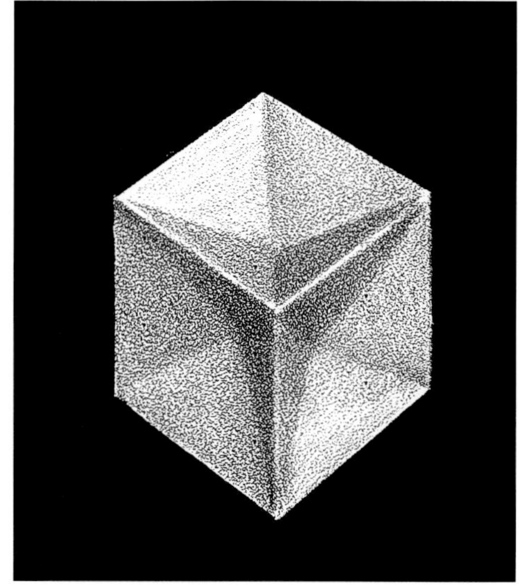

the Hollow-sided Figure

He could *reason* that we were dealing with a cube-shaped, mathematically precise form. Its sides were at right angles with one another, were equal, flat and reflected the light in three shades of tonal values. He could further know it was a *cube* because its planes ran perspectively, giving its form depth in its various slants and angles.

When the *sphere* appeared, the likely emotional response to the round form with the light softly graded and distributed symmetrically over its curved surface would be one of pleasure. A *static condition* may have been felt in its concentric symmetry. The observer could, perhaps, feel a desire to touch it, stroke it or cup it in his hands. It would relate to many normally pleasant familiar things: balloons, oranges, bowling balls, basket and beach balls, tree ornaments, a baby's head shape. In other words, a *sphere shape* would probably arouse pleasant reactions.

The student could consciously *reason* that it was a *pure sphere*, since the reflected light on its surface diminished equally toward its edges. If lines of longitude and latitude were to be drawn upon it, as on a global map, its mathematical sphere form could be identified perspectively as well.

The student, when he is confronted with the *hollow-sided form*, might desire to know how these *empty* forms, with their sucked-in appearance, came about. He might try to relate them to familiar images: hollow molds, honeycombs, caves, chuck holes, craters, empty bowls.

As he watched *the cube grow into a sphere* during the second demonstration, his feeling might be that the increasing size of the form from cube to sphere indicated a radiating *force* within, growing from the center outward in every direction. The form's movement and expansion would probably induce a pleasurable excitement in him, as if he were watching a toy balloon being blown up.

One could reason that the form's expansion was caused by an inside pressure that was greater than the outside atmospheric pressure.

Seeing Form

Form is revealed to us if we separate a cast from its mold. Their *contact surfaces*, surface "skins," as it were, are thereby made visible. In a *cast* we see that skin from the outside; looking into the *mold* we see that skin from its inside. This means that when a sculptor makes his three-dimensional pieces, he can approach the skin from the outside or from the inside, toward that contact area between the two. He can work by *adding* clay, piece by piece toward that outside, or he can chip away, piece by piece of stone inward from the outside toward that skin *interface* between the two. The ultimate surface can be reached from either side, if the sculptor is able to *visualize* the end product clearly.

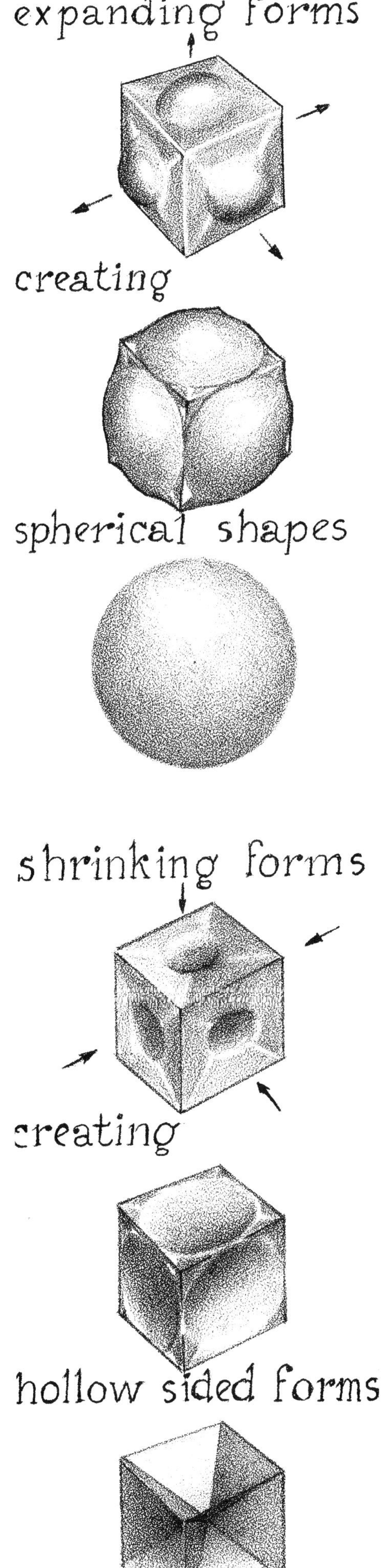

Man's Ability to Visualize

Example 1

If we were to consider the skin of the expanding spherical form as imaginary material that could grow and in time overreach and envelop us, this would place us *inside* the sphere where we would see its hollow surface surrounding us. We would be *inside* the sphere's mold. Thus a *reversal* of its spherical outside cast would have taken place. Like the mathematician, we too learn to *visualize form* (in this case the sphere) as the contact area between one spacial convolution and its opposite.

Example 2

A mathematical formula in the third power is the product of abstract thought. It can actually be made visible, *plotted out three-dimensionally,* and used to make a cast in plaster of Paris. Such models can be seen displayed in museums and university mathematics departments. They can also be found in the field of computer application.

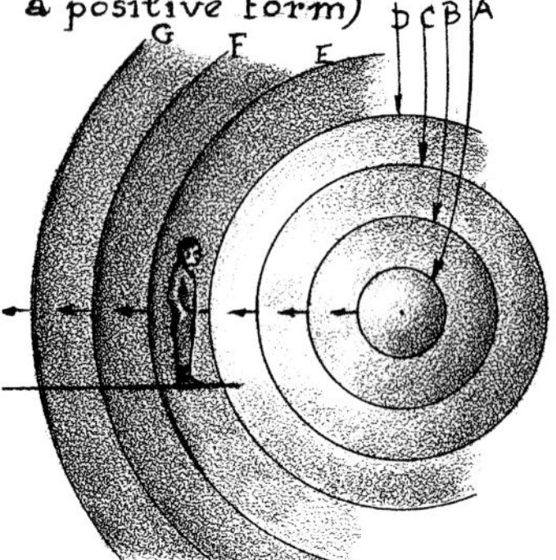

next he finds himself inside the growing sphere E. (he then sees a negative form) E, F, G shown in crossection

plaster cast of a formula in the 3rd power plotted out in space

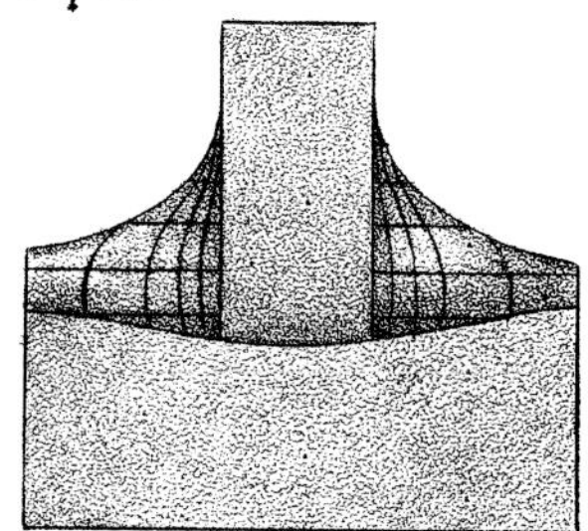

front view

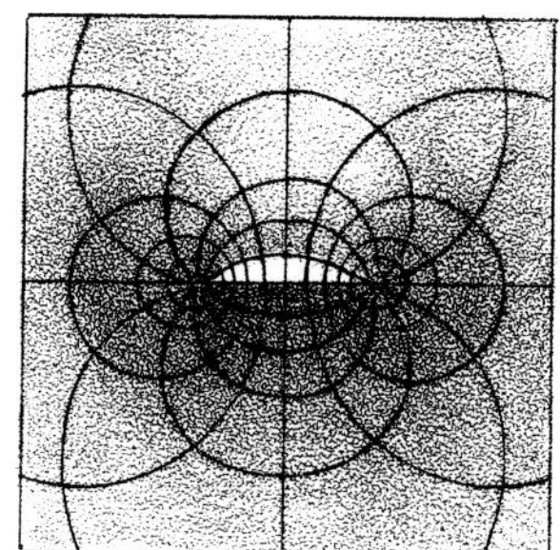

top view

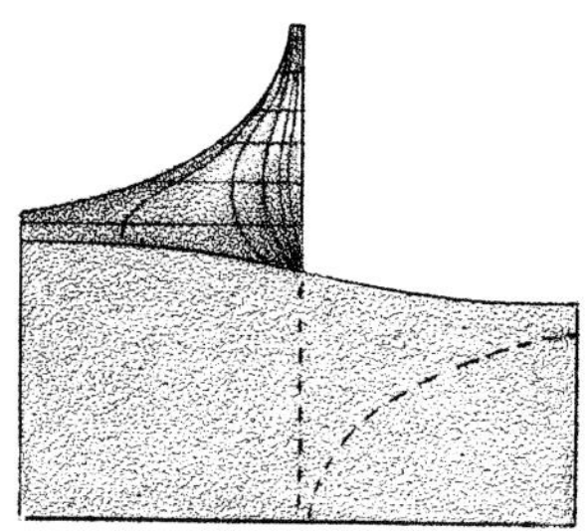

side view

Two identical casts of such three-dimensional formulas can be placed in reversed fashion in assembly, as shown in the illustration. This demonstrates that one cancels out the other at their contacting surfaces. In this way we can learn to *visualize form* and *think of the contact area as "skin" between one spacial convolution and its opposite (or their interface).* (See figure.)

Definition of the Word "Form" in Sculpture

Form is the contact area between one spacial convolution and its opposite. Examples: a cast and its mold; a pudding and a pudding form.

In *sculpture* it is that *interface* between cast and mold that is expressed three-dimensionally.

The demonstrations show that *pressure* variations in the instrument create different form characters (qualities) that cause different emotional reactions.

Terminology

When the pressures inside and outside the cube are equal, a state of "at rest," equilibrium, or *neutrality* exists. A *neutral* form has a character *midway* between positive and negative.

When a higher pressure creates the sphere, it gives it a *positive* form quality; and a lower pressure in the hollow, collapsed cube produces a *negative* form quality.

In addition, we see that different form qualities produce different emotional reactions. The key to *form* qualification can be stated thus:

> A pressure in the demonstration instrument higher than that of the outside atmosphere creates a *positive* external form, while negative pressure in the instrument (a pressure lower than that of the outside atmosphere) creates a *negative* external form. A neutral pressure, when pressure inside and outside the instrument are equal, results in a *neutral* external form.

Note on terminology: The qualifying terms *positive, negative* and *neutral,* when carried into the fields of philosophy and esthetics, have meanings that also range between opposites; beautiful and ugly, desirable and undesirable, attractive and repulsive . . . all connote opposites in qualifications and reaction. In the field of art, the quality "beauty" is normally deemed desirable and adds pleasure, whereas "ugliness" subtracts from it.

Form theory suggests then that *positive* form *adds* pleasure and *negative* form *subtracts* from it.

Spherical surfaces of forms in sculpture express positive qualities which, as a rule, are aesthetically desirable, pleasing or beautiful.

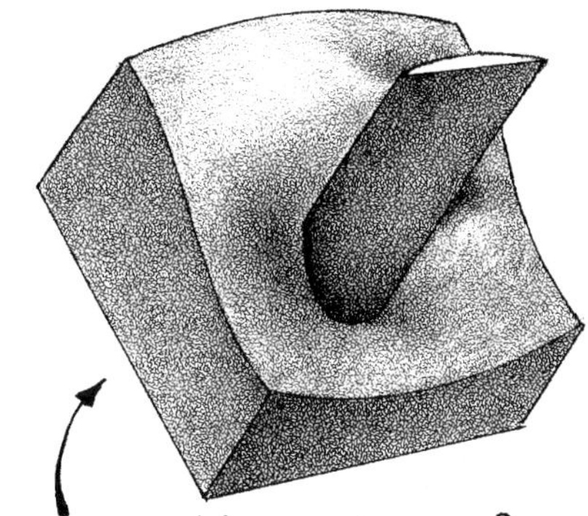

perspective view of a mathematical form (a formula in the 3rd power

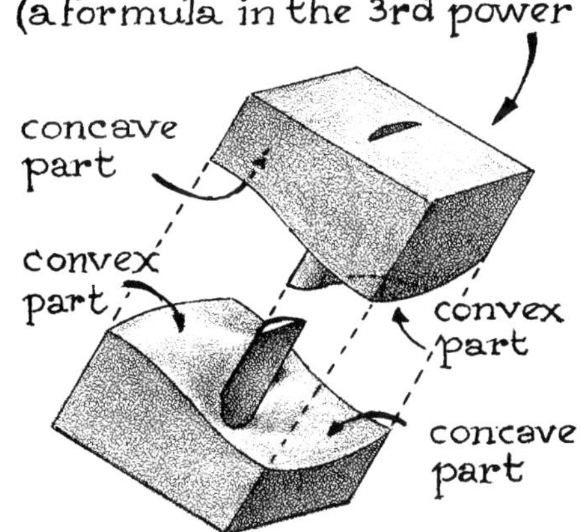

Neutral planes in sculpture inject a feeling of equilibrium suggesting ambivalence, passivity and lifelessness. When they dominate the composition, the viewer may feel a less warm emotional interest; often he will not feel one way or the other. For this reason, flat backgrounds and flat-surfaced bases for pieces of sculpture are desirable since, being neutral in character, they do not alter the feeling of a composition but simply set it off.

The term *negative* when describing forms in a composition refers to all hollow surfaces and also to the empty spaces between the protruding parts of the composition. Such empty spaces subtract from the positive and neutral character in sculpture compositions.

The Reversal Factor

Our ability to *think* about as well as *see* form can be thrown into momentary confusion when optical illusions occur.

Observe the illustration of the sculptured portrait with its cast and mold side by side. A photographic print made with a single light source from above, shows both cast and mold looking alike. In one form the light seems to be shining from below, and in the other it seems to be shining from above. An optical illusion takes place, caused by the *reversal factor.*

If we look, with one eye only, at the *mold* in the picture, it does not look hollow. Instead, a reverse surface seems to pop out and come toward us. The seemingly protruding image looks as if it is lighted from below instead of from above as it was when the photograph was actually taken. Knowing that the picture was taken with the light coming from above, we can only *reason* that the mold must be a hollow form and not a protruding one.

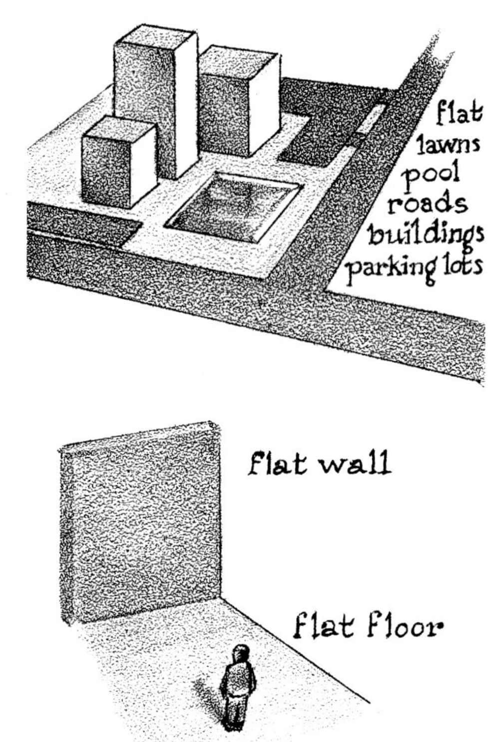

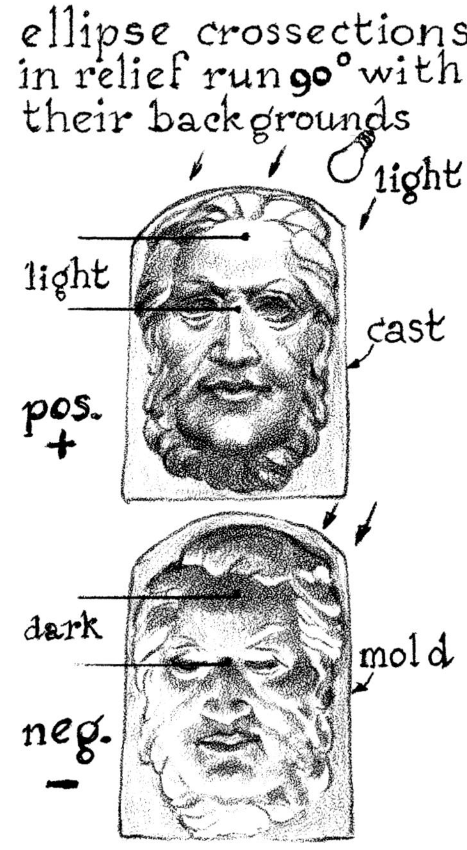

Similarly, the single eye of the camera sees no depth in the way that two eyes do. Therefore, only light, by *reflection*, reveals the various light intensities, which in turn give the illusion of depth. This reversal of thinking or seeing three-dimensionally when dealing with casts and molds becomes apparent when we visualize, for instance, a hand-fitting glove, or a foot and footprint.

Optical illusions can trap us in confusion, in which one element can switch into its opposite, not gradually, but instantaneously. This reversal factor occurs more often than we think. Hate can become love and love can become hate. Images are instantly reversed in a mirror. Printing type is reversed when inked and printed.

Infinity and the Reversal Factor

Although man cannot visualize the *infinite,* his reasoning can *direct* him toward it along lines of logic. The illustrations show how he can proceed to understand infinity conceptually through *instrumentations* that correctly direct his understanding.

First Example

The instruments are a piece of blank paper, a ruler, and a pencil.

Draw one straight line A across the paper from edge to edge, then another straight line B1 which intersects the first one at point *P1*. A chosen point a on the second line B will act as rotation point for line B1 which, when rotated, will make intersection point P1 move to our right-hand side to *P11* and *P111* and ultimately cause it to disappear from our field of vision. If we continue line rotation, there will be an instant when line A and line B1 run parallel, but if line B1 is rotated around point *a* still further to *B1111*, we will see that the point of intersection has returned into our field of vision, this time coming from the left side (the *reverse* side).

This demonstration leads to a *definition: two straight lines run parallel at the instant that they intersect in the infinite.* It demonstrates also that in this process of reasoning we accept the term *infinite* as an abstraction nearest to our understanding of the word *absolute*: something that we cannot grasp with our hands, as it were, but which we are able to conceive of in a process of reasoning.

It is by *direction*, therefore, that the student can reach farther and farther into the unknown toward infinity, where the reversal factor triggers a reverse direction from the very end to our starting point *zero* moving inwardly or outwardly, to the left or the right, into the past or the future, upward or downward, backward or forward, etc.

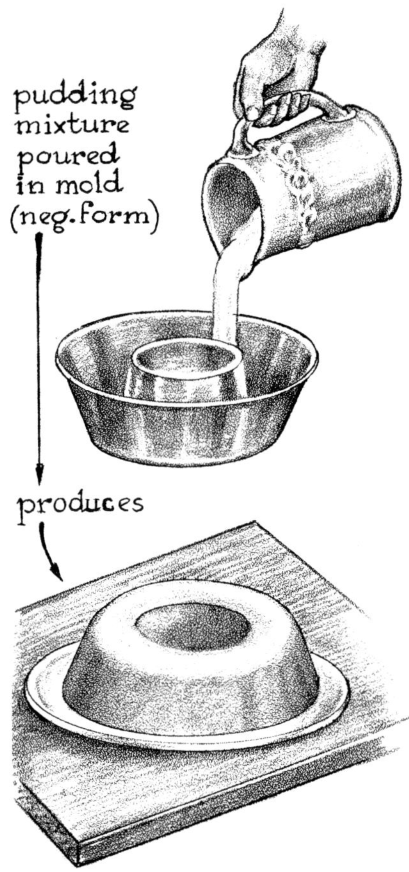

the pudding, a positive form

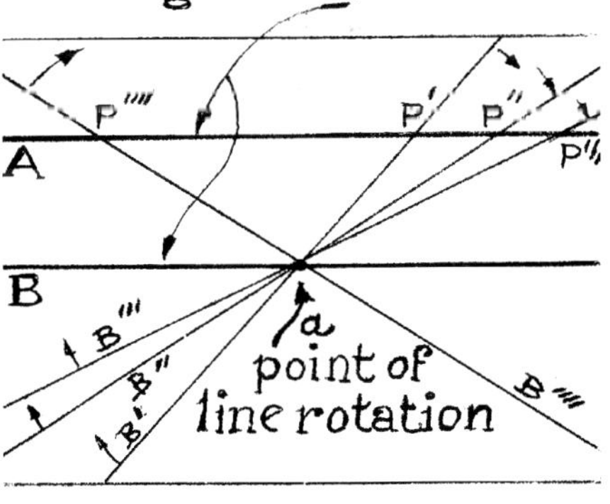

Three-Dimensional Example

The person blowing a bubble sees the outward unfolding
of form growing endlessly larger. The form is *positive* and
radiates in all directions towards the infinite. Then,
instantly reversing itself, it completely *surrounds* the
figure, who sees it now as a *negative* form.

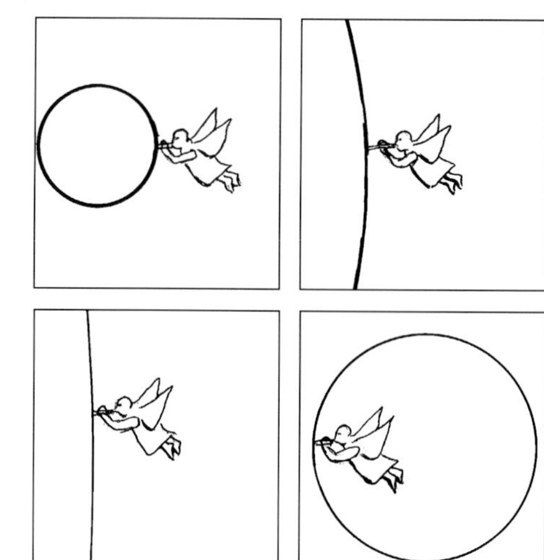

Emotional Implications Arising from the Theory of Form Concepts

In daily life, we often experience emotional reactions
upon seeing various form qualities.

For example, consider a gathering of people in which all
seem lethargic, bored, pessimistic, dull and hopeless.
Suddenly someone enters, full of spirit and vigor. He
may be full-bodied with rounded cheeks and in fine
health. He is stimulating, enthusiastic, optimistic and full
of creative ideas. He seems to fill the room to overflowing
with an excess of energy. He brings desirable *positive*
qualities to the *negative-neutral,* undesirable condition in
this depressed atmosphere.

Another example: When we see an ill person with
sunken cheeks and chest, a body that is hollow and
collapsed, skin over bones, we are affected emotionally.
The situation arouses a desire to "give" from our own
energy enough to restore health or at least establish a
neutral condition.

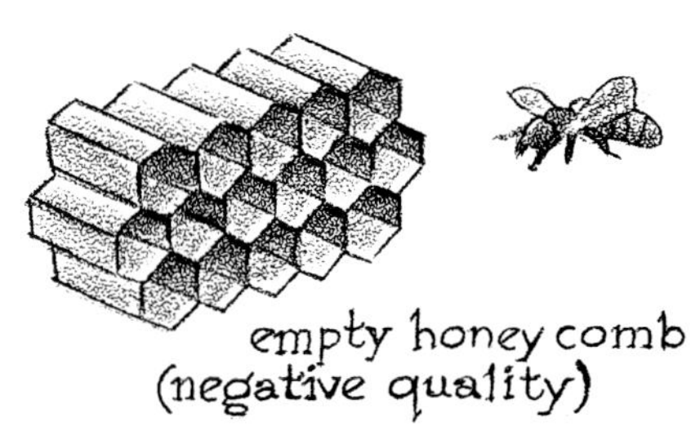

empty honey comb
(negative quality)

Sculptural forms that have hollow surfaces create
negative reactions, as in the collapsed cheeks, which
relate to the collapsed cube planes of the demonstration
instrument.

Imagine entering an unoccupied apartment building
where the hollow or negative spaces echo one's footsteps.
In its dim light we feel lonely and sucked in: the opposite
of feeling full and alive. The walls seem neither to give
nor take, because of their *neutral* character, which results
in one's emotional feeling of being spiritually in
suspense. We feel that we cannot get out of this place fast
enough.

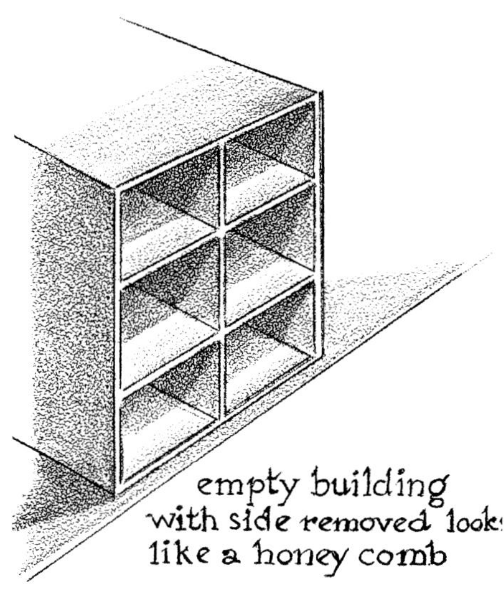

empty building
with side removed looks
like a honey comb

Form Theory tells us that looking at *negative* forms seems
to make us *feel* in *negative* terms, even if a sort of morbid
fascination may attract us. Empty, unfinished buildings,
open honeycomb cells, volcanoes, deep wells, caves, etc.
arouse *negative feelings* as if something is "lacking;" and,
of course, such a mood can be deliberately created in this
way if the artist sees fit to do so.

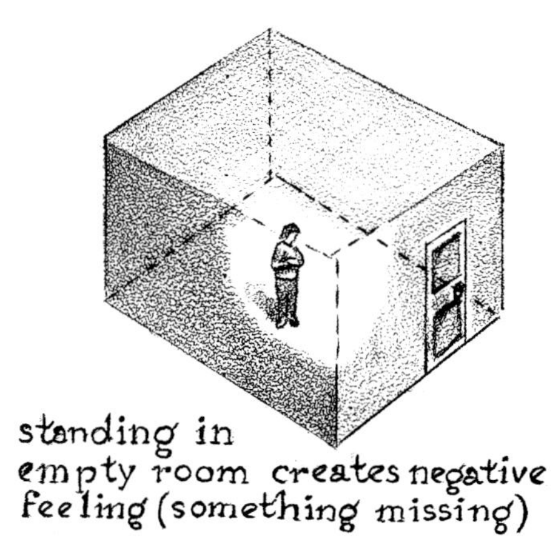

standing in
empty room creates negative
feeling (something missing)

An example of transfiguration and metamorphosis: Consider the person who is blowing a soap bubble. He feels that the single bubble is a beautiful thing. But when two bubbles join together, the combination injects a new element. A *neutral flat plane* between them detracts from the pure positive character of the single sphere. As more bubbles join together, they ultimately become foam, with only a positive texture over an unshapely mass. In the process of seeing the transfiguration of a single bubble into foam, our emotional response to form becomes more and more complex. The experience creates progressively a *blend* of feelings, until we lose track and witness the final formless mass.

Dictionary definition of the word *transfiguration*: to alter radically, to glorify, to change an outward form of appearance, to make glorious and idealize. Somewhat similarly, the word *metamorphosis* means the passing of one form or shape into another.

Should the meaning of the word *transfiguration* leave us in a state of suspense and desirous of a more satisfactory means to measure its value, modern instrumentation by way of the camera can come to our aid, allowing our eyes to pictorially witness nature's phenomena of transfiguration.

one soap bubble

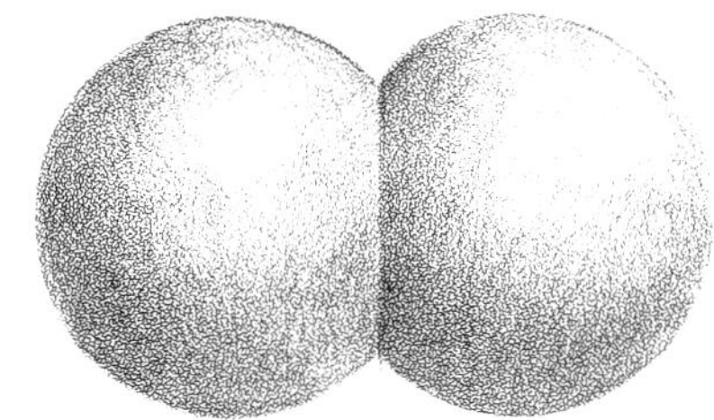

two bubbles

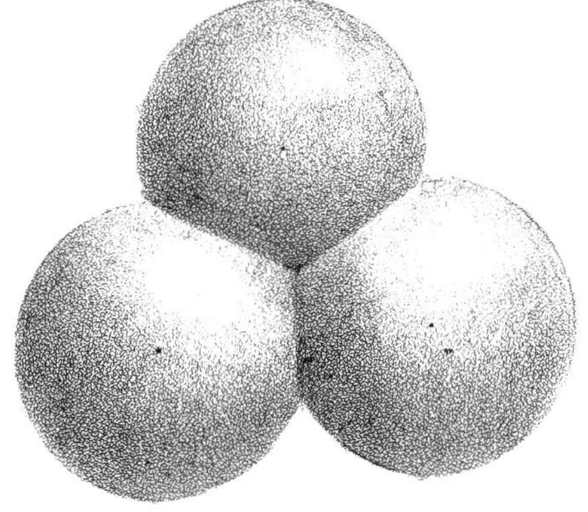

three bubbles

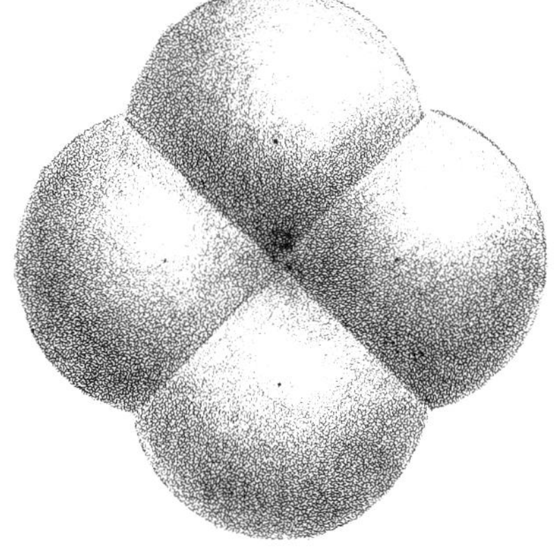

four bubbles

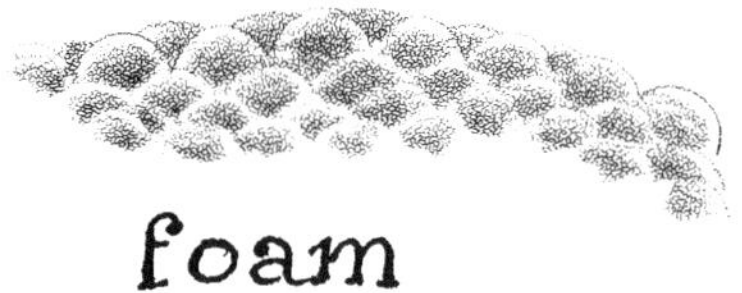

foam

Using the Camera as a Tool in Form Study

Demonstrations show that instrumentation can make abstractions *visible.* This can be seen in the camera recordings of light refracted from water drops. (See the space convolution photo illustrations at right.) We can see nature's invisible forms through these light refractions. These invisible forms, discovered and recorded by the camera, can help the artist, if he feels himself walled-in by the storytelling qualities of the real, visible world, to extend his power of visualization and to remove possible mental blocks that may hold him back from conceptual thinking about the abstract world.

When the camera, out of focus, is directed at a series of drops of water that are close together (condensed on the bottom of a piece of glass) and which sparkle in the sunlight, that sharp, direct light refracts them into three-dimensional intersections in the camera's focal plane. Those images will move at the slightest change of lens positioning, enabling us to watch one isolated portion of the design become its own opposite as the lens travels. The camera thus makes visible that which we have tried to understand in our approach to abstract thinking. We come to see that when a visible curvature flattens out and reaches the infinite, it suddenly reverses itself into its opposite. As indicated before, though man cannot visualize the infinite itself, his reasoning can *direct* him along lines of logic toward it.

Recordings of *spacial convolutions* can be used by the student in order to increase his ability to visualize form abstractions. In his attempts at seeing forms in his mind's eye, he may well succeed in cultivating clear visions of what he wishes to carve or model, without needing actual models. A sharpened ability to see things in his mind's eye helps him to create visualizations of what he *feels.* As a result, his work may well radiate the "mood" of that feeling in the sculpture form assemblies he produces.

Philosophical Implications

In sculpture, *mood* has come to connote the *blend* of all the separate and various forms with which man has shaped his compositions.

In my opinion, since nature's forces reach man's perception demonstrably through Form Theory, man's creations can be no more than his rapport with those forces as expressed through his art.

Remember, when we speak of the arts and sciences we do well to search for the truth directly and indirectly, with a universal yardstick that reaches inwardly as well as outwardly toward infinity, encompassing all that is negative and all that is positive, in combination. Truth, being all-encompassing, leaves us no other choice.

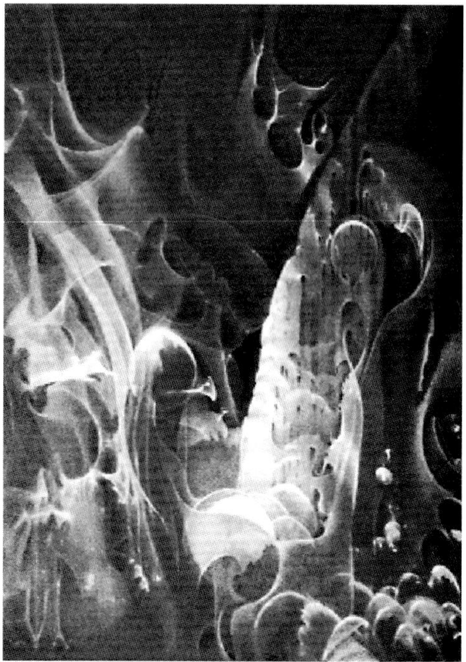

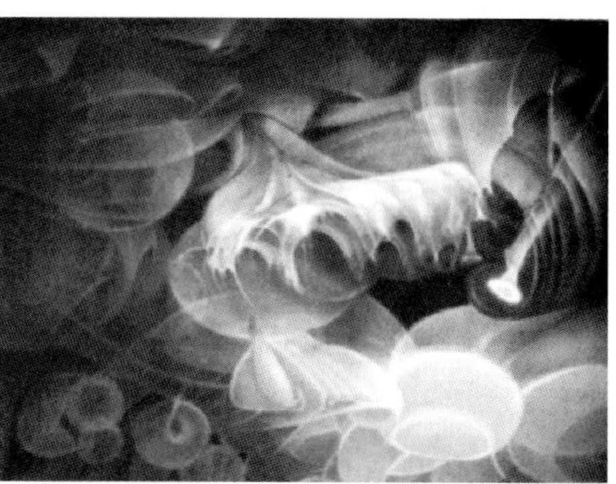

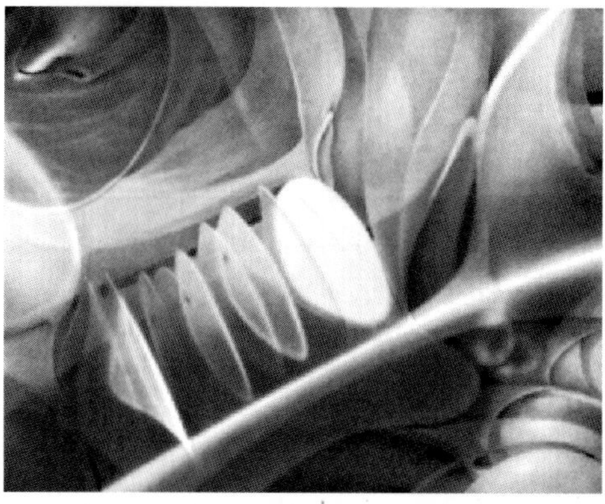

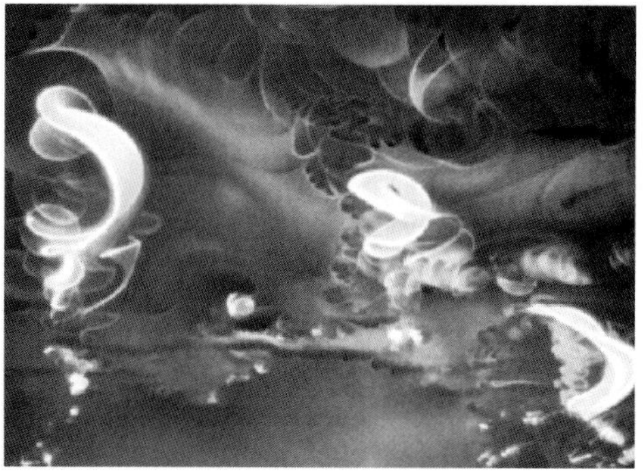

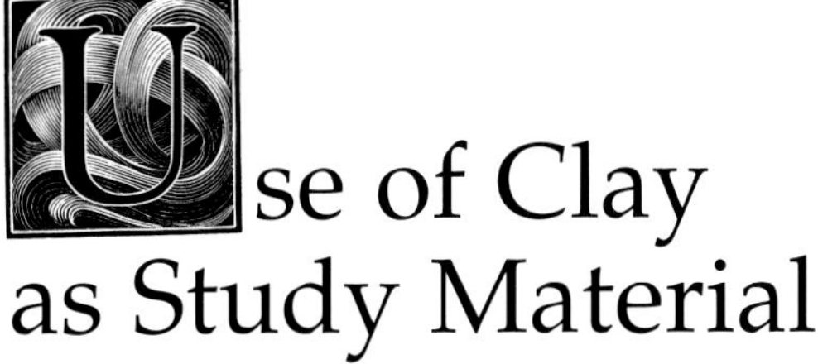

Chapter 3

Use of Clay as Study Material

The two major kinds of clay used for modeling are *Plastelina*, an oil base clay of such quality that it never needs reconstituting and grows better with use (see testing as shown), and *water clay*, which is cheaper and useful as a study material but needs upkeep.

Reconditioning Water Clay

The ideal consistency for water clay is soft, but not so soft that it sticks to the hands. Should the clay become too dry to model, it must be allowed to become absolutely *cork dry* before it can be reconditioned by soaking in water, since water will not penetrate the surface of partially dry clay. Once dried, it acts the way hard, dry earth does when it absorbs the first rains of the season. The water will make the surfaces open and will gradually seep through layer after layer until all of the clay has fluffed up. A smoothed clay layer is often used as a sealer in water storage pools.

When I worked to earn my tuition as a monitor in the Chicago School of Sculpture in 1930, I devised a way to save myself the grueling work of keeping the clay in perfect modeling condition.

In the classroom was a two-compartment, zinc-lined clay bin soldered water-tight. The dried work-pieces in the class were taken apart, dried completely, then broken up into walnut-sized pieces. One half of the bin was filled with these, then quickly flooded with hot water until the water covered the mass up to the top. Half an hour later all the water was absorbed and, taking off my shoes and standing bare-legged in the clay, I jumped up and down with my feet, utilizing the weight of my body, until the clay was evenly reconditioned and ready for use. Meanwhile, the next batch of discarded clay would gradually be collected and dried in the other half of the bin.

For very large projects (ten feet tall or larger), the clay model had to be enveloped each night in a balloon-like cotton sheet. To keep the model moist, clay and sheet were sprayed with water. (In the old days we used oil-cloth for smaller pieces. Today plastic is used and the clay figure itself wetted down just before wrapping.)

How to Model in Clay

Illustrations overleaf demonstrate the procedure.

Note particularly the importance of *avoiding* the temptation to use hand and finger movements that *scoop* the clay. Instead, the *acquired* technique is to

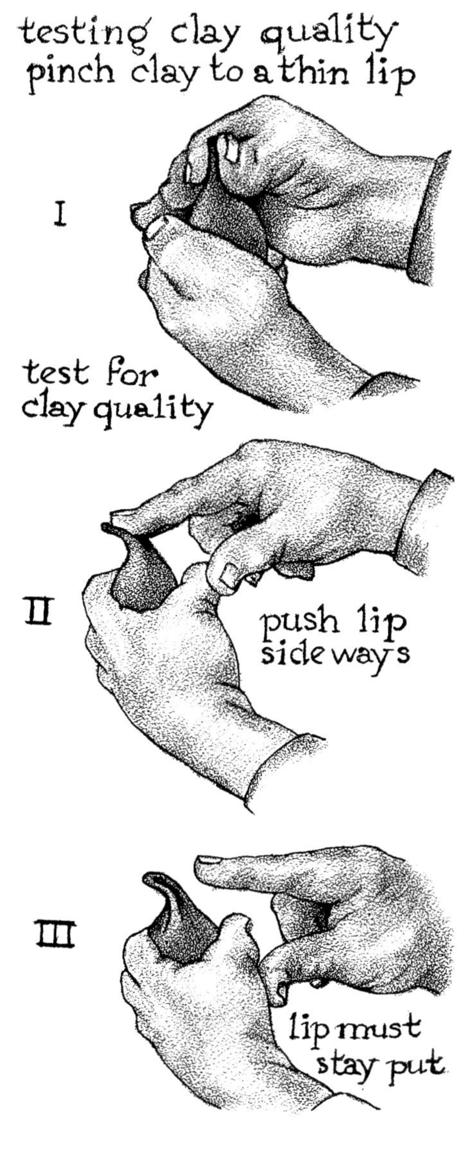

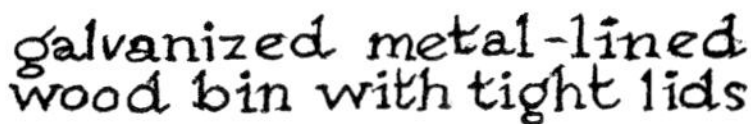

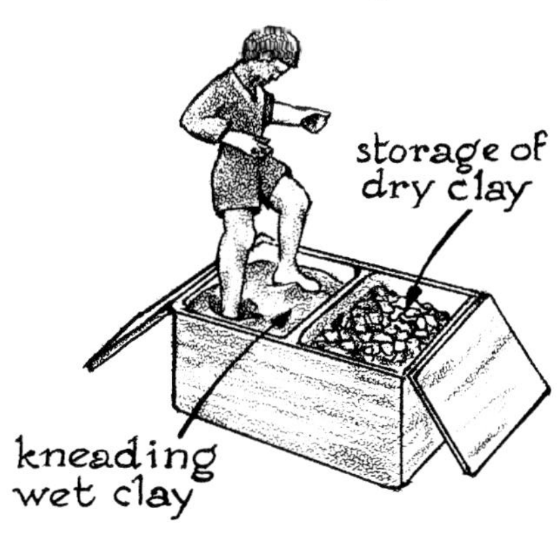

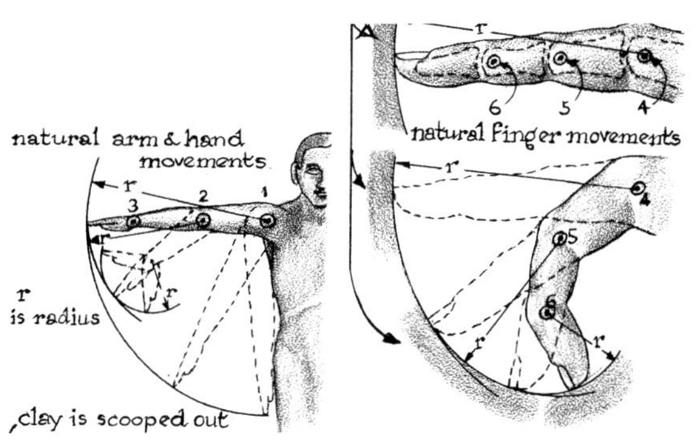

move the hand and fingers in a *rolling motion* (which also should be used when manipulating modeling tools). This is a "key" movement when modeling.

Once this acquired technique has become second nature, building up with *clay pellets* will prove to be a direct and time-saving way of working. This method is demonstrated in the photos of sculpture portraits (see page 25). This method was accepted by such old masters as Michaelangelo, whose over life-size, marble **Day** was first sketched in a small clay figure in this manner. Some claim that this clay sketch was done by a student *after* Michaelangelo's finished marble. Either way, the modeling technique in that period seems to be the same as recommended today. Once the method has been perfected, the resulting clay sketches become accurate for measuring, when one is duplicating and enlarging projects.

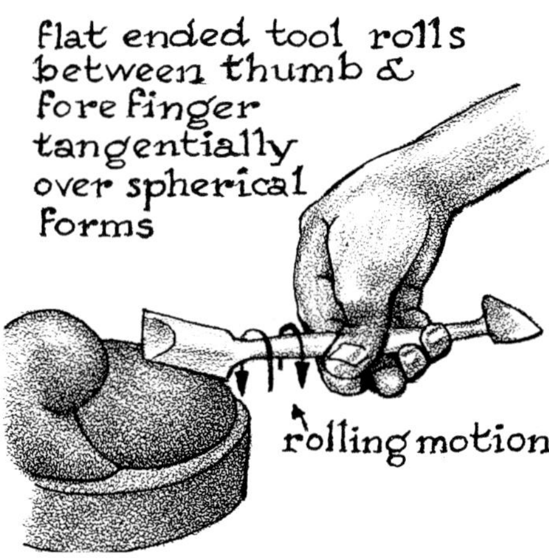

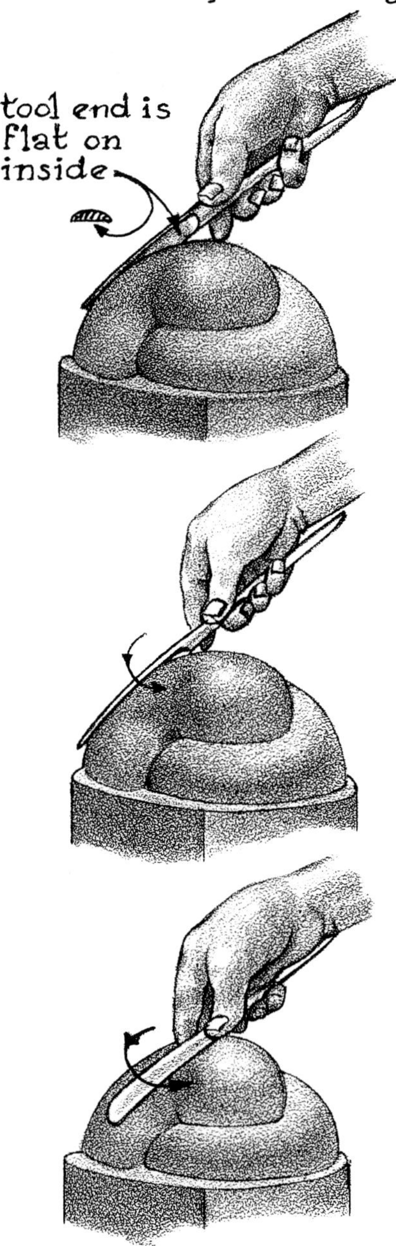

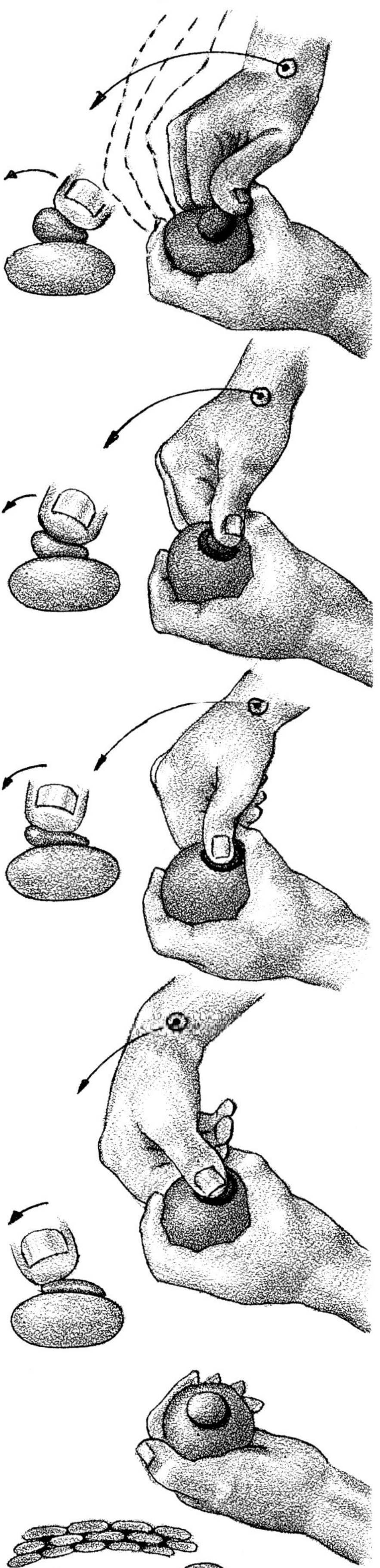

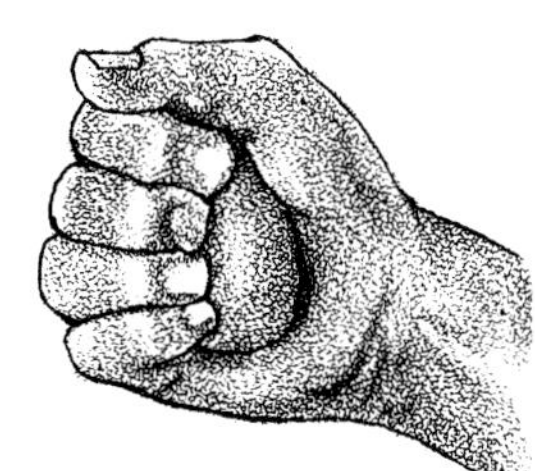

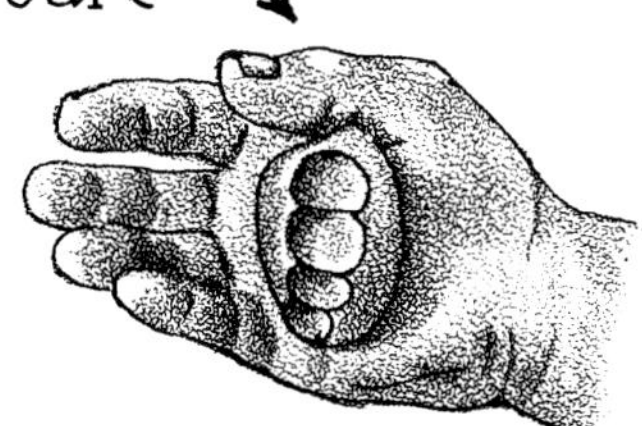

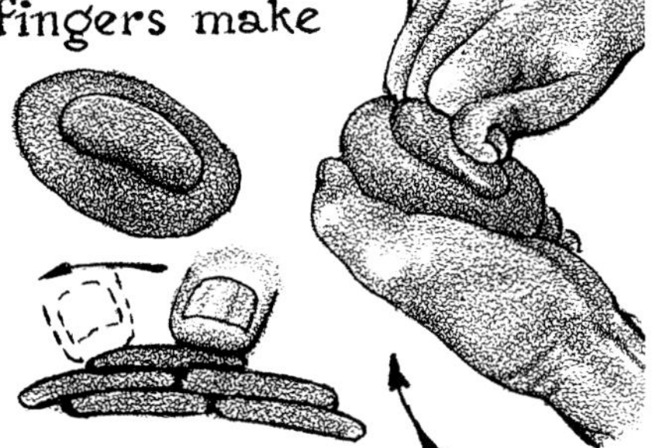

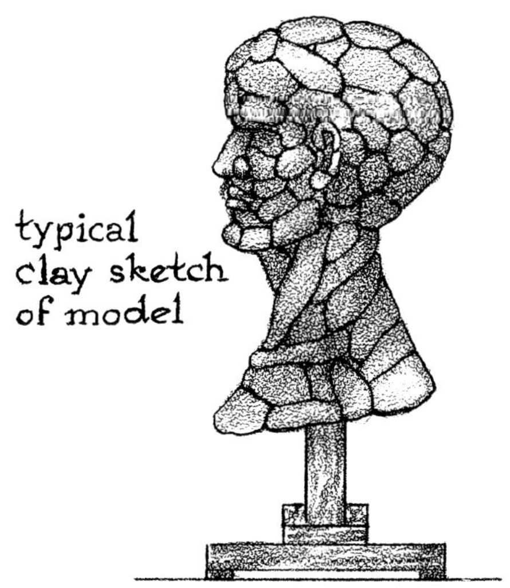

clay pieces are pressed down
just enough to make them
stick together without
smearing all into a smooth
surface

this final sketch, if
correct in all features
is accurate for future
needed measurements

How to Model the Human Figure

A practical armature is used. The aluminum sculpture wire cable is bent to meet the recognizable silhouette lines of the figure. Clay is applied to fill out the required areas step-by-step. The size of the pellets are gradually reduced the closer one gets to the final surface.

This procedure in modeling the human figure should be practiced extensively in life classes until the student overcomes the obstacles that may confuse him. Practice and more practice, self-discipline and persistence will reward him in the end. The sooner he reaches the point of control in clay modeling, the longer he will be able to cash in on the facility it gives him for the remainder of his life. No longer will he be hampered by hit-and-miss guessing. Once this modeling skill has been mastered, the final step begins: the study of human anatomy, geared especially to the artist's need (see chapter 16).

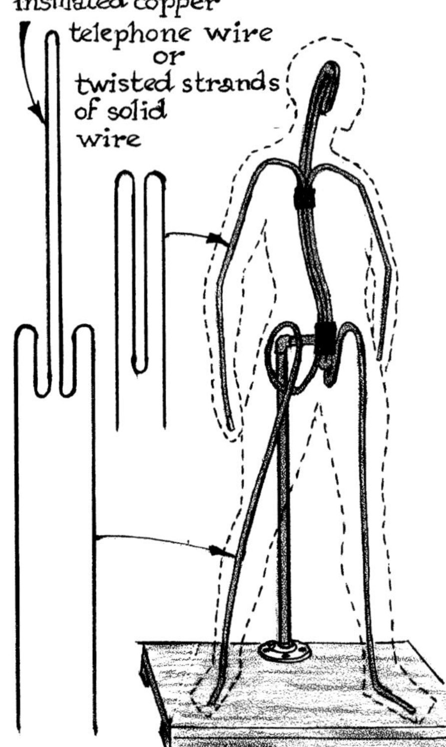

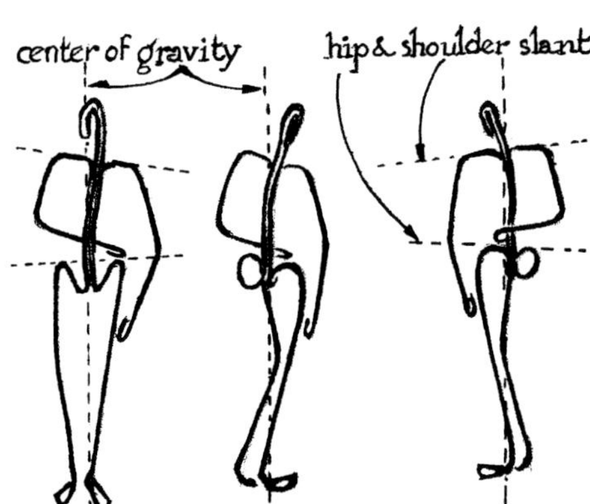

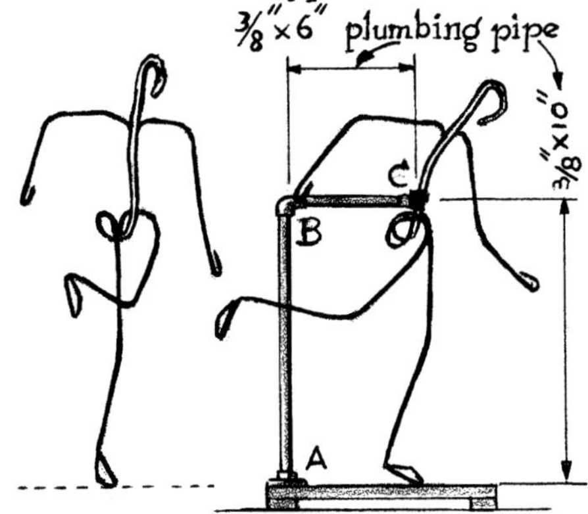

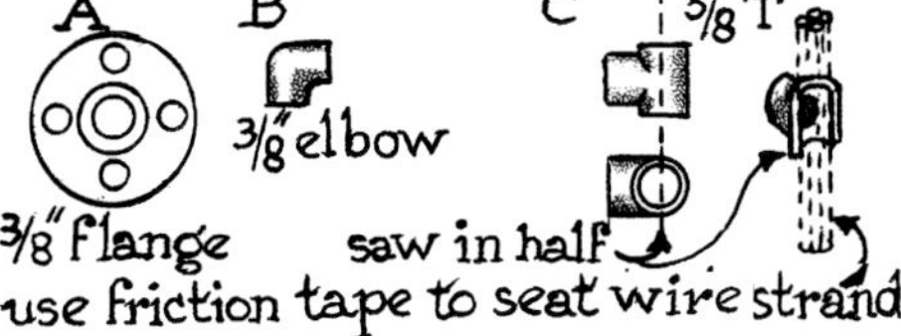

Warning against Taking Shortcuts

The student may be tempted to take a big lump of clay and squeeze it this way and that into shapes resembling the final model. He will be inviting trouble since such actions will result in time-consuming repairs of errors spread all over the figure. It is a waste of time to model complicated human body forms this way, especially when the body stance is asymmetrical. In the *big-lump* squeezing approach, no matter how we try to repair mistakes, each one affects others adversely. Modeling by squeezing the clay suggests that we have not as yet understood what clay, as material, demands of us: that we should *let it grow from the inside out*, as opposed to stone, which is worked, chip by chip, from the outside inward.

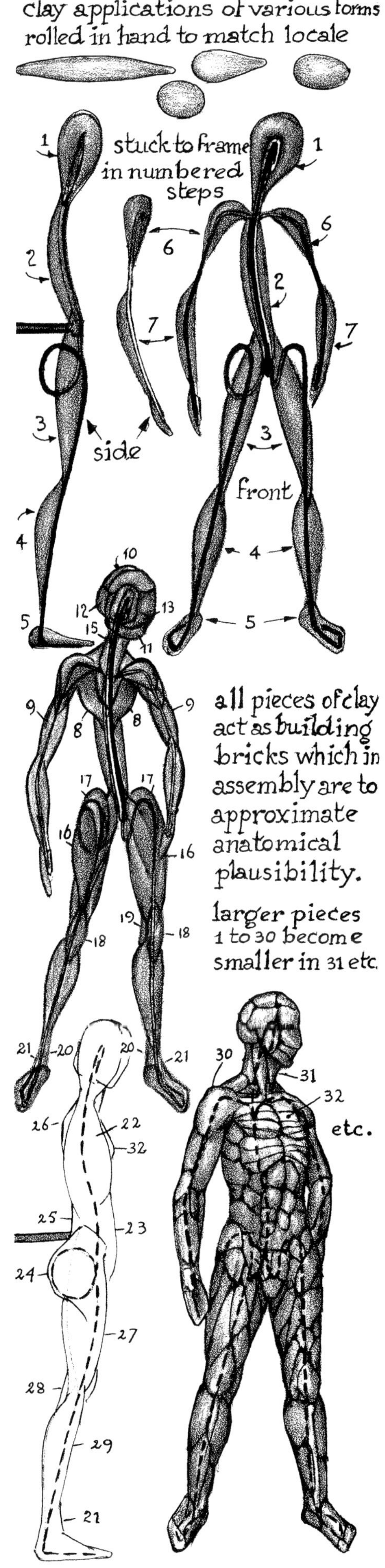

Making Clay-Modeling Tools

The wooden tools used are simple and quite easy to make. Pear wood and most close-grain fruit wood, Toyon, and Madrone are good types of wood from which to make clay modeling tools. Useful wood varieties can probably be found in your own locale, as native plants or in nearby orchards. All citrus wood, for example, is very good, as it is fine-grained and strong.

Once the tool is dry, correctly shaped, and sanded down, it should be sealed. Although moisture from water clay swells up the tool's surface during modeling, which seals it against further water penetration, it is a good idea to dry it once more and sand it down gently with a fine-grain sandpaper. Heat the surface over a flame (just short of scorching), then dip it in olive oil. This causes the oil to penetrate in a vacuum action as the surface cools, drawing the thinned oil into the wood pores. You can meet your needs inexpensively by learning to make your own tools.

The only complication in the making of wire-end tools is how to anchor the wire into the tool shank. (See illustration on next page.) Wire tools are used to remove clay. Grooves can be cut into the ends and used to create the texture of the claw tool used in stone carving.

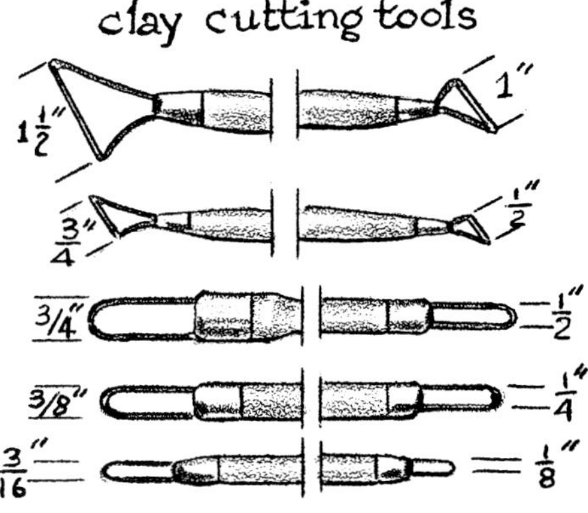

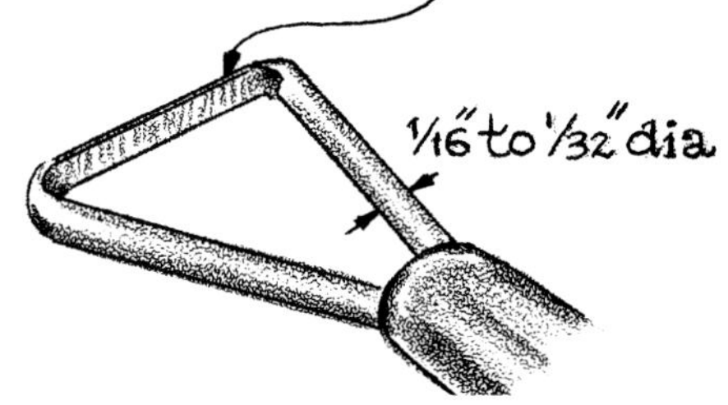

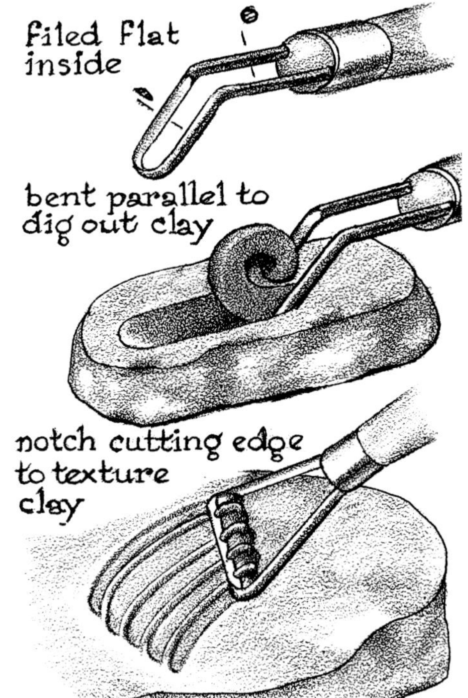

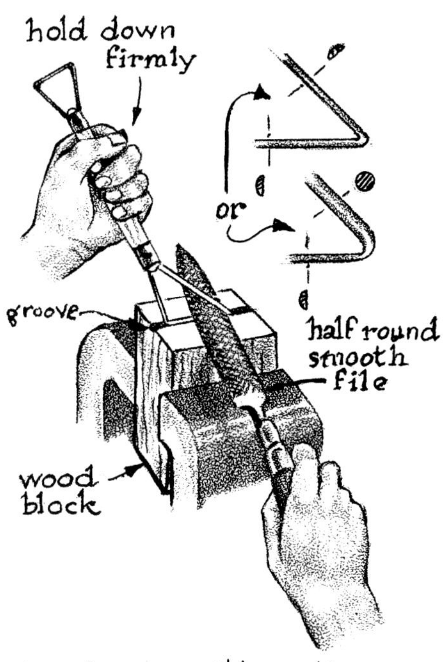

assembled tool placed
in groove & filed with
sharp cutting edges
hold down
firmly
or
groove
half round
smooth
file
wood
block

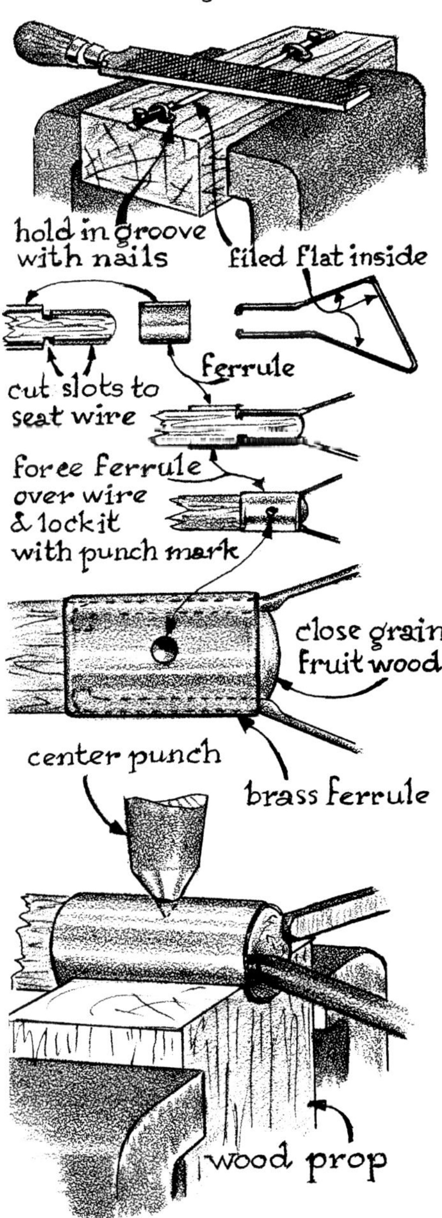

bend wire with 2 pliers
after filing
hold in groove
with nails
filed flat inside
cut slots to
seat wire
ferrule
force ferrule
over wire
& lock it
with punch mark
close grain
fruit wood
center punch
brass ferrule
wood prop

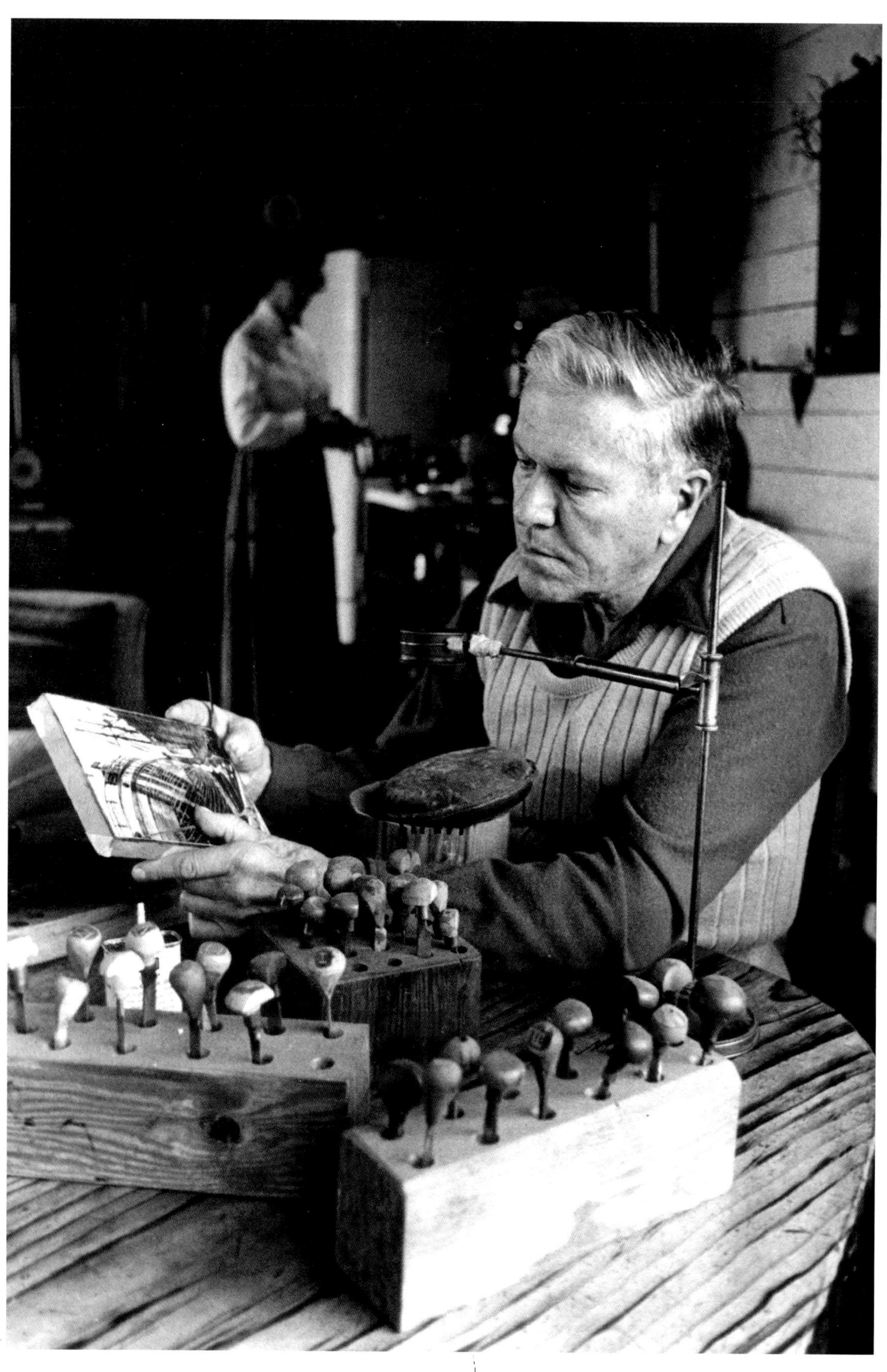

Alex with one of his fine engraved wood blocks and with a selection of 30
or more hand forged gravers.

ompound Forms, Three-Dimensional Perspective, Textures & Design

Compound Forms

When several dynamic forms spring from one base and their variously directed extensions are assembled, they create compound forms with compound surfaces. Many illustrations show details of the human body as *compound form assemblies* (faces, joints of arms, legs, parts of the torso).

Single muscles and fatty deposits make up form combinations of body parts that are anatomically recognizable. Throughout this book, examples show variations in compositions that use *dynamic abstract* forms. Once an artist clearly understands *Form Theory*, he can see endless possibilities in composing.

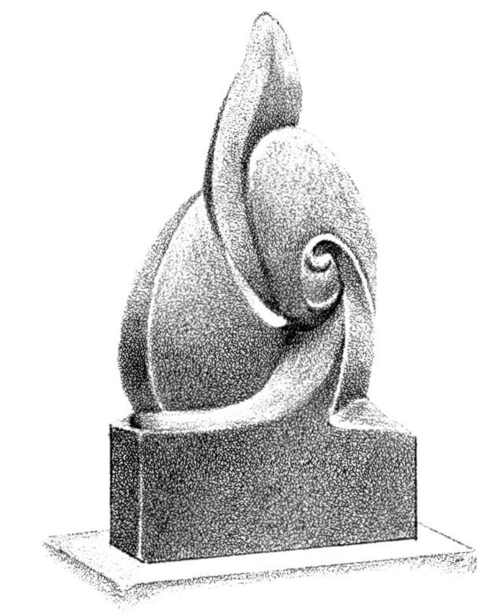

assignment: carve from a 1½"x 6"x 11" piece of wood three abstract forms with positive planes on 1 side & neg. on reverse

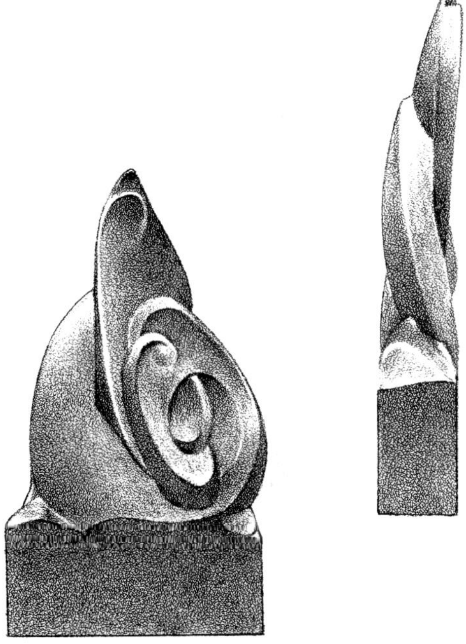

forms are dynamic & plane texture is neutral
uncarved part of the block acts as the base

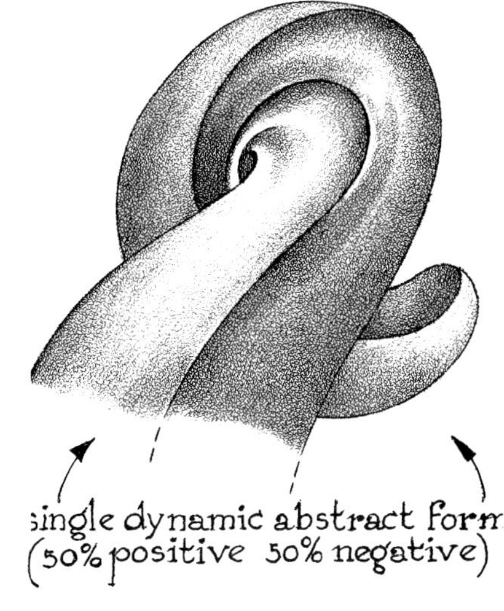

single dynamic abstract form (50% positive 50% negative)

Among the human body's compound form interweavings and interlockings, the individual forms in an assembly maintain their own character, although each one in these blends may flow from the same beginning.

Overlaid skin should not "eat" into individual form walls (see illustration). Picture a skin spread thinly over the muscles and fat deposits, like a clinging wet garment.

Warning: We must learn what the correct forms *below* the skin look like and understand these positions and relationships of muscles, fatty deposits, tendons, and bones; and how hair, skin and drapery may cover them.

Drapery over Body Forms

When the human figure calls for drapery in a composition, the clay modeler too often makes the figure look as if it had fallen into water and emerged with the cloth clinging to the skin. Its streaky crisscrossing folds exaggerate the drapery effect, and the anatomy of the body shows too obviously, which distracts from the *mood* the artist aimed to evoke. Beautiful body forms are most aesthetic when they are *subtly suggested* under nonclinging drapery.

Example: *The Triptych* (page 123). This low relief carving in lemon wood demonstrates how its spiritual mood is enhanced by the suggestion of only the most essential body forms and stance below heavy drapery. Here the drapery is like a blanket hanging tangentially over the protruding portions of bodies underneath it. Body parts suggest their unseen extensions. As a rule, such suggestions are enough to maintain and communicate the *mood* of the body as desired. Paradoxically, "hiding can become showing." (In order to convey reverence, this piece demanded subtle body forms. No jarring physical exaggeration was allowed to interfere with the subject's storytelling, spiritual quality.)

An Experiment as an Assignment

Make a model of a nude in clay and pour over it a fairly thick mixture of plaster, being sure to reach all the smaller cavities. The result of this coating is a much softened figure that subtly reveals all that it was meant to express; and it is often more beautiful to the viewer than the original explicitly detailed display of body parts, no matter how anatomically correct and sharply modeled.

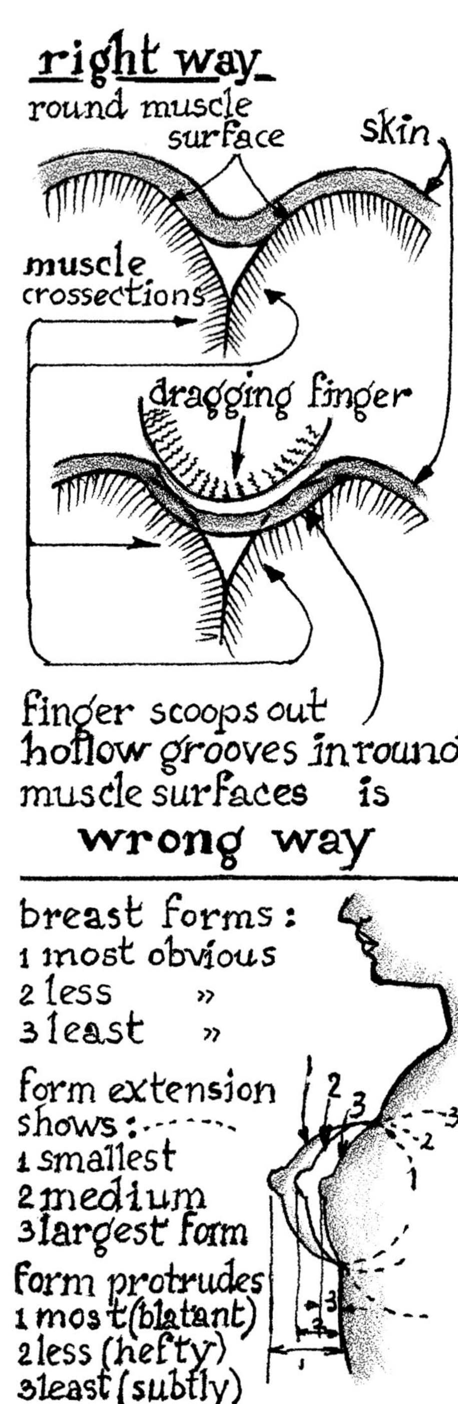

Compound Form Combinations in Abstract Form Assemblies

1. The upside-down hull of a ship shows its *positive* form extensions along the rib lines, which are infinity-directed. The hull forms between stem, midship and stern, and all find their origin in the keel.

2. In the low-relief carving of a box lid in tropical hardwood, various *compound forms* in the stylized face allow free play with plausible anatomy, all form detail interweaving and interlocking (page 45).

Compound Forms Combined with Three-Dimensional Perspective

Form perspective in a pyramid shown lying on its side can fool the viewer's eye. Various cross sections, in our successive views of these forms, seem to move farther and farther away to a vanishing point (the tip of the pyramid) at the horizon. This form perspective principle gives the sculptor a chance to create three-dimensional optical illusions that he submits to the viewer (e.g., as in the composition *Abel*, described on page 50).

Textures on Form Surfaces

Unpolished, smooth, dull surfaces are *neutral* in texture. In dull white they show form at its best under overhead diffused light. Highly polished white surfaces, on the other hand, acquire shiny or reflecting highlights which detract from the form itself.

Many beginners in clay modeling spend too much time creating elaborate rough textures on form surfaces. Impressed by the tool tracks on stone carvings, they often copy such textures using notched clay-modeling tools. Some imitate other materials: cloth, fish scales, wood grain. The lesser-talented modeler may try in this way to enhance his work with eye-catching textures, which can be an attempt to cover up form mediocrity.

Very rough textures tend to obscure good form, which, in turn, causes a loss of intended mood.

During direct carving, the wood-carving gouge and stone carving chisels leave their natural tool textures.

In stone carvings, the cutting edges of the fine-tooth claw chisel may leave a velvety surface appearance (see *Ondine* on page 122). Michaelangelo's *Victoria*, in which the man's face is left unpolished, is an example.

When hired craftsmen/duplicators made 19th century marble carvings, they would often be instructed by their artist employers to *texture* the base with the one-point tool to make the statue appear as if it were done in direct carving and had arisen out of the block carved by the artist himself. But the duplicator, because he lacked the inherent spontaneity of direct carving, could only leave a stilted regularity of texture on one part of the statue: its base.

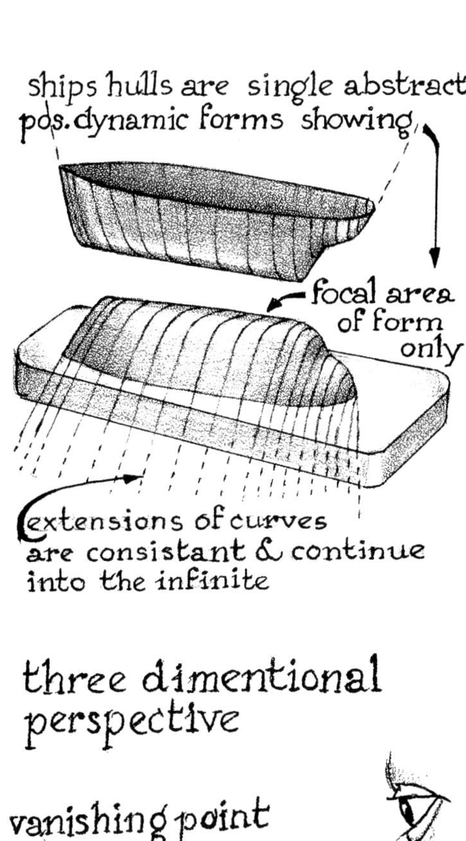

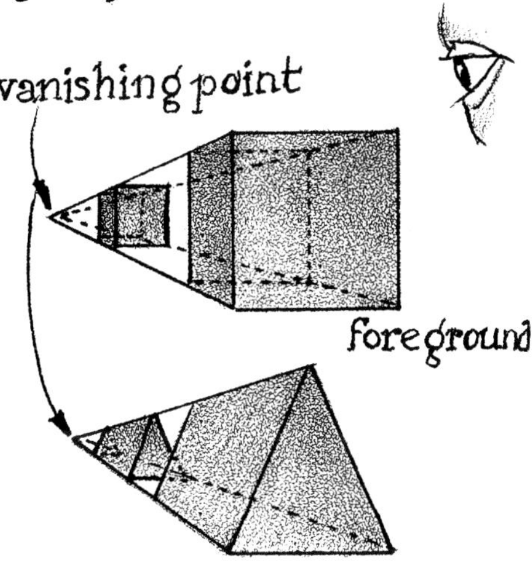

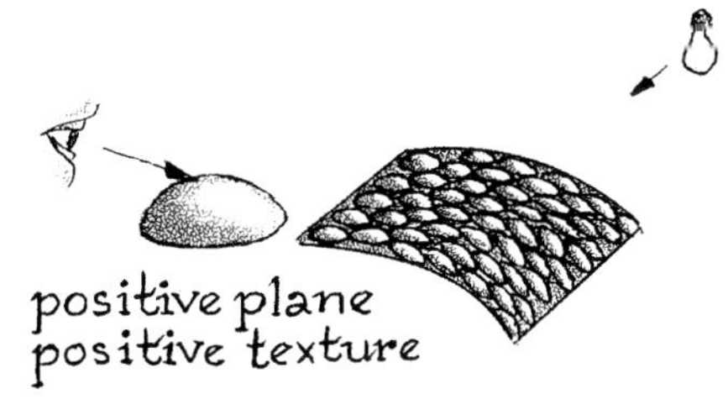

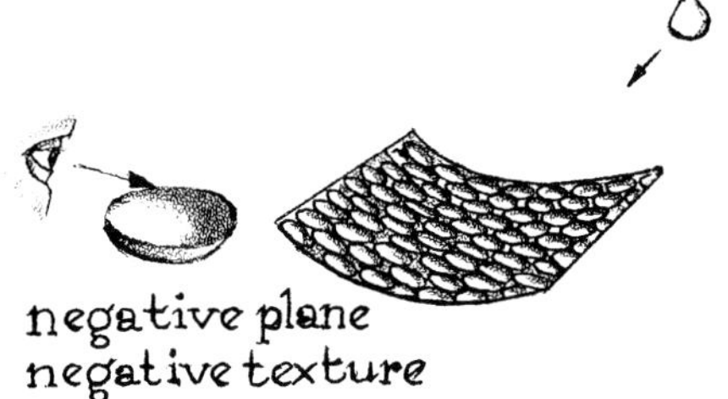

Design

This is a word misused, abused, and overrated by most artists and art critics, who consider it an art cure-all.

I find that "design" is simply an automatic spin-off from inherent and inborn talents, an unstudied ability applied to self-expression in all art media. Inventive design application may serve in the making of industrial and commercial artifacts and utilitarian products: packaging, automobile shapes, household gadgets. The more attractively a thing is "designed," the greater its sales value.

Natures designs are seen in cloud formations, gnarled tree trunks, sand-blasted rocks and weatherworn driftwood. All have resulted from the workings of unseen self-governing forces.

Page 22 (regarding spacial convolutions) show *nature's* designs made visible by the camera. These could be a gold mine of design sources for those who are drawn to kaleidoscopic-type phenomena. In these, the meaning of the word *design* may find a more tangible concept, and its range of possibilities may be greatly extended.

I once witnessed a Javanese woman batik-designer prepare a cloth for a scarf. Her black "lining" pencil kept contact with the material until she had filled every portion with design patterns. Muslim mosques are extensively decorated with patterns in geometric arrangements as fill-space where walls, columns and floors seem to have tempted the artists to leave no space unfilled.

The student should consider whether his art studies warrant a special study of design. He too may come to the conclusion that emphasis on design study as a serious art specialty is overblown. In art endeavors, design is an ever-present integral part of the process; there is no need to treat it separately.

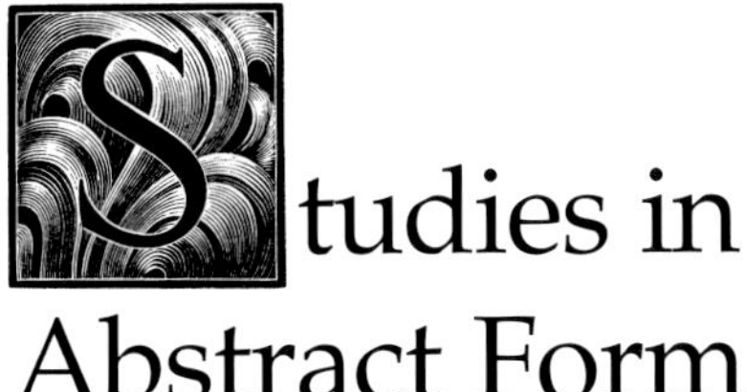

Chapter 5

Studies in Abstract Form

The making of abstract form compositions (those without any storytelling quality) may trouble one student more than another. He should make it his first effort to overcome that difficulty. It may seem impossible not to think of familiar, recognizable things; ones that tell you, "I am a flower . . . a bunch of grapes . . . a horse. . . ." Just trying *not* to think of recognizable things opens an unknown world in which one can become at first lost or confused.

The familiar things we see around us can be thought of as *form assemblies;* each *single* form, separate from the rest, constitutes one *abstract* of that assembly. Such parts (forms) are the study material referred to as *forms per se* or *form for the sake of form.* The aim is to inject the maximum esthetic value into each abstract form, multiplying that value in the final assembly.

An infinite variety of such forms can be observed. The example shows that an unopened leaf-bud or flower is actually an assembly of single petals or leaves, each separately looking like an abstract form; they are perhaps unrecognizable when detached from the whole, but when fitted together they make up the *assembly* we call a flower or bud. In a similar way, a segment of a watermelon, as a portion of the whole, is an abstract form maintaining the *form character* of the whole.

If at first your visualization and inventiveness are lacking, keep examining the tangible world all around you, and gradually your creative ideas will ignite to shape assemblies of forms in endless variety.

In these studies, discipline your thinking. Should you find yourself confused, break off your thoughts at that moment and, before proceeding further, retrace your steps until once more you feel you are on solid ground. As a rule, your first successfully completed composition will leave you better prepared for the next one. If you are working with a teacher whose constructive criticisms call for adjustments, carry them out carefully.

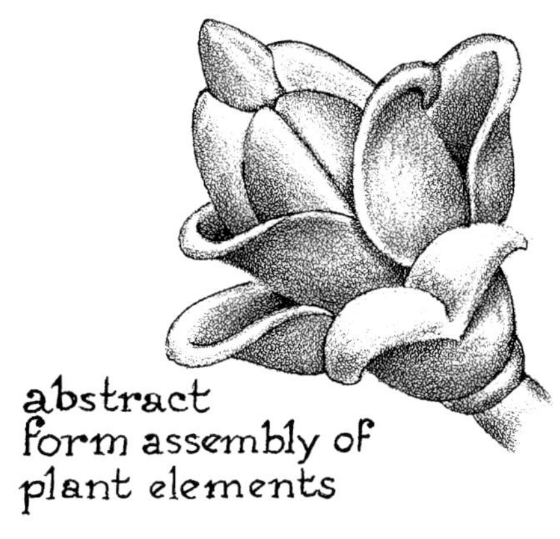

abstract
form assembly of
plant elements

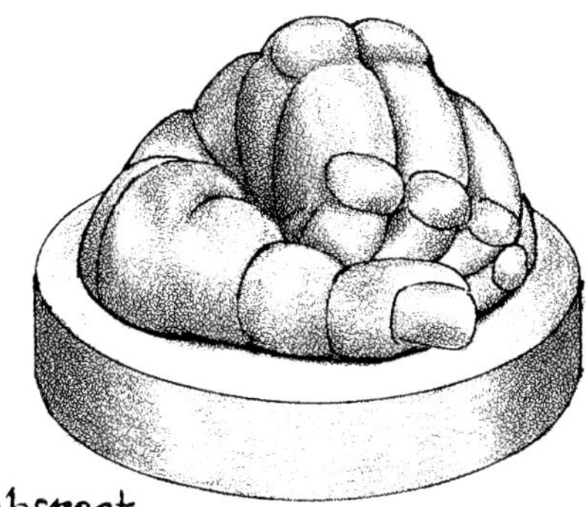

abstract
form assembly visualized
below the skin of a hand
(disregarding anatomy)

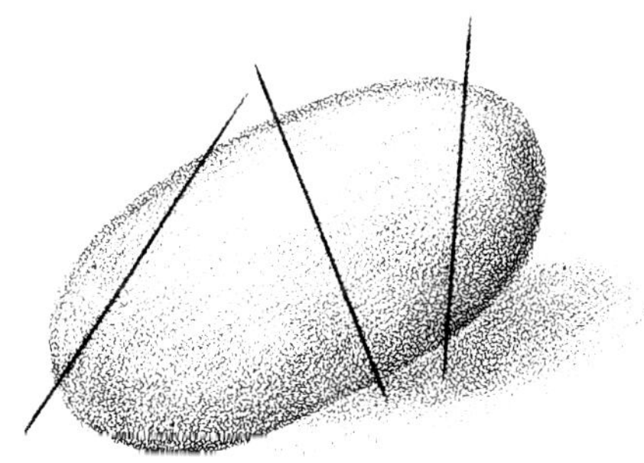

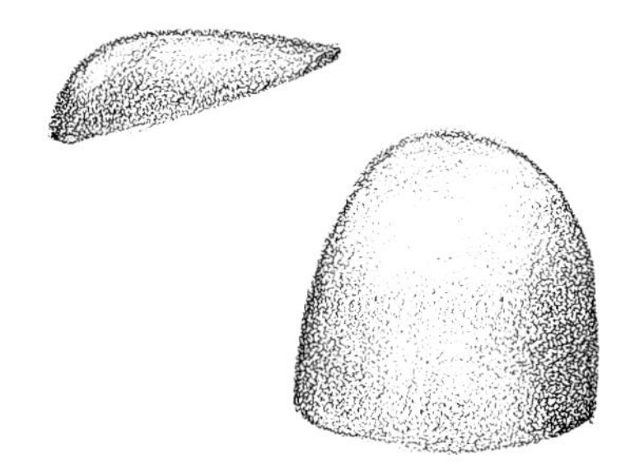

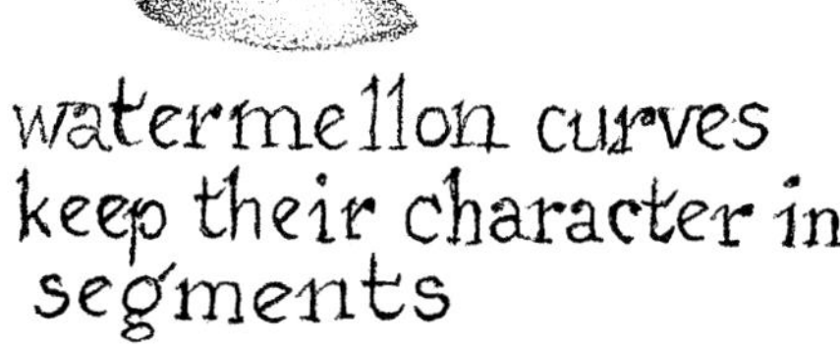

watermellon curves
keep their character in
segments

Study Assignments in Abstract Form
Modeling Clay Used as a Study Material

Use water clay or oil-based Plastelina of a light gray color and medium hardness.

Water clay is less expensive, but it needs to be kept moist, especially when it is used in great quantity. (See illustration.) It is most responsive to the touch when it is softest, just short of sticking to the fingers.

Plastelina of good quality grows better the more it is used because use causes its granules to become finer and finer. It is long-lasting, takes little upkeep, and is best when kept clean and at room temperature. It is more expensive than water clay but, in the long run, it is worth the investment.

As explained in Chapter 3, page 23, it is important that the *natural* hand movements be *avoided* when clay is modeled into spherical forms. Correct hand movements, once acquired, become second nature to the modeler.

At first, no clay modeling tools are to be used. It is only when the final surface or minute detail is worked on that tools should be used as shown.

General requisites for all of the following assignments:

a. The forms should not be separated from one another. (They should intersect one another sharply.)

b. The forms are to have *consistent* curves and direction and maintain continuity of character.

c. The forms in assembly must belong together in such a way that the withdrawal of one would not leave the rest out of balance and unsuccessful as a single form composition.

d. When viewed at eye level from all around, one form should at no time be entirely blotted out by the others.

e. The final surface texture of the forms is to be smooth (meaning dull and neutral).

f. The base should set off the composition, as a frame does a picture.

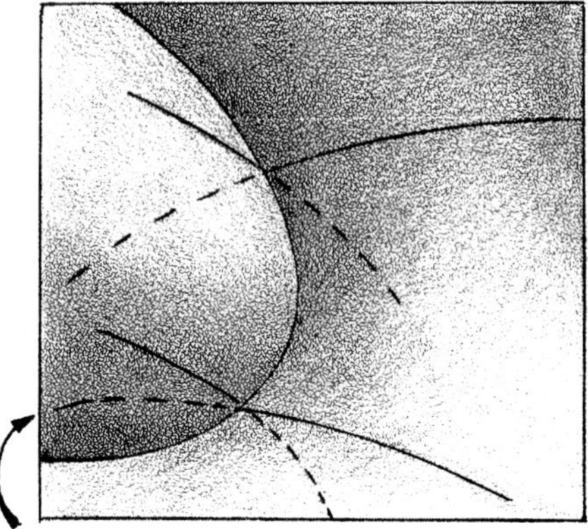

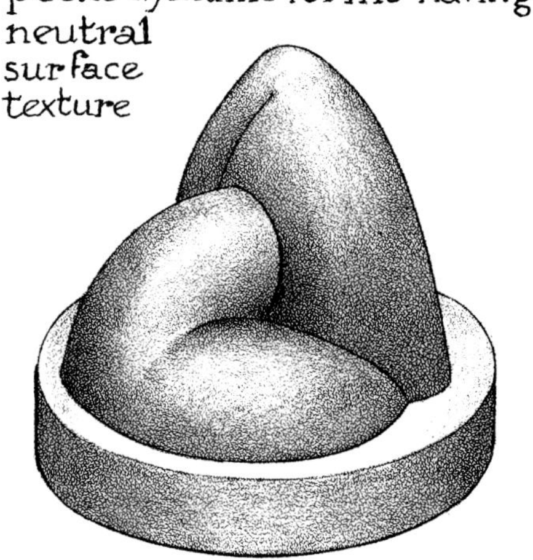

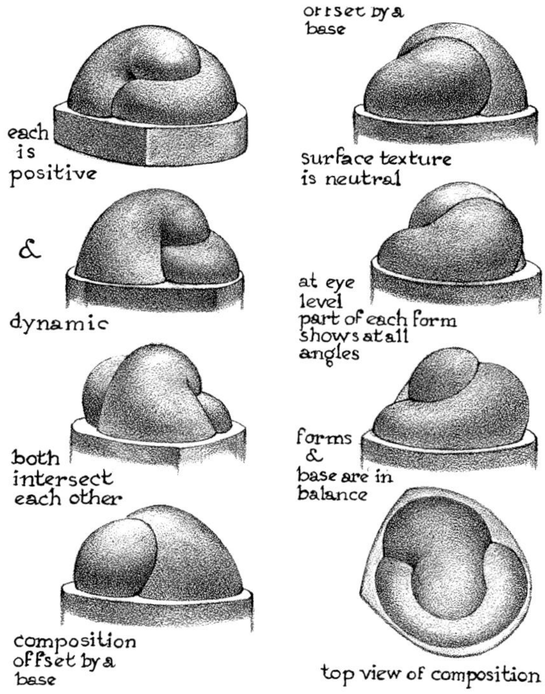

Positive Forms

1. Make a composition of *two* abstract forms placed on a base. Each form is to be *positive* and *dynamic* in character, both having the same bulk. Follow the general requisites for all assignments.

2. Make a composition of *three* abstract forms set off by a base. Each form is to be *positive* and *dynamic* in character.

The illustrations aim to clarify how to proceed. But the student should use his own ideas of form shapes and make them as different as possible from the ones shown.

The student will soon be able to criticize his own work through self-teaching. For example, he will learn that the greater the number of single forms there is in a composition, the more difficult it is to see the forms, or their parts, from each viewing angle. With this knowledge he will be better able to create compositions that will be viewed from all around, such as group figure statues and sculpture in public parks. The idea should be to give the viewer the desire to walk around the sculpture.

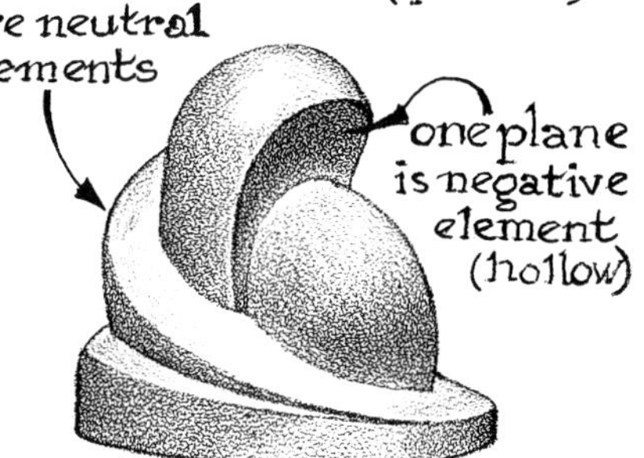

each form is
predominantly
positive

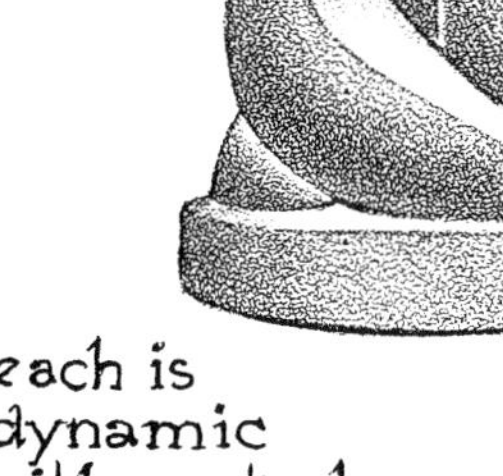

each is
dynamic
with neutral
surface
texture

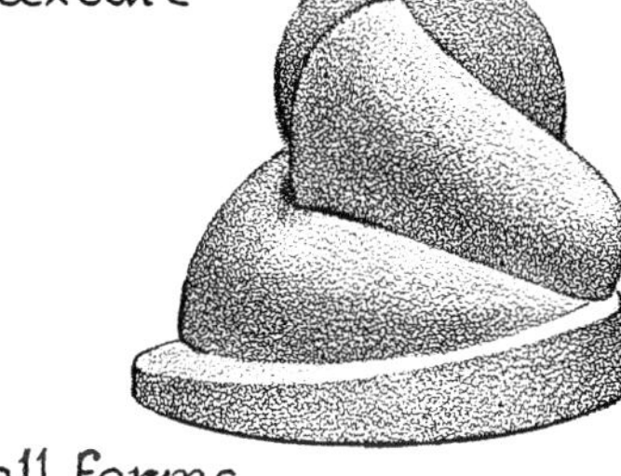

all forms
intersect each
other

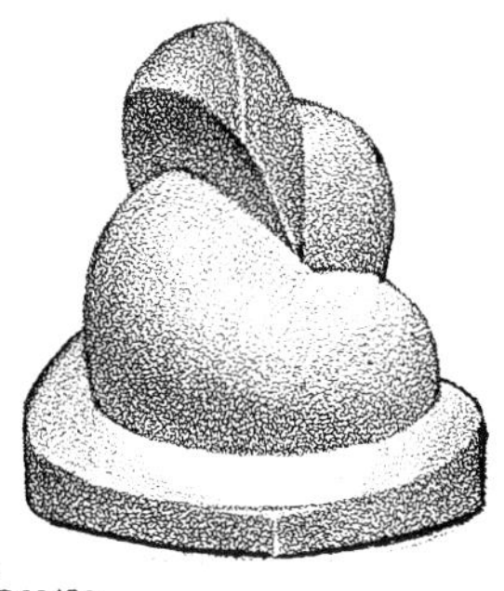

one form
becomes partly
the base

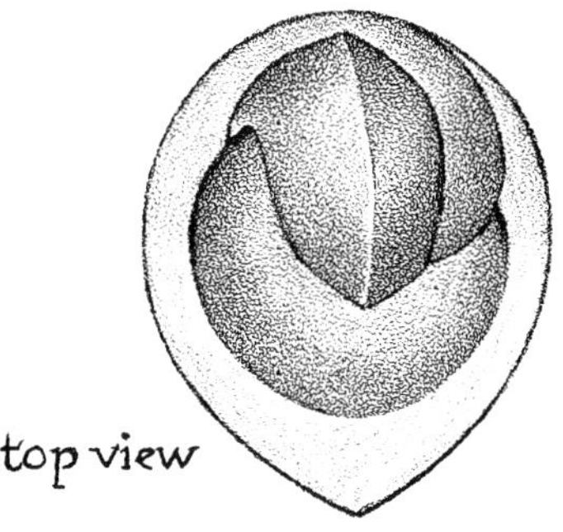

Second Series of Studies

Positive and Neutral Forms

1. Make a composition of *four* abstract forms placed on a base: *two positive* and *two neutral*.

2. Continue making compositions, each time adding one more form.

Reviewing Your Studies

At this point, place all of your study compositions in a group for viewing. This gives an opportunity to compare the pure character of the *positive* form assemblies with the character of the *positive-neutral* ones and to weigh the difference in *mood* each creates. The process sharpens one's judgment of how to alter moods by adding or subtracting form character so that either the *positive* or *neutral* will dominate. Thus it is possible to arrive at the right "blend," one that creates the desired mood and affects the emotional reaction of the beholder.

Third Series of Studies

Positive and Negative Forms

1. Make a composition of *three* abstract forms: *two positive* and *one negative*.

2. Continue to make compositions, successively adding single forms. The resulting form groupings create "blends" of positive and negative form characters.

Fourth Series of Studies

Positive, Negative and Neutral Forms

1. Make a composition of *three*, equal bulk, abstract forms: *one positive*, *one negative*, and *one neutral*. Continue to follow the general requisites.

The sample solution shown in the illustration indicates that the blending of the three different form qualities creates a mood markedly different from that of the previous study compositions, which had blends of only positive, or only positive and neutral. This should encourage the student in this phase of his studies because his awareness of these mood differences can help him to eliminate guesswork when he endeavors to express his feelings in sculpture compositions.

Example: A form-quality blend of 20% *positive*, 45% *negative*, and 35% *neutral* results in a mood in which the negative aspect prevails, though not overly much.

Guidelines in these studies aim at eliminating guesswork (accidental results). We learn what to do and what not to do when carrying out stated requisites. However, during all our work, individual taste naturally accompanies our activities. No matter how well the assignments have been accomplished, they are bound to reflect the student's taste.

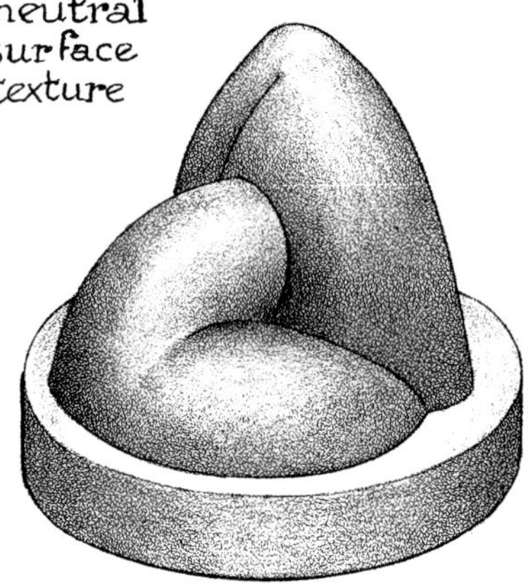

composition of 2 abstract pos. & dynamic forms having neutral surface texture

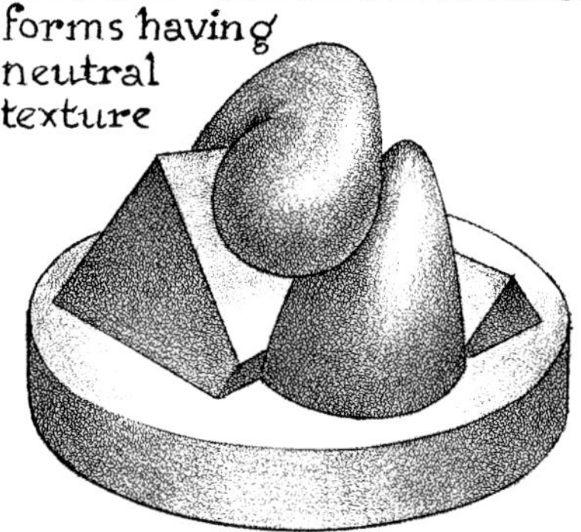

2 abstract pos. & dynamic forms & 2 abstract neutral forms having neutral texture

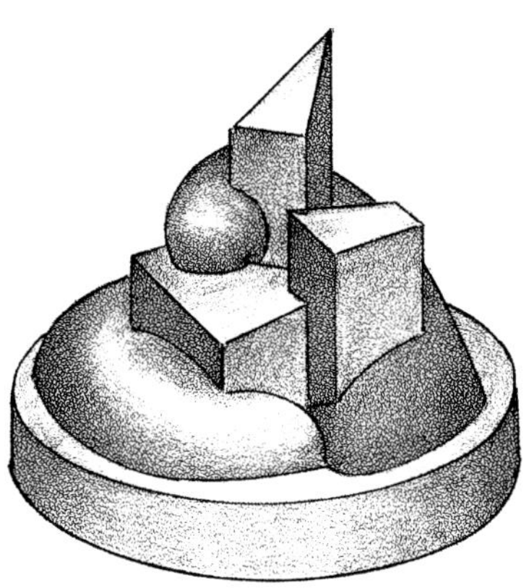

2 abstract pos. & dynamic forms & 3 abstract neutral forms having neutral texture

3 abstract pos. & dynamic forms & 2 abstract neutral forms having neutral texture

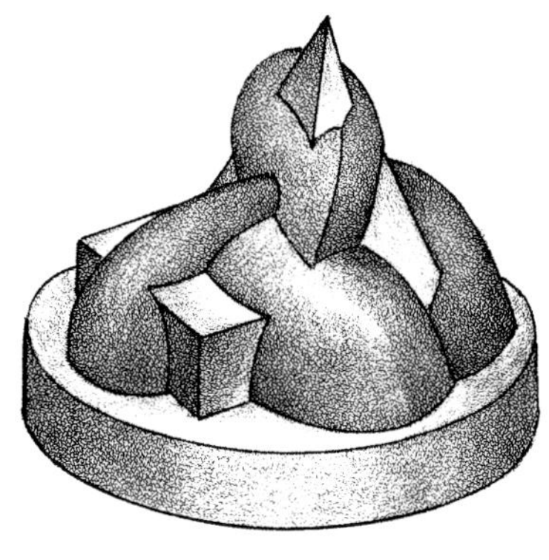

base is not part of composition & only acts to offset it

Four or More Abstract Forms

1. Make a composition of *more than three positive* abstract forms.

2. Make a mixture of *positive-negative* form qualities in a composition of *more than three* abstract forms.

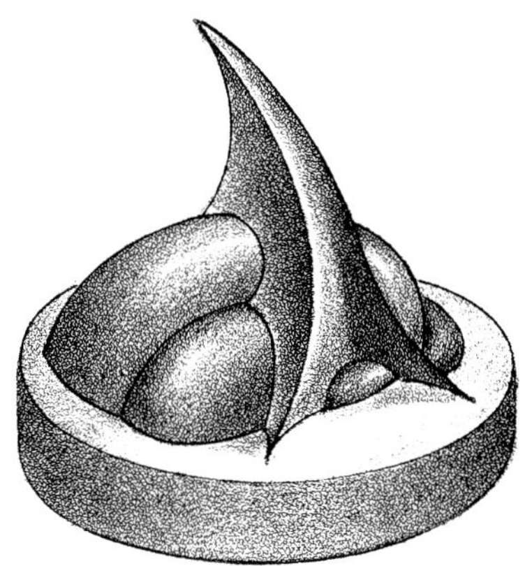

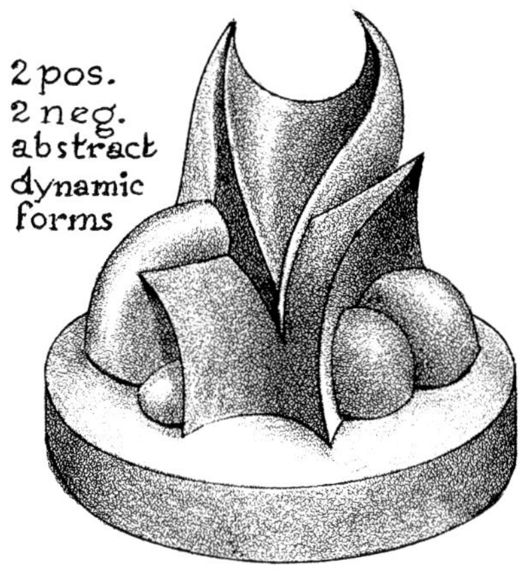

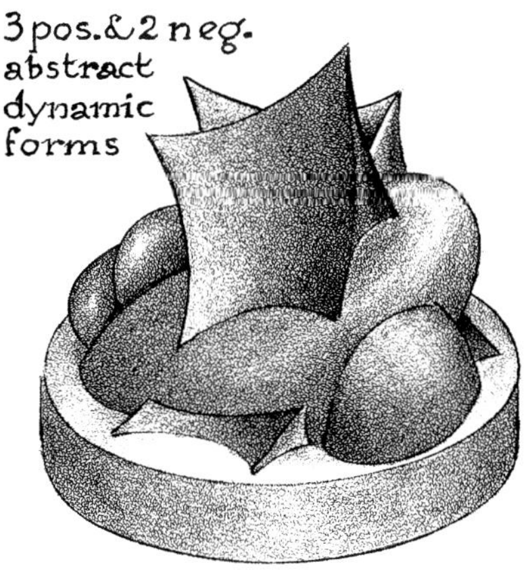

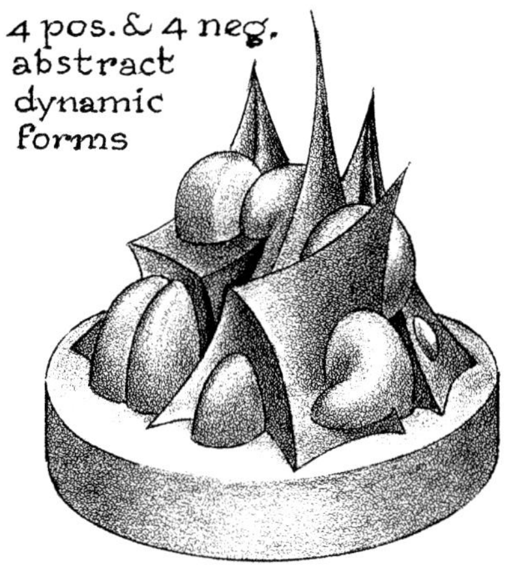

An Unlimited Number of Abstract Forms

1. Make a composition, with abstract forms assembled to suggest a subject.

The "story" it tells should emerge only gradually. Instead of letting all be seen in one glance, leaving nothing to the imagination, the artist can give it a greater scope of feeling and interpretation. The intent of this study is to teach restraint in presenting the subject.

Example: The composition titled **Meditation** suggests a kneeling figure in an attitude of contemplation. The five views show the grouping of anatomically plausible parts and their locations in the human body. The composition proves to be in perfect balance from every angle. It reveals a full range of light and dark tonal values as well.

Specifically, we see the head-neck-shoulder combination as having *positive-dynamic* elements, different from arms, trunk, and limbs. The resultant blend of character in form detail aids in evoking the intended mood of this piece.

Visualizing the Composition

Note that the neutral-surfaced detail of *Meditation* is shaped by curved ribbon-like planes which in themselves suggest dynamic aspects. Such "ribbons" inject a feeling of form, defined as the contact area between one space convolution and its opposite. Objects of bent sheet-metal fall into this category.

Empty spaces between protruding form details constitute negative elements in a piece. Imagine a transparent membrane enveloping the whole composition tangentially to all protruding parts; this aids one in seeing the empty spaces, which influence the whole mood. This same device can be used to visualize all other compositions in order to facilitate analysis.

The student must learn to be more aware of visualization during composing so that the fullest possible range of form understanding is always at his fingertips.

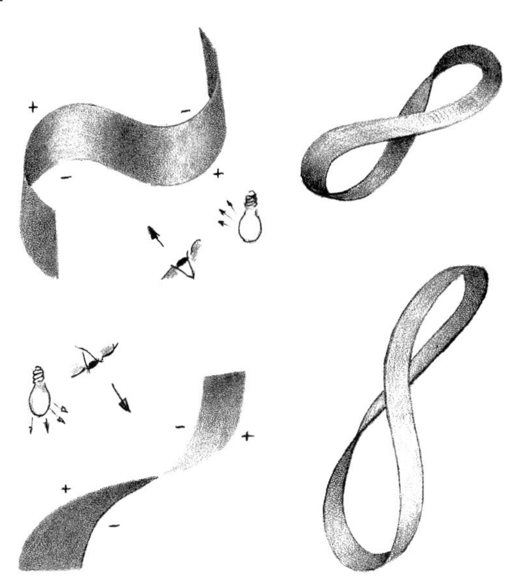

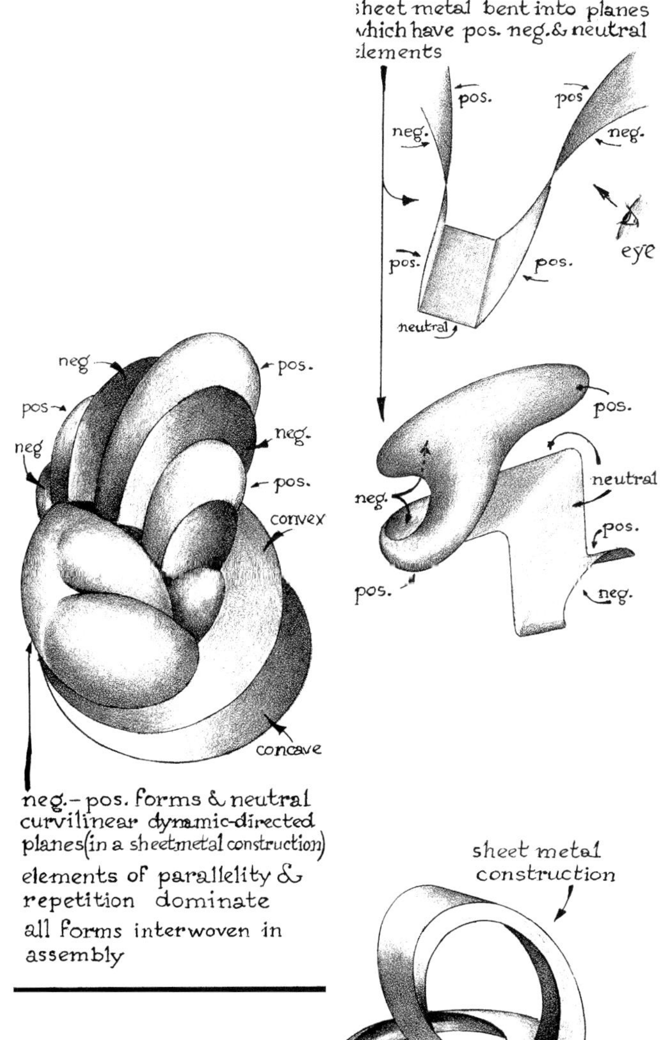

Realistic Subject Matter

1. Make a composition which reveals an *entirely realistic* subject, but use only *abstract* forms in its assembly.

Example: ***Monday Morning Wash***. In this composition the body forms are anatomically recognizable though somewhat stylized. The space beyond the legs has been filled with abstract forms to suggest "atmosphere," as opposed to being filled with props such as a tree stump, bush or similar device to steady the composition. We accept this solution readily as reinforcing the physically weak spots of the material at the base. In this case the base consists of a combination of a laundry basket, a bottle, and the atmospheric fill-space, none of which detracts from the main impression of the subject.

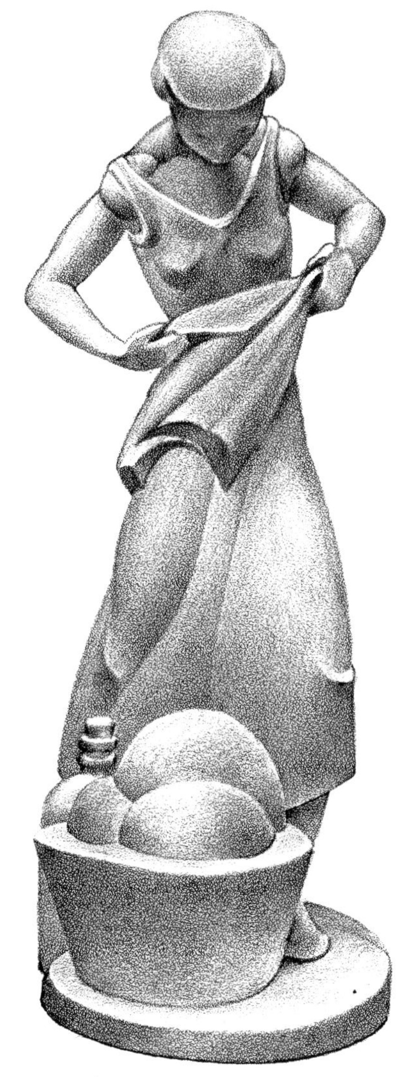

subject title:
monday morning wash

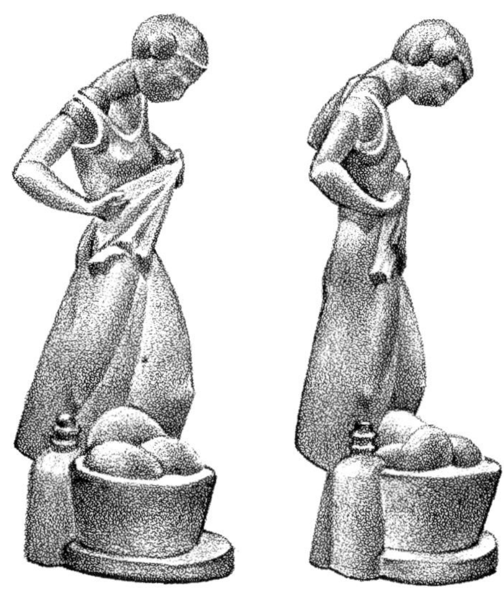

maximum number of forms
must show from any angle.
surface texture: neutral

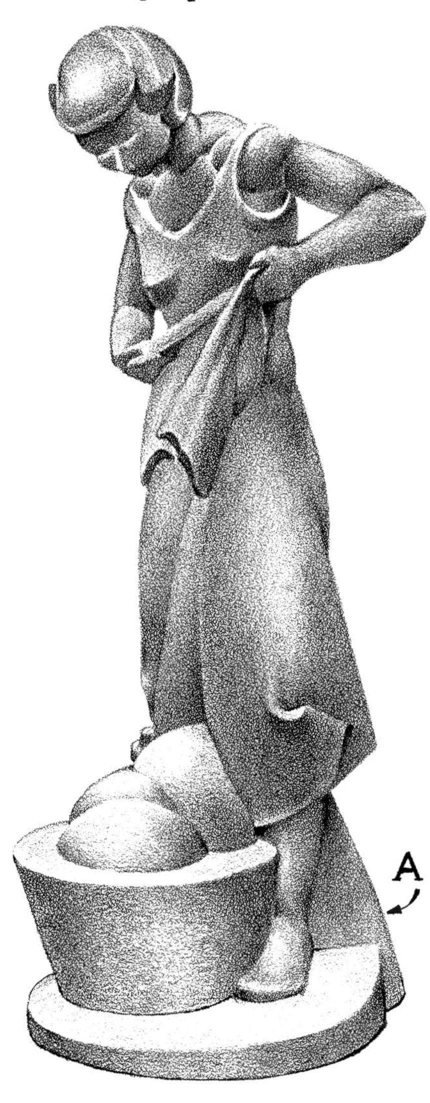

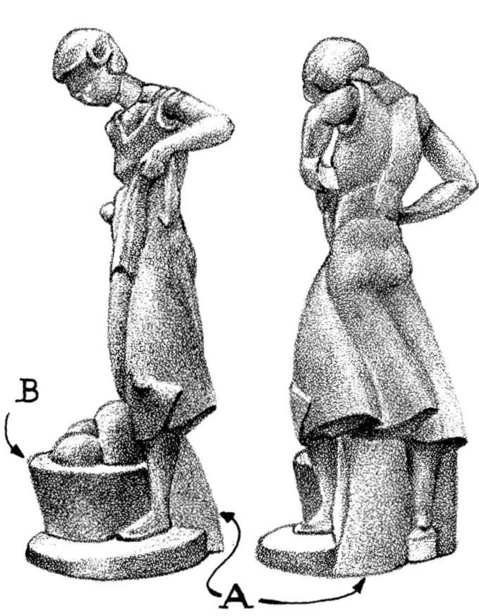

form A fills a space to balance
the bulk of B (laundry & basket)
without distracting from the
composition's subject matter

Caricature

Giovanni Boccaccio's **Patron Saint**. With such exaggeration, it is contrast rather than subtlety that tells the story. Each single abstract facial form is kept anatomically plausible. The lecher's grin is emphasized by distortions of the nose and mouth. The eye wink is stressed by the local protrusion of the pupil and the slant of the little pupil facet, which causes more reflection. The hair is kept in individual form masses, to aid blatancy still further.

Box Top. The carving in choice hardwood could have been modeled as well in clay and later cast, without losing the sculptural appeal, as long as the *form* quality was established.

Camel's Head and Broach. The exaggerated stylization in such works as these underscores the growing flexibility of the sculptor, who can shape all the forms he uses in his work in any material he chooses within the confines of odd branch sections, mill blocks, small choice pieces of rare wood, etc.

The following notes and observations will aid the student in form analysis, techniques and skills, with which he can develop the basis of his three-dimensional artwork.

Surface, Textures and Colors

Sculptures can be textured in various ways (see Chapter 4, page 33). If a sculptures surface is highly polished with scintillating highlights or is rough, the quality of *form per se* may suffer, especially when the surface is imitating various material. If it is unpolished but smooth, the surface should be dull and light in color.

In all work, dull white surfaces tend to show best the maximum range of three-dimensional forms, particularly when *lighted correctly;* the subtle gradations between the lightest light and the darkest dark are thereby revealed. This also points out the difficulty of showing form at its best when surfaces are black, very dark or of uneven color (striped, spotted, etc.). A light color or patina can overcome these handicaps.

Subtlety

The student can learn how to *suggest* what he wants to express rather than tell the story with obvious exaggeration. Subtleties in form, though often difficult to create, will make room for actuality to come through *gradually,* allowing the viewer to enjoy the unfolding recognition of conceptual elements.

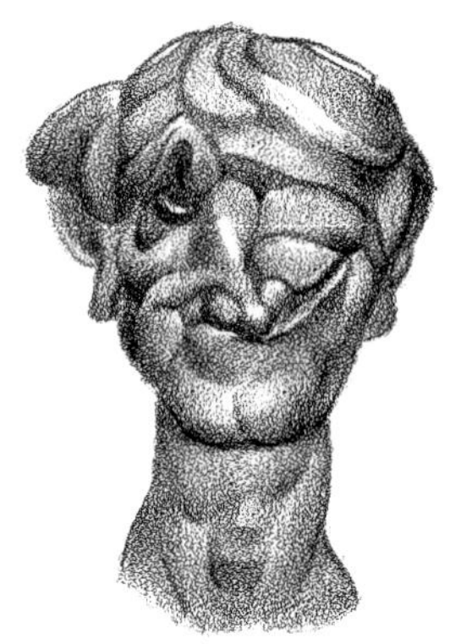

Giovanni Boccaccio's
Patron Saint

caricature exagerations
of facial & hair forms

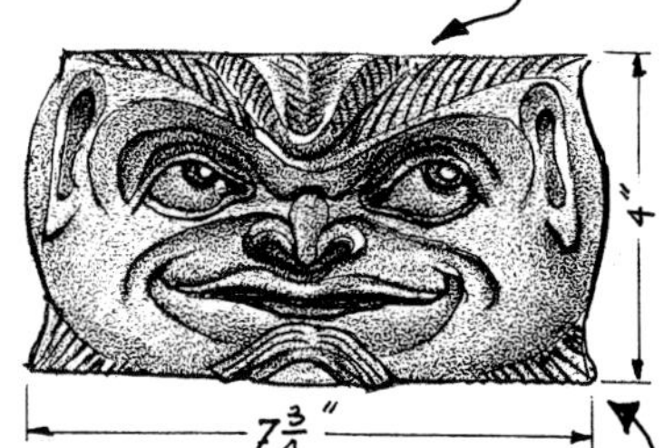

box top in tropical hardwood 3" thick

low relief carved with engraver style gouges, sanded down & polished afterward

stylized camels' head in sequoia redwood

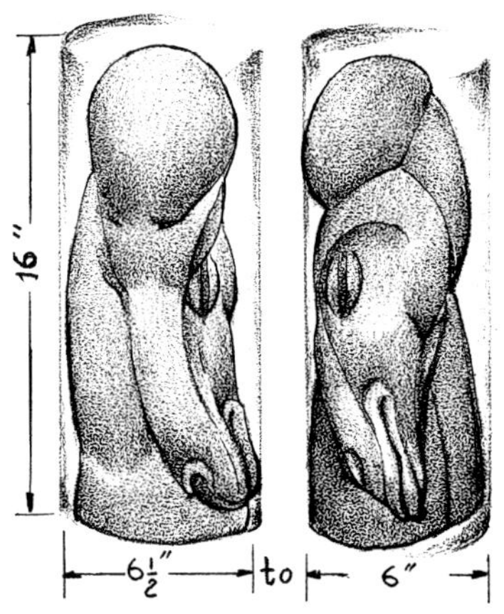

this size & over carved with hand hammered gouges first & finished with small engraver style gouges

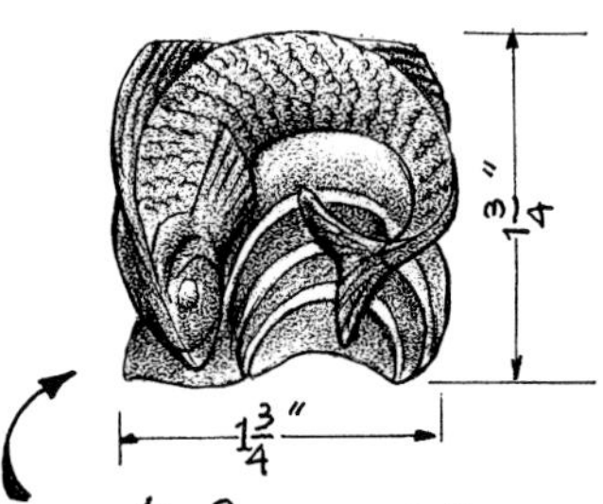

low relief carved brooch in manzanita wood 3/8" thick

Facial Forms

There is an infinite variety of human faces, and each has different forms of fatty deposits, under the skin, that subtly influence facial expressions. No two human beings have such material distributed exactly the same. These differences give the sculptor the opportunity to use his inventiveness, as long as the form assemblies fall within anatomically plausible limits.

If he wishes to distort, for further emphasis, he is free to use artistic license. In the making of caricatures, for instance, there is much leeway (using correct anatomical knowledge) for the artist to shape the forms into exaggerated facial expressions.

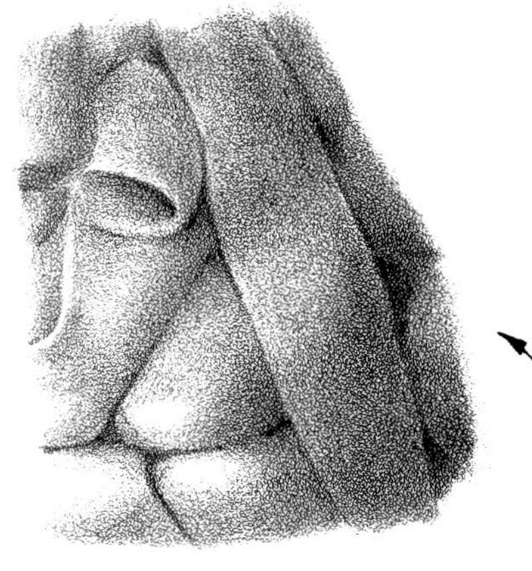

modeled in clay with neutral texture

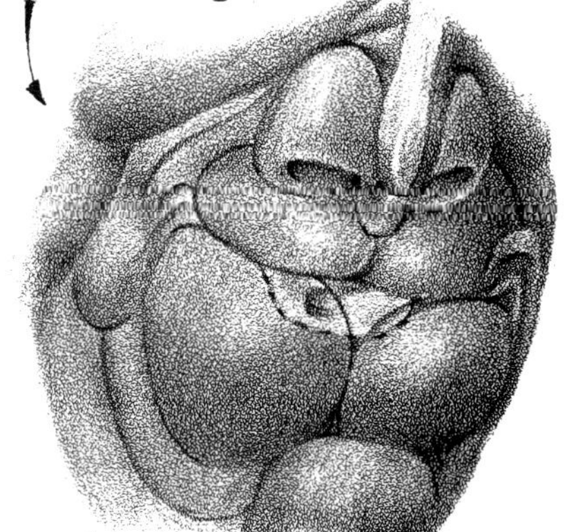

dominating forms below skin

modeled in clay or

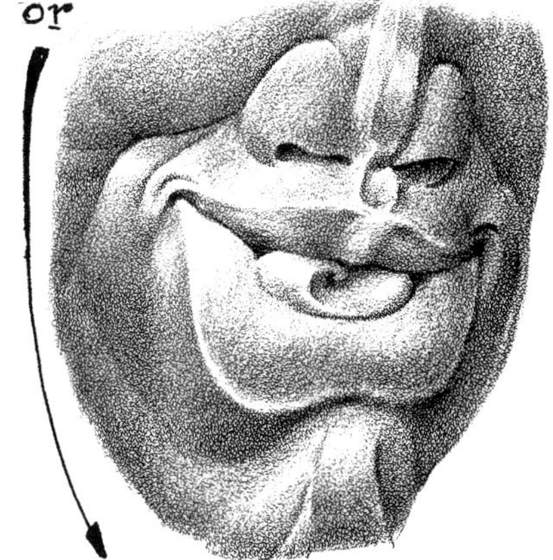

carved in wood with neutral texture

Plaster Casts as Models

The illustrated eye details from a plaster cast of the face of Michaelangelo's *David* show its basic forms. Casts in plaster of Paris of that face are used in art classes to acquaint beginners with facial forms in general. Once the modeler can retain three-dimensional memory of facial forms, he will find that, in all his inventive applications (based on his knowledge of abstract forms, in combination with realistic facial forms and anatomy), he will be able to easily work out otherwise puzzling form-groupings.

Gradually the sculptor/modeler becomes more at ease in his "map-reading" of body forms, which, in their assembly, make up all of the human figure. With the struggles for dexterity behind him (as the pianist masters his keyboard), he can freely sculpt facial expressions as varied as those of all the people he meets.

Photo Data

Keeping a scrapbook of photographs selected from magazines is useful in cultivating memory retention of three-dimensional images of faces, bodies, abstract mathematical forms, etc. These photos can be re-examined from time to time, especially in order to study three-dimensional interpretation through tonal values. In this way, the repeated impressions become a kind of *photo-memory* data bank, leaving their residue in our mind.

It may be questionable whether an abundance of *photo-memory* is essential to the artist. My own experience has sometimes made me wish I had more of it. But in reality, when the urge to say something three-dimensionally was strong enough, there was a compensating factor; the *residue* of the images I was exposed to in my life's experiences proved sufficient, so that I could do without actual visual aids of any kind. Whatever impresses us enough to leave *some* stored visual memory can most likely be released subliminally when needed.

A Popular Misconception

It is a common notion that a student is imitating his teacher's ideas or style, particularly if the teacher's work has strongly influenced him. If he has *unconsciously* imitated his teacher, it is likely that he is only trying to perfect his skill and insight as a student.

In my own experience as a teacher, I was happy to witness that, in time, when talented students achieve the teacher's skill, they emerge with their own distinctive and individual touch, recognizable in all their work. That touch can be regarded as the artist's "signature," making an actual name signing unnecessary.

If the creative urge is strong, and if what one has to say is worth saying in one's own way, a personal and distinctive individual *style* inevitably comes about.

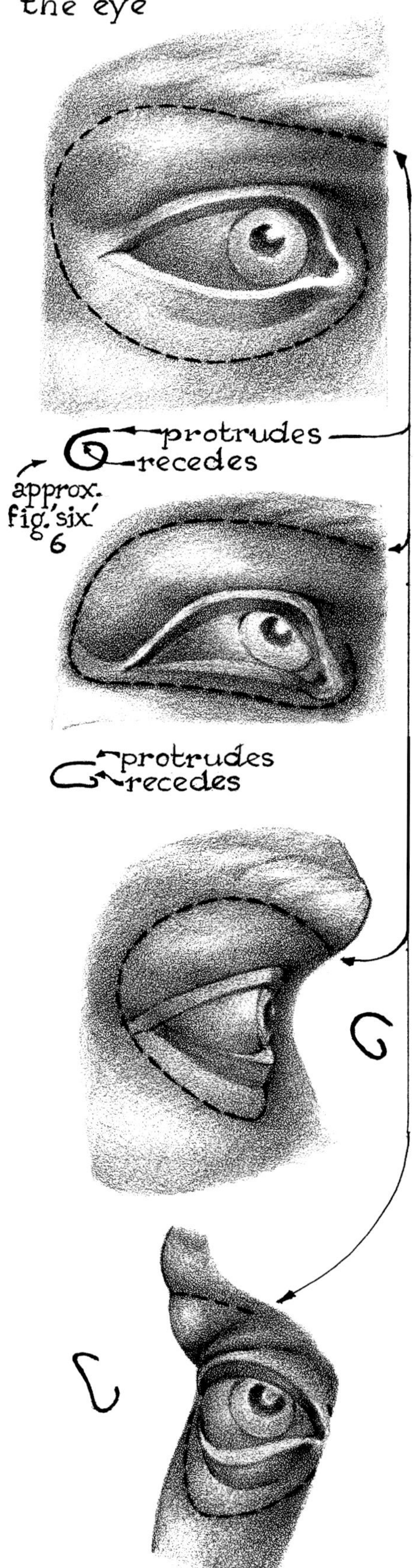

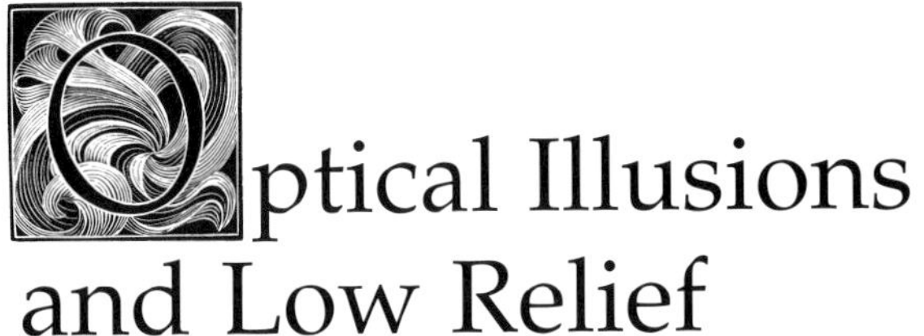ptical Illusions and Low Relief

The illustrations explain, through descriptive geometry, what happens when a stovepipe damper is rotated from open to closed. Its projections form ellipses between circle and straight line. This same concept can be applied using a cross section of the human head instead of the circular damper.

Shown are projections between the full third dimension and the flat base upon which the low relief is shaped with elliptical cross sections. Since low relief creates optical illusions of the missing dimensions, we refer to it correctly as "fooling the eye" (in French, *trompe l'oeil*).

Low relief work is more difficult to do than full round sculpture.

Assignment

Life-Size Profile in Low Relief

Make a life-size profile portrait in *low relief*, no more than 2″ thick. Use a flat metal base or shellacked wooden board upon which a 2″ thick clay slab can be attached.

First, using a wire-ended, clay modeling tool, cut away excess clay around a scratched-in silhouette of the portrait (as the illustration shows). Let the light shine on the work from above, shearing by the clay surface to show the modeling in detail.

Throughout the exercise, follow the elliptical stovepipe projection principle closely; cut away with the wire-ended tool all excess clay lower than the 2″ thickness of the portrait so that an elliptical cross-section remains, as shown. The edge of the profile should arise from the base under right angles. The resulting form then shows that the actual elliptical surface envelops the finished portrait tangentially. Flat-ended modeling tools indicate their slants at any tangent point to the overall elliptical surface of the form assemblies. (Follow the illustrations.)

Another way to model a low relief portrait is by *building up* with clay pellets.

First, outline the silhouette or profile on the base. Then stick small pellets of clay on to it, one after the other, within the required thickness of 2″.

As with the first method (cutting away clay), building up with clay requires *visualizing the head cross-section* in projection (as with the slanted damper in the stovepipe), the dimensions ranging from 0″ to 2″.

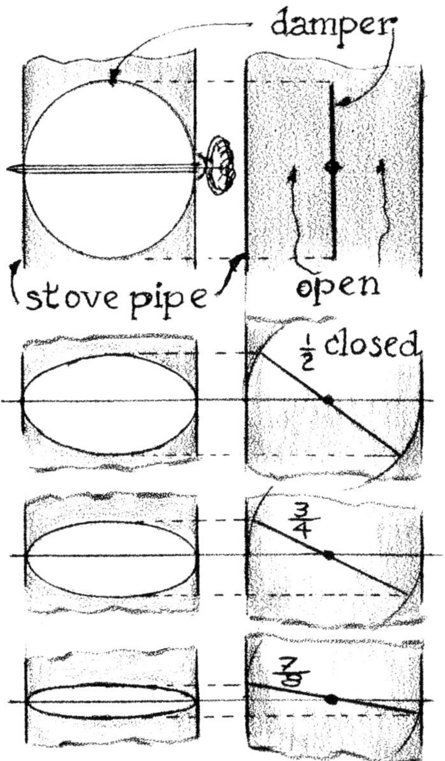

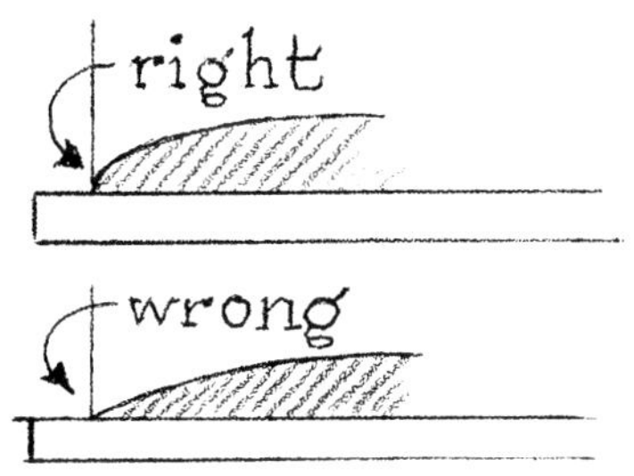

Although the illustrations clarify this principle in relation to relief work on a flat background, it can be applied as well to areas of full round sculptures where there is a lack of material. Many examples of such sculptures (pages 121-125) showing the blend of full round and low relief should demonstrate the great advantage that the sculptor has in applying this principle.

Full Face and Three-Quarter Frontal Face in Low Relief

Facial symmetry in a relief portrait requires correct geometric placement of forms and should be apparent when the work is viewed from any angle. In a *full face relief* portrait, the nose protrusion requires inventive treatment using optical illusions to prevent it from sticking out more than needed.

In a *three-quarter face relief* portrait, the slightest misalignment of the nose will cause it to look askew in relation to the central dividing plane of the head. A simple test shows if all is correct: hang such a three-quarter portrait on the wall at eye level and walk in front of it, back and forth, without taking your eye off the portrait. If the nose seems to move out of alignment during viewing, correct your misjudgment as the illustration shows.

Correct Lighting

The setup in the illustration shows how direct light should shear along the work to accentuate the form details. Darker shadows result in very shallow areas. Such light will accomplish this better than diffused light. A little experimentation will reveal the most favorable type of light and location.

Clay Condition for Relief Modeling

For very low relief and small work, it is best to use a stiffer clay. Soft clay yields too easily under the slightest tool pressure.

On a hot day, oil-based clay should be cooled in the refrigerator from time to time in order to stiffen it and make the wire tool-end more effective when cutting or scraping, especially in the finished stages of the work.

Different Uses for Relief Work

Thin modeled relief in water clay can be carefully cut off the board and transferred and bonded to the round surfaces of clay pots. It is surprising how modeled faces can be lifted and bent this way and that, without losing much of the modeling, in spite of some inevitably distorted features. In a similar way, decorative clay ribbons may be transferred and applied to pottery. Various tools made to accommodate the modeler are shown.

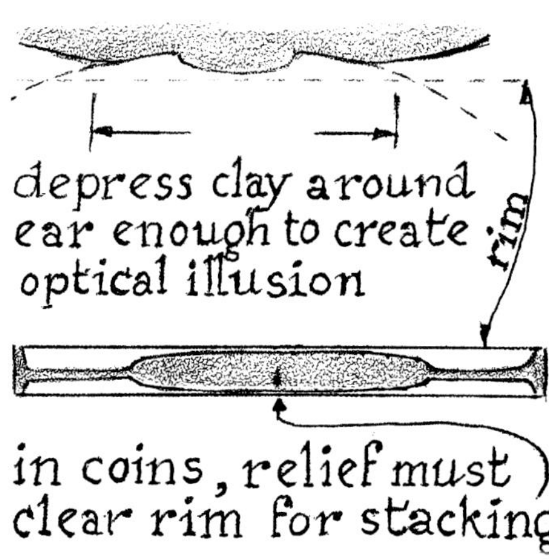

Modeling Coins and Medals

These are modeled in relief in a stiff clay. Raised letters, especially, can be modeled easiest in hard oil-based clay. To remove the clay piece, you may cut it with thin wire from the base. In very low relief, the harder the clay the better it stands up for casting. For example, casts that are made in a very hard dental plaster will hold up during machine-type pantograph enlarging or reducing work (as in the making of dies and matrixes for the striking of coins and medals).

Some sculptors are so attracted to the very low relief work of medals and coins that they decide to specialize in it. Needless to say, the lower the relief, the greater the skill required to create the maximum illusion of the full round in the undersized third dimension. The slightest discrepancy will show up as a detriment. Many mediocre low reliefs are simply scratched-in drawings, which leave mere ridges and grooves without sculptural quality.

About coins, it should be noted that the rim must be slightly higher than the highest point of the relief so that the coins will stack without touching the relief.

A practical advantage of relief work is its easy duplication by means of casts, dies and matrixes, since there are no undercuts. The modeler and sculptor who decides to make it his sole activity can undertake commissions for commemorative medals, portraiture and the like, needing little equipment. Inexpensive duplicating materials can be used, leaving greater margin for earnings. Pantograph cutting machines can cut matrixes for medallions and coins from larger hard-surfaced castings. Libraries list fabricators in this field.

Distortions

Optical illusions are a form of distortion that are usually not disturbing to the viewer, who seldom is aware of them. All seems to look natural and is quite acceptable. The artist can apply this relief skill to full round sculpture surfaces also, especially when he wishes to produce subtle moods in facial expressions. Quite often, full-round sculpture benefits from relief treatment, which can be used to make up for local lack of material

High Relief

This challenges the sculptor's ability to crowd many figures into limited space: all seemingly full-round figures, not separated, but not looking as if intersected by one another either.

The high relief technique has been used throughout the centuries, and can be seen in many varieties of stone in the friezes of classical buildings and temples, in the marble and ceramics of the Renaissance, and in contemporary architectural decorations. Students have ready access to examples by way of photo reproductions of high and low relief in library books, and they should

Negative Relief Carving

This is a technique of carving or scraping depressions in a flat slab of plaster or wood that then can be used as a mold. The resulting cast from such a mold possesses a surprisingly clean-cut and sharp positive quality that is difficult to obtain in any other way. The explanation is simple. Visualize the natural finger and hand movements that "grasp" and dig away material, leaving negative imprints. Casts of these automatically give their opposite *positive* quality forms.

This technique is especially suitable for the making of rotary (wheel) molds, which, when rolled and pressed onto strips of clay, dough, putty, etc., make decorative beading out of them. Examples are the cookie molds carved in wood.

Three-Dimensional Perspective

One can *deliberately* compact form assemblies when wishing to emphasize, subdue or eliminate body parts, to the advantage of the artist's intent for the composition. They may be hidden from view or made to disappear into the form mass of the total sculpture.

The bronze panels of the Baptistery doors in Florence are good examples of the use of three-dimensional perspective. Photographs of Lorenzo Ghibertis **Porta del Paradiso** unfortunately tend to distort the parts of the bodies that come very close to, or are farther from, the lens, showing them progressively larger or smaller.

My composition of the biblical **Abel** in bronze is an example of the use of perspective in sculpture. The back of **Abel** shows the maximum dimension of the torso gradually diminishing perspectively downward. The extension of the left leg is left to the imagination, disappearing from view unnoticed and not missed when the composition is seen from any angle.

The intent was to show the lifeless right arm massive over the right knee next to the lifeless head (with grotesque negative open mouth) suspended from the downward twisted neck: all representing a "slain" Abel. Any part of the body not contributing to this mood of the slain man was subdued or eliminated and is not missed.

In the figure of **Cain**, which was carved in Verde di Prato, the face is hidden in the rest of the form assembly. The pose of the body, rather than the facial expression, gradually communicates the mood of the guilty slayer.

The examples of **Cain** and **Abel** demonstrate a control method of stressing two opposite values and moods, while maintaining subtlety. Three-dimensional perspective is just one more tool the sculptor can use to communicate his ideas and effectively serve his intent.

Illustrations of carvings in this book show the wide range of application of perspective and optical illusion combined.

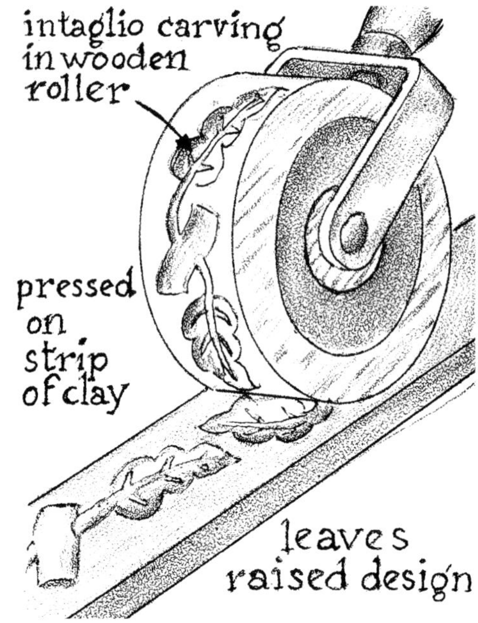

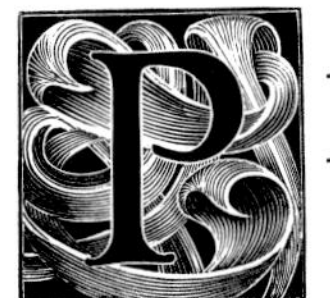# Plaster Casting

As a rule, when a study in clay is to be cast in plaster, *a waste mold* is made. It is called a waste mold because once a cast is poured into it, the mold is chipped and thereby lost.

Plaster acts in the same way as cement, setting up hard within a certain time period. Setting time for casting-plaster (plaster of Paris) should be between 15 and 20 minutes, long enough so that the sculptor does not feel too rushed during his handling of it.

Many studios show the telltale signs of unskilled mold-makers. I have seen plaster splattered all over the room, even on the ceiling, because students feel rushed, are inexperienced or lack control in the handling of plaster.

Mixing the Plaster

My own casting procedure may differ from others, but I offer a few variations with possibly useful new twists.

Use a slightly flexible plastic mixing bowl rubbed inside with a little candle wax for easy cleaning.

Size up the clay model to gauge the approximate volume needed to cover its surface with the first layer. This layer is tinted *blue* with laundry bluing so that, as the mold is chipped away, you will be warned that you are getting close to the surface of the cast.

Into the blue water in the bowl, sift evenly between the fingers scoop after scoop of plaster. As it settles on the bottom, layer after layer, it will reach the top, showing little peaks of dry plaster here and there on the surface. Stop and wait until all dry spots have become water-saturated, as they suck up the water like blotting paper through capillary action.

Only now is the mixture gently stirred into an even consistency. Be careful not to create air bubbles since they will cause air pockets in the cast. Vibrate the bowl and contents, and if any bubbles do arise, skim them off.

Making the Mold

Follow the illustrations closely, observing the hand positions when applying the plaster over the model in an *upward* motion, directing each dollop of plaster inwardly as it flows off the hand. Continue, one dollop after another, round and round, to cover the whole surface.

If small areas seem to remain uncovered, do not try to *push* the plaster with the fingers, because the slightest touch onto the clay below will show the mark later. Tilt the whole piece onto its side, wet plaster covering and all (assuming the study is well-secured on its base), so that the small uncovered spot is better exposed. Let a drop of plaster-mix fall on it. To help spread and cover

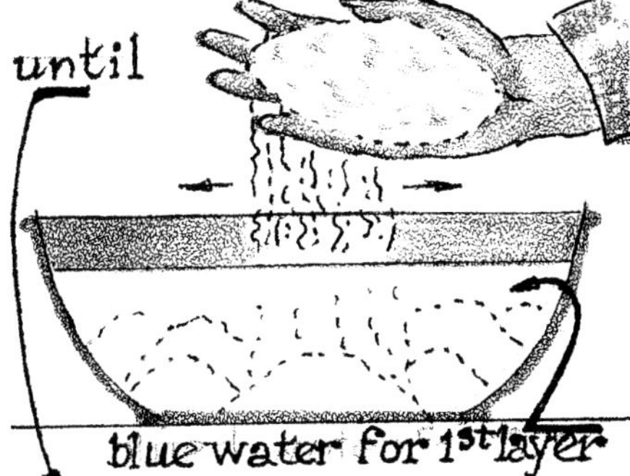

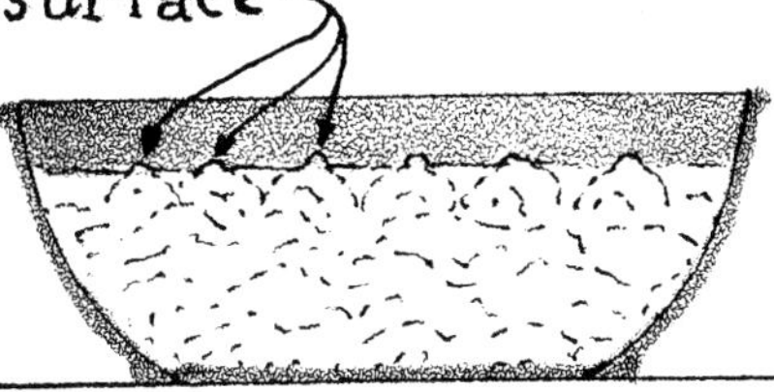

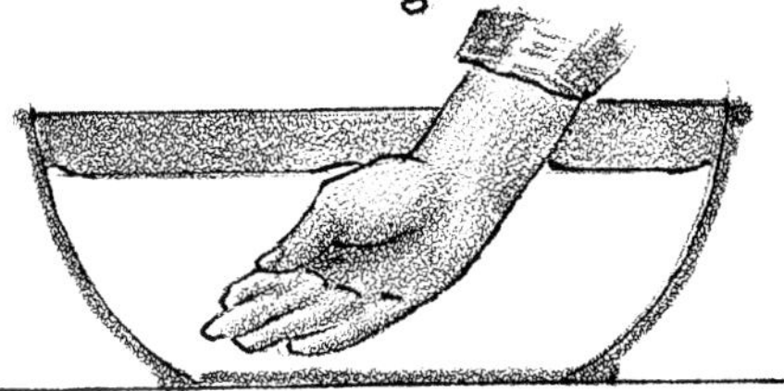

without wasting time:
pick up a blob and in an upward motion let plaster slide off, laying it on the clay surface, all around

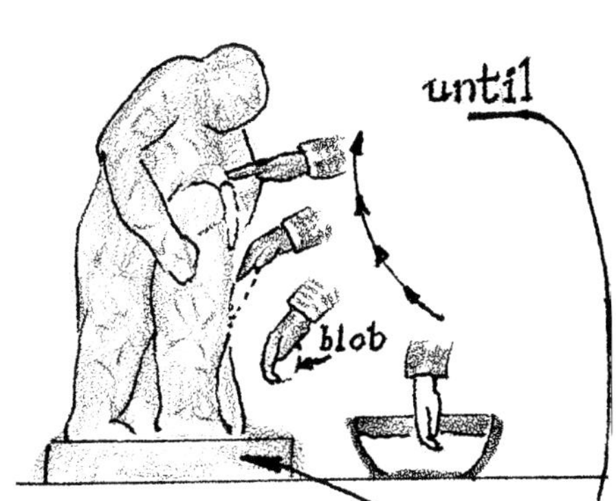

whole surface is covered with its 1st blued layer

2nd layer in plain white plaster stengthens mold for handling

aim to make waste mold thin but strong enough

it, bring your mouth close and blow over the drop in the direction needed. This way the spot is covered without fingers injuring the clay below.

When the clay is completely covered, thicken any thin areas to at least 1/8". Do this gently so the added weight will not cause the plaster to pull the first layer off. Let the blue layer harden while making a batch of white plaster mix for the second layer. Apply it in the same way to finish the mold.

One learns through practice, observing how plaster behaves during the few minutes between its liquid, semi-liquid and solid states.

If all preparations are well-planned and set up to meet eventualities, and the hand manipulation is easy and relaxed, the beginner's nervousness will become self-confidence, with increasingly successful results. But, *beware of overconfidence!* I found myself tripped up by it when I undertook a demonstration before a group of fellow students in the classroom.

An elderly student had made a portrait study in clay. She had worked over it for weeks, and it had become her great pride. Unfortunately, the result of her efforts was a poor portrait. But, in charity, no one said so when she wanted it preserved and cast in plaster of Paris. It was this piece that I used to demonstrate plaster casting to the group.

I first made the two-piece waste mold from a batch of fresh plaster. When it was set and separated, I removed the clay model with a wire-ended tool. Then I cleaned and water-soaked the reassembled mold, swished a soap solution in it as a separator, and was ready to mix the batch of plaster for the cast.

However, finding that I was out of fresh plaster, I resorted to using some old stuff left over from a year ago. It looked fresh and had not solidified, so with this I poured the cast. It did not set up hard in the normal time and, scratching the plaster with my nail, I found it only medium hard. Nevertheless, I went ahead and began carefully chipping away at the mold.

The onlookers were eagerly watching every step. There was a thrill of excitement when the first blue appeared, and then a clear area of the white of the portrait became exposed. The maker of the portrait was breathless as her artwork began to appear. All watched intently as the face was uncovered, and soon the whole head stood revealed.

The neck was now the only part still to be chipped free. Since there were no undercuts on the neck, I figured, why not deliver one well-aimed blow between the mold's two parts to separate them? The lady was spellbound by this magic treatment of her work the others were fascinated by the boldness of my master stroke to come.

But then . . . the crisp blow, acting suddenly like a guillotine, severed the head from the neck, and I swiftly caught it as it fell just before it hit the floor. "Think nothing of it," I said glibly, "because we now have an excellent opportunity to demonstrate how easly the two parts can be bonded together, while at the same time the neck can be reinforced, and without showing a seam."

I was surprised at my own sang-froid. The dumfounded look in the lady's eyes expressed "reversal" emotion: changing from consternation, to relief, then to admiration at the performance.

It was my over-confidence that had spoiled my judgment regarding the state of the plaster of Paris, and that last whack of the hammer was my undoing.

Needless to say, before making a new mold and cast with fresh plaster of Paris, I also added a central reinforcement to the neck, a shellacked steel rod.

A Simple Two- and Three-Piece Waste Mold

Make the mold as the illustrations show

The inside of the mold should first be shellacked (thinned down with some denatured alcohol). Keep brushing the inner surface until it becomes a little shiny, which means that all the pores of the plaster are closed.

Brush over the inner surface a separator compound to prevent the poured cast from sticking. Several separator materials can be used: olive oil, salad oil, soap solution, etc. An excellent old-fashioned one is a 50/50 mix of melted candle wax and kerosene. Cut candle wax in slivers. Place them in a can floating in a pan of boiling water until the slivers melt. *WARNING: TAKE THE CAN AWAY FROM THE FLAME BEFORE ADDING KEROSENE!*

When the mixture has cooled, the wax remains in suspension as thin, microscopic flakes. Pick up some of this mushy wax with an old shaving brush and apply following the steps shown on page 54. Remove all excess with the brush, which should be squeezed free of the remaining mixture to prevent its leaving depressions in the cast's surface.

Soak the mold in water, before pouring plaster, to prevent surface holes in the cast.

Very often, in spite of all precautions taken when coating the inner surface of the plaster mold with shellac, minute unsealed spots will remain that may later act to suck water from the plaster of the cast, leaving little pinholes on the surface. To the artist's dismay, he will find beneath these pinholes larger air pockets that will require patching. (It is a mistake to think that such air pockets were air bubbles already in the plaster mix during the pour.) To patch them after the cast has been freed from the mold, use the pointed knife-end of a steel plaster tool, as shown, and cut a little open crater through the pinhole. Follow the steps shown, which should leave the repaired surfaces without any visible blemish.

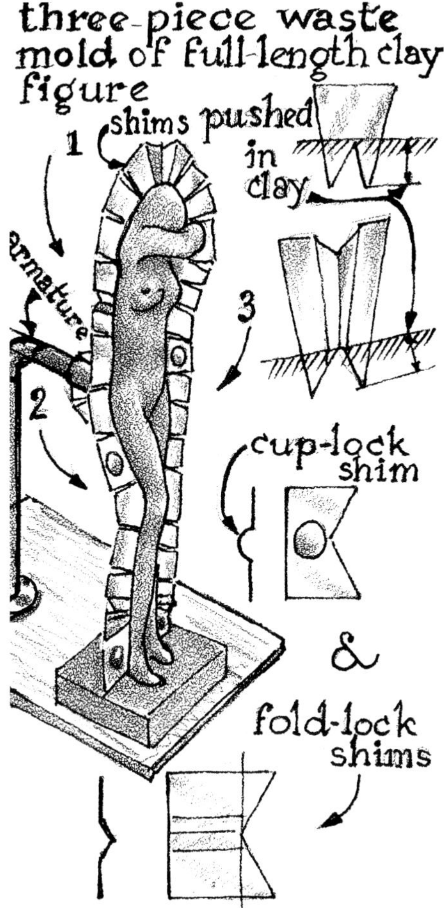

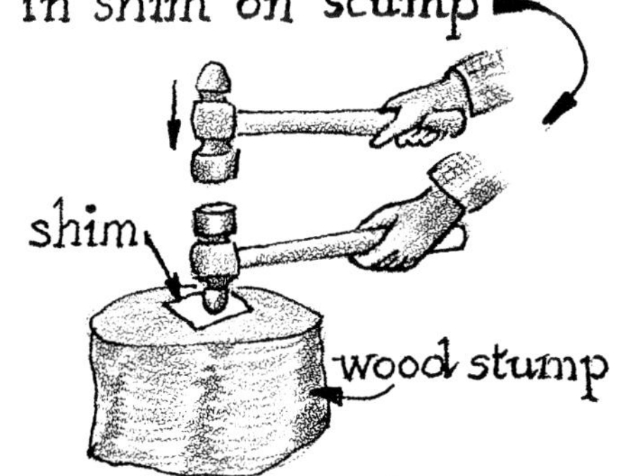

how to prevent air
bubbles in plaster
surfaces of castings
dry plaster mold

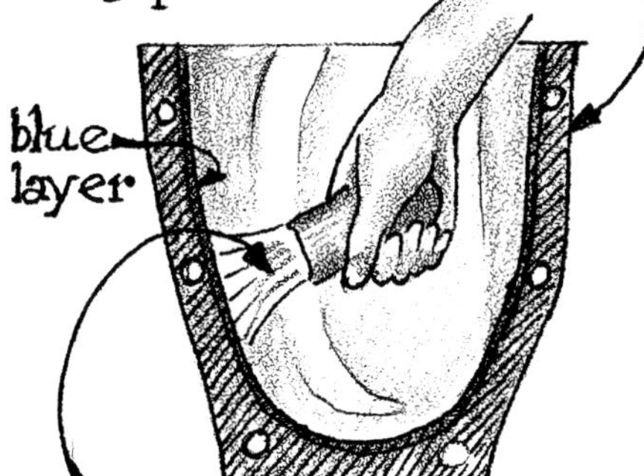

brush-on separator-
compound on shellacked
surface

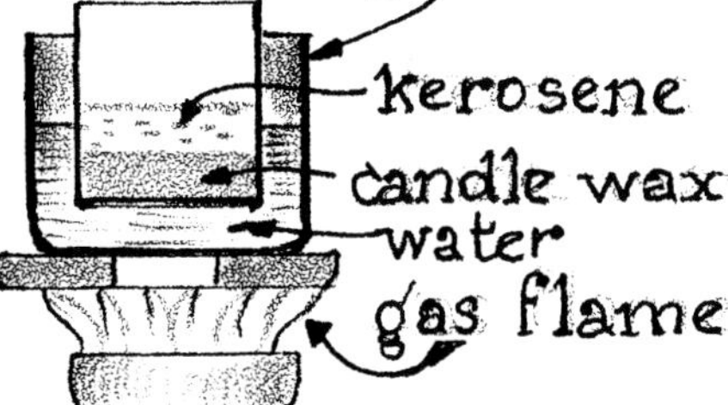

after wax has melted
add its volume of kerosene
away from flame

only then pour plaster
for the cast

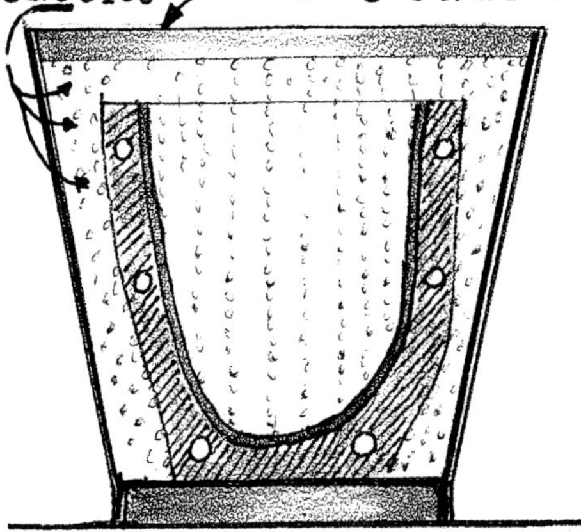

vibrate bowl to make
air bubbles) in mix rise
to be skimmed off before
pour)

pinholes in surfaces of
plaster casts have air
pockets below,
open them into crater pockets
with steel spatula cutting end

fill pockets with drops of
water hanging
from soft brush

until

plaster around
is saturated &
only then pick up a dollop
of plaster mix with wet brush
or end of spatula filling
pockets full

next:

a clean wet brush
wipes off excess plaster just
before it sets up, flush with
statue surface

after setting, scrape off with
knife edge to retouch further

warning:

the mix that is to fill the wet
pockets should just begin to
set-up at moment of filling

this insures repair plaster
hardness will be the same as
the cast hardness

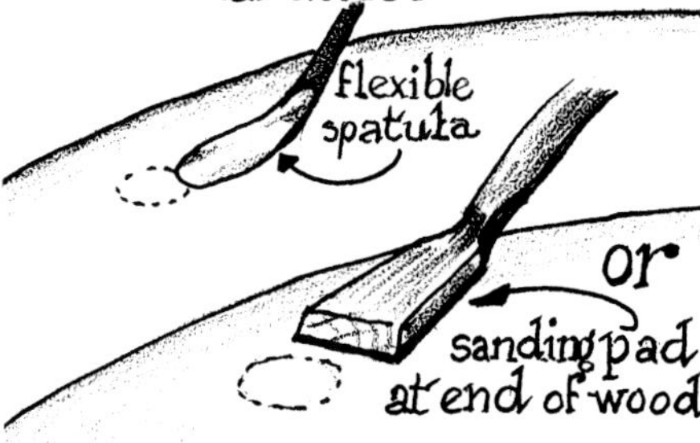

retouching is eased when
all repaired areas are of
same hardness as the cast
and cork dry

Chipping off the Waste Mold

The illustrations show the chisel movement and the chisels slant at various angles to the surface of the mold. With a light hammer, gently crack the plaster with light, short, high-velocity taps (rather than slow driving blows). Be careful to keep the chisel edge from reaching the surface of the cast lying just under the blue layer. As a rule, the blue and white layers do not bond much, so as the outer white one is cut away it exposes more and more of the blue below it.

When, next, the blue layer is carefully knocked away and the surface of the cast becomes exposed, one feels the excitement that comes with "sculpting" rather than modeling. It is this excitement which becomes infectious to onlookers because the process is a speedy one compared with real carving in stone or wood. Watching the "chipping off" of fairly large casts is spellbinding, as the roughness of the surrounding mold is removed and the delicate final surface underneath is revealed.

Large Casts

The photo illustrations (page 125) show a section of a steel-reinforced plaster mold of the armored knights in Lorado Taft's sculptures that flank the entrance of the state capitol in Baton Rouge, Louisiana.

The casts were made and assembled for the stone carvers who, on location, would point them up and carve them in Indiana limestone. The reinforcement steel safeguarded the handling of the plaster mold parts in transit.

All reinforcing bars; steel, wood or other, are held to the mold surfaces with blobs of hemp (or sisal) fibers dipped in plaster. This method is so simple and effective that most sculptors who do a lot of clay modeling use it as a practical method around the studio for connecting things together, whatever they may be. It is somewhat similar to a welder's habit of tacking together this and that "in a jiffy," and creates a bond strong enough to stand much stress.

Sometimes a clay modeler becomes so engrossed by this clay-plaster activity that he abandons earlier intentions to carve in stone or wood. This is a pity since stone carving, although dealing with bulk and weight, is not much more cumbersome than working with heavy plaster molds and casts.

chipping off a waste mold

successive chips 1–7 expose blue layer

white layer

cast

chip after chip exposes more & more of the blue layer

chisel pressed against finger with light taps cracks off blue layer

fingers' flesh acts as rubber to lift chisel upward for each next tap, thus only cracking blue layer

once casting surface is cleared locally, chisel held under right angle will crack off successively a-b-c-d-e-f etc. using snappy blows instead of driving blows

injuries caused by too deep chisel cuts must be scraped clean

before filling with plaster mix in pre-wetted cracks to insure bonding

reinforce molds if needed with wood or steel bars attached with hemp fiber dipped in plaster

pry off after cast has hardened

Piece Molds

The step-by-step procedure illustrated covers most of the recurring problems.

All mold sections must be planned so that once cast, they can interlock against shifting and also be disassembled easily. Follow the illustrations showing how to avoid undercuts and secure the accuracy of all fittings.

In the past it was essential to have absolutely perfect piece molds to secure exact duplicates of the famous sculptures of the old masters. One of the reliable tests for such accuracy was, and remains, that no cast would need any retouching by whatever means. Proof of perfection and accuracy could be found in the telltale signs given by barely visible hair-thin plaster seam marks on the casts at the meeting places between the sections of the mold. They would reveal the slightest *shifting* of the mold parts, which would distort the original form quality and be unacceptable to the artists as well as to the purchaser of the duplicates.

The advanced student can take pleasure today in looking at the perfect casts in plaster of works made by the old masters, in museums here or abroad. Remember: The *forms* of the original and the duplicate are identical.

making piece molds in plaster
each piece must come off easy one by one when taken apart while all pieces must interlock during casting

for this composition three pieces are needed
dividing lines are where clay strips border each piece

clay strip

bend strip along marked dividing line & prop up strip with crumpled newspaper on wood board

nail sidebord on wood base flush with cast base

next: shellac & grease surfaces of all parts to be disassembled later

after casting first piece remove clay strip & turn assembly over for casting 2nd piece

twirl knife-end into plasta to shape cup-lock

first piece

one clay strip is needed to pour second piece

after it is cast

clay strip is removed & lock-cups cut in second piece border; cast third piece

next: disassemble & soap surfaces & re-assemble the 3 pieces for final cast

finished cast

Flexible Molds (Glue and Rubber)

The value of flexible molds rests on their flexibility, which allows for undercuts that would otherwise call for piece molds.

Making a Glue Mold

The glue mold technique is the historical forerunner of all modern methods that use rubber, gelatinous and plastic molds for multiple cast-making of bronzes, cast stone, and plastic statuary.

This book offers the historical glue mold technique only, leaving all other methods up to manufacturers and sellers of modern compounds replacing glue. No doubt their recommended techniques in turn will be adjusted for ever-growing improvement in the years to come.

Hide or bone glue in dry chip form is heated in a double boiler with a minimum amount of water for some hours, until it has melted to a thick honey-like consistency. A little carbolic acid is added to the water if the glue mold is to be used over a long period of time, to safeguard the glue against mildewing.

The plaster model is rigidly and firmly secured to a base so that it cannot shift its position.

A 20″ model that has been cast in plaster is shellaced thoroughly and rubbed with an oily-type separator compound to prevent the glue from sticking to the surface.

For a figure about 14″ to 20″ high, the thickness of the glue mold will be about 3/4″.

Make 3/4″ thick strips of clay about 1″ wide and 20″ long and press them, one at a time, next to one another onto the surface of the figure, until it has been completely enveloped. With fingers or tools, smooth them all together to an even thickness. The aim is to eliminate all undercuts that might have remained, so that over this mantle a plaster housing can be cast in two parts.

This housing may be lightweight but reinforced with hemp fibers for strength (as illustrated). The parts should have *lock* locations to prevent shifting.

Now disassemble and remove the clay mantle, clean the plaster figure's surface, and re-coat it with an oily separator compound.

Prepare for the pour of the glue. The principles of hydraulics should be understood because we deal here with a pressure of liquid on the walls of the vessel, exerting a force that is much greater than we may realize. It was my underestimation of this fact that led me into trouble at one time.

Imagine my loft studio over an old carriage barn on a very hot summer day. I had shed clothes to swim trunks and bare feet. A group of my fellow students and friends were watching, with keen interest, the "master" demonstrate how this job was done. I definitely was

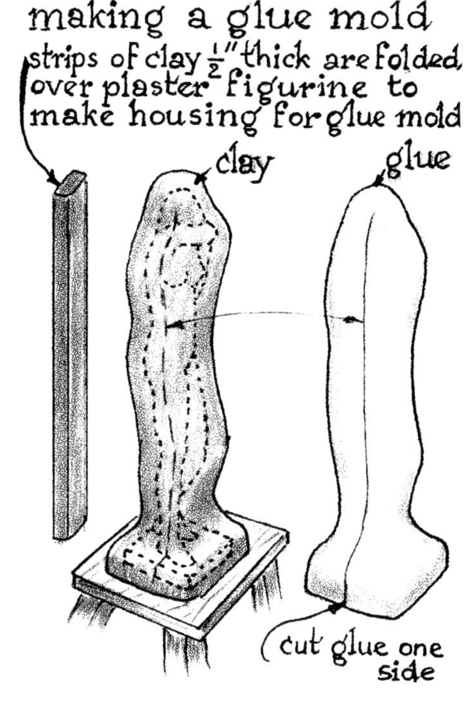

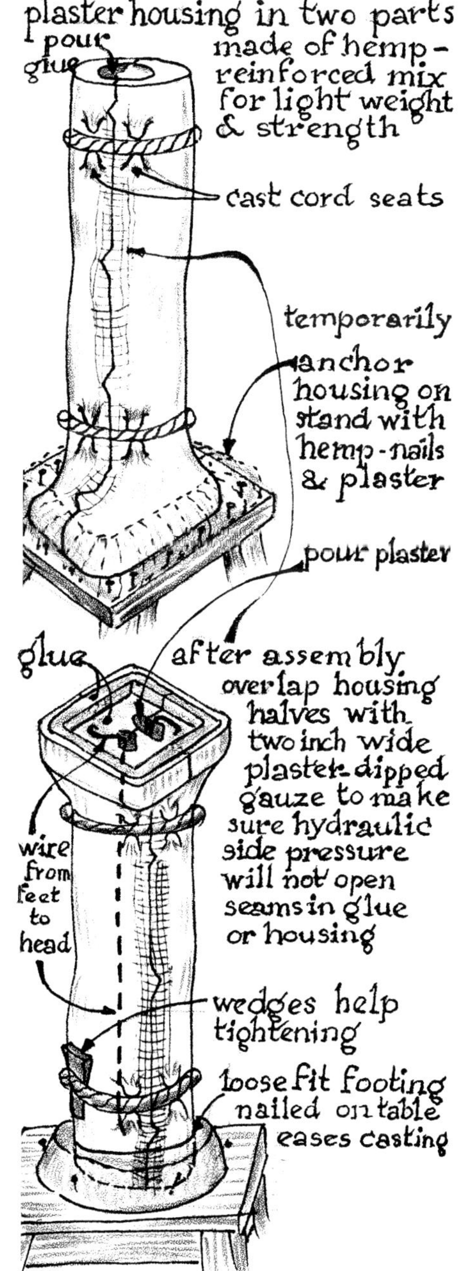

self-confident, if not cocky, and enjoying the attention of an admiring audience. As a student I had a reputation for my combined engineering background and sculpture talent. Therefore, I could not fail in this type of project.

When about one quarter of the glue had been poured into the prepared mold, an onlooker piped up . . . "Alex, I see a little glue coming out a seam here." Undaunted, I put down the glue bucket, saying, "Think nothing of it," and descending from my perch, yanked a hunk of clay from the pile and jammed it over the leak; I then resumed my position and continued pouring. Soon another person, on the other side, pointed out another drop oozing from the mold's seam. I got down to plug that one.

But in the meantime the first leak had found its way between clay plug and housing and was dripping on to the floor. I pressed the first plug a little firmer with more clay, attended to the second one, and, a little puzzled, began to pour once more.

I was certain that I had tied the two interlocking housing halves together very firmly with strong cords and tightening wedges. But by now several new leaks were showing up and dripping on the floor, which was covered with protective newspapers. As I scurried about adding clay to leaks, my feet picked up the glue and then picked up newspapers and all other chips and odds and ends from the floor. Suddenly, we all realized that things were completely out of control, and the scene became one of hilarity at my madcap appearance and losing battle.

This irreversible situation left me with no choice but to lift the whole mold, partly filled with glue, and pour the glue back into the bucket to start all over again, next time better prepared with mistakes corrected. Because of the hydraulic side-pressures, which I had overlooked, it was necessary to bridge the seams with strips of gauze dipped in liquid plaster. This would not only hold the halves together, but seal the seams as well.

After pouring the glue in the mold, let it stiffen overnight. The plaster gauze strips can easily be ripped off and the housing halves separated.

Using a greased knife, the glue mold is next cut open along one location, as shown. It can then be *peeled* off regardless of any moderate undercuts.

Casting Plaster in a Glue Mold

The major handicap of glue and gelatin molds is that when plaster sets, it heats up enough to melt the glue and gelatin wall if it is not peeled off the plaster in time. This means that the craftsman must time himself exactly, in order to intercept *over*-heating, and quickly disassemble the mold at just the right time.

I once witnessed a very impressive handling of casting with glue molds by a true master in this field. He was an Italian plaster-caster who had learned his trade in the traditional way, from father to son. In many countries during the 19th century, humble folks would buy inexpensive plaster statuettes for their homes. Other articles too, such as cheap toys, piggy banks, etc., were popular as plaster casts.

The craftsman I watched in his workshop was casting six "piggy" banks, this time in the shape of elephants. Even without many undercuts, they still required glue molds for easy mass production.

The six assembled molds stood on his long bench, and he was ready with a batch of creamy plaster mix. He poured into the first mold enough to coat the inside with the first layer. Then he picked it up and gyrated it deftly in mid-air. This clearly revealed his visualization of just how that liquid was flowing inside the mold. He did not just haphazardly distribute the liquid plaster, but caught the gravity flow of the liquid in its natural tendency to pull off where it had already covered the inside surface. Thus he "cushioned" the down-flowing plaster without any abrupt halting movements. It was a spellbinding performance for those who understood what was at stake inside the mold!

As soon as he judged it ready, he poured the excess plaster back in the bowl and very gently placed the first mold back on the bench. Without a second's loss, he repeated successively the same operation with all six elephants down the line, emptying each bowl at the finish.

Next he mixed enough plaster to add the second layer. By this time he figured that the first one had set enough and could now receive the second layer. Very carefully the second layer was added to each following mold and, behold, when he filled the last one, every drop of the plaster had been used.

By this time the first mold was setting up, just short of overheating. He quickly placed it in the upright position, separated the housing halves, deftly peeled the glue mold off and plopped it back into its housing to keep it from warping.

So he continued, one after the other, and there stood six steaming elephants, perfect and unblemished! My memory is one of an immaculate workshop where not one morsel of plaster was wasted or spilled and where the shelves all around displayed his finished products ready for the market.

Let the modern reader and student be reminded that the *craft* of plaster-casting at one time ranked equally with all other esteemed crafts: carpentry, blacksmithing, furniture making, house painting, etc. The village trade school was the backbone of the future self-employed master craftsman; he was a part of the country's guild system.

In those years, a well-furnished house was rarely without decorated ceilings with plaster cherubs and ornate, complicated moldings originating from a wide stock of molds for the customer's choice. Well into the 20th century this kind of ornamentation of house interiors persisted. And, who knows; it may be revived again.

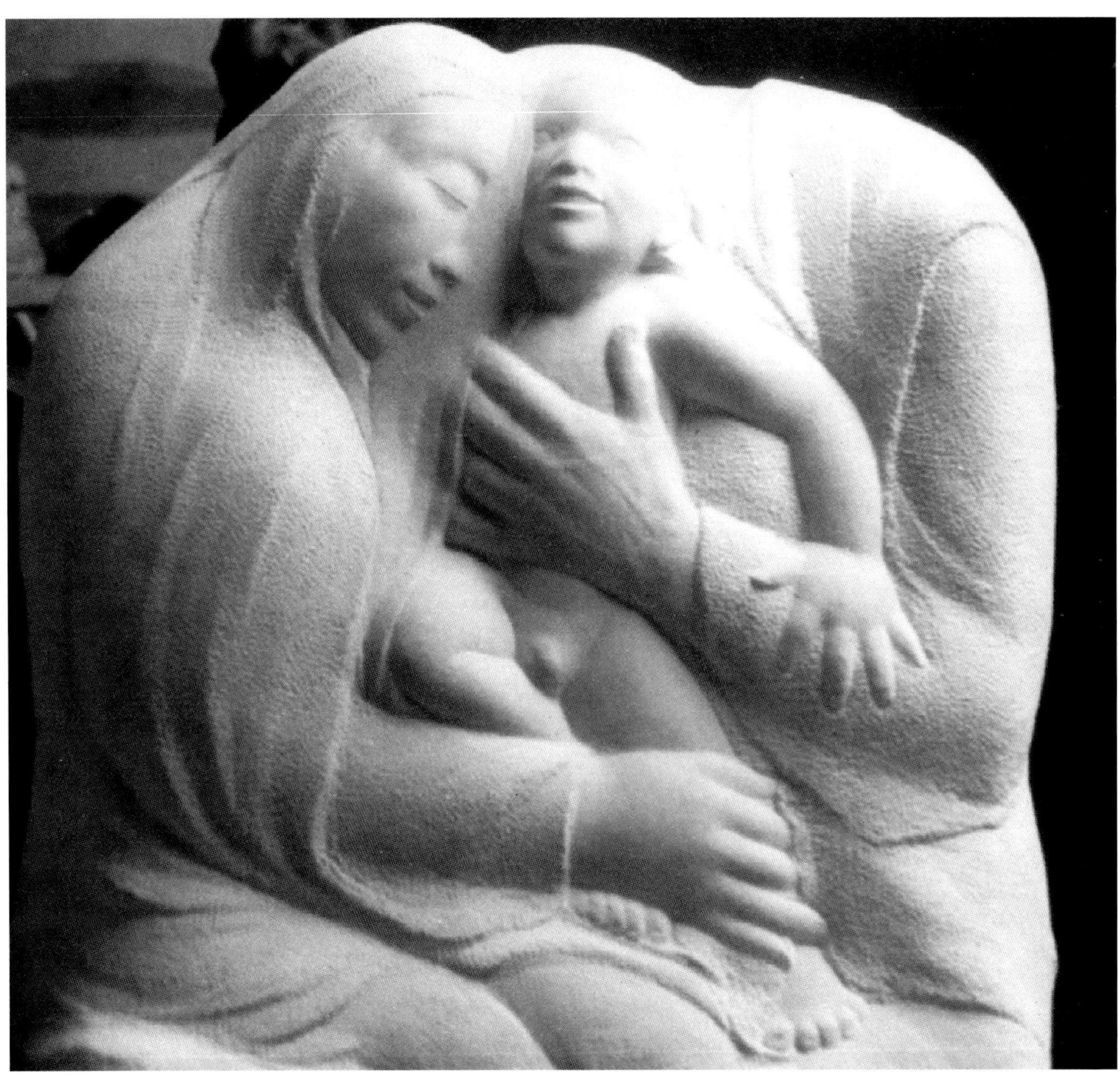

"The Future"
Life-size Sandstone

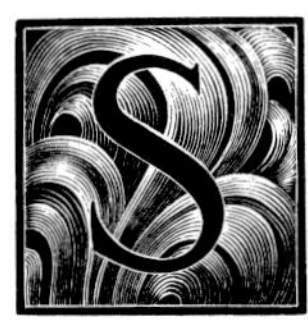

Chapter 8

Stone Carving

A safe beginning in learning to carve in stone is the making of duplicates from plaster casts, using measuring tools.

Advantages:

1. No anxiety about misjudgments while learning.

2. Getting acquainted with the same tools that will be used later in direct carving.

3. Increasing one's range of stone carving know-how.

Disadvantages:

1. Dependence on measuring devices, which tends to become a setback to natural eye-sighting ability so necessary in direct carving.

2. Missing the exciting creative aspect of direct carving.

My own disciplined learning and long years of practicing stone carving have given me a wide range of stone carving facility. From my experience I hope to provide the student with the much needed data on how to begin his first attempts at stone carving.

It is his option, based on the degree of the aspirant sculptor's inborn talents and aptitudes, whether he should begin first with direct carving or with the making of copies.

My first teacher, Mr. Zimmerman, at the Lorado Taft studios in Chicago in 1930-31, taught me the use of the "pointing" instrument (often referred to as a "pointing machine"). (See illustration.) It transfers needed measurements "A" from the plaster cast to the stone. When freehand carving between the measured points begins, finer and finer teeth claws are used, followed by flat chisels, rasps, abrasive papers, and, for polishing, a crumpled lead ball and emery powder with copious flushing with water for a final sheen.

Making Duplicates from Plaster Casts

This type of duplicating was prevalent in the 19th century as the favored method of reproducing clay compositions in marble.

A cast in plaster was made of the clay model; it was then turned over to hired marble carvers for duplication. These experts would deliver the finished marble duplicates to be signed by the artist, if he approved of them and considered them accurate.

There was an outpouring of thousands of these marble statues, copied in this manner. Their telltale *clay* character showed, and they looked like *petrified* clay, as, for example, does Rodin's marble pieces. These can easily be identified as duplicates by the numerous pinpoint spots left on their surfaces where the pointing instrument overshot the depth measurement a little.

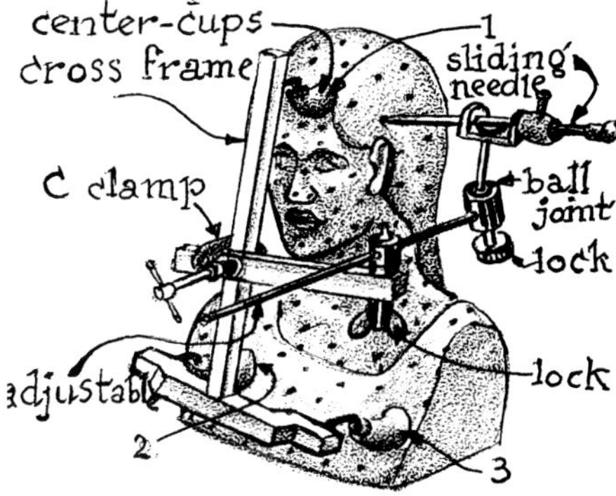

to reach identical measure of cast
all marked points cut this way
prepare for final surface carving by sighting only

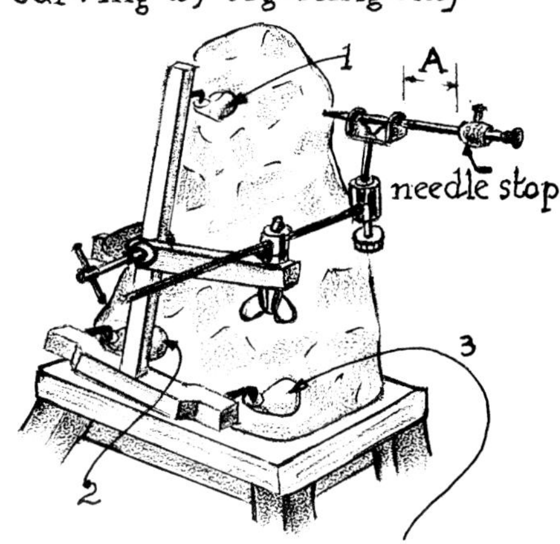

1-2-3 positioned identical on cast & stone

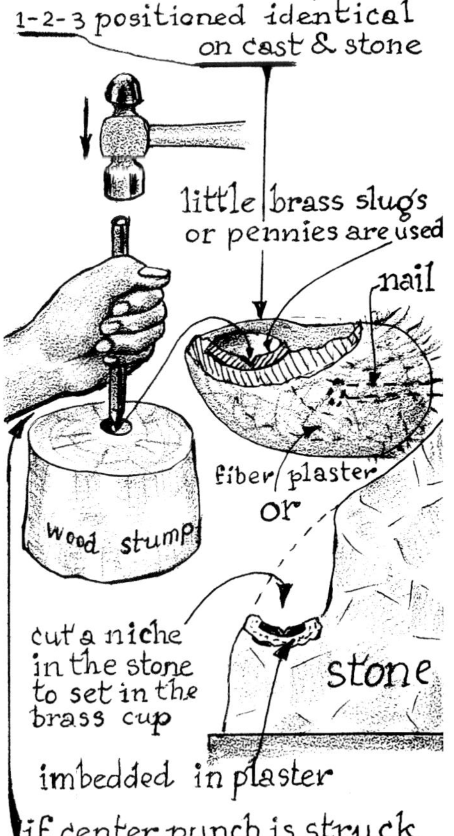

if center punch is struck hard enough on wood base slug will bend in cup shape

Stone Carving Tools

WARNING: WEAR GOGGLES AT ALL TIMES!

The one point. This basic chipping tool is used to
"rough-out" the statue. Depending on the angle
between tool and stone, a larger or smaller chip will
crack off. The size of the chip corresponds to the size
of the crater on the stone surface. If the stone is
homogeneous and evenly hard, remarkable control
and judgment in chipping is possible. The aim is to use
only the one point for the *entire* roughing out of the
composition, before any refining begins with the claws.

Follow-up tools. *Claws* are tools with two or more
points. Each point of the claw actually does what the
one point does. Claws reduce the stone surface to a
finer and finer texture. The greater the number of teeth
in the claw, the less time it will take to establish a
"finished" surface. The sculptor may not even wish to
smooth the surface any further.

Sharpening Claw Teeth and Retempering

Claw teeth wear fast and need resharpening often.
The teeth become flatter and flatter until their spacing
grooves almost disappear. Just before that happens,
anneal the tool (heat the working end to a barely visible
heat glow, then cool it slowly in ashes). Clamp that
softened end in a vise, and place a hacksaw blade in
the remaining groove to maintain correct spacing. Next,
re-cut the grooves on each side, deep enough to follow
up with the file, as illustrated.

Two methods of restoring hardness of teeth are
suggested:

> 1. **Quench hardening.** Once the teeth have been
> restored, heat 1/4" of the restored working end
> dark cherry red in the fire and quench it in water.

> 2. **Tempering.** Polish the re-filed surfaces on a
> buffer after the quench, so that oxidation colors
> will be clearly visible during tempering. Draw to
> *straw color* over a blue flame and quench at that
> instant.

Tool Sharpening in General

*WARNING: ALWAYS WEAR GOGGLES WHEN
MOTOR GRINDING!*

Motor dry-grinders can sharpen tools quickly if the
tool's temperature is kept cool by frequent quenching
in water. Although water grinders safeguard tool
hardness, they are slower.

One can learn to use electric motor dry-grinders safely.
It takes a little practice but does save time and effort. I
often let a whole batch of dulled tools accumulate, then
sharpen all, one after the other, and am ready to start
the day.

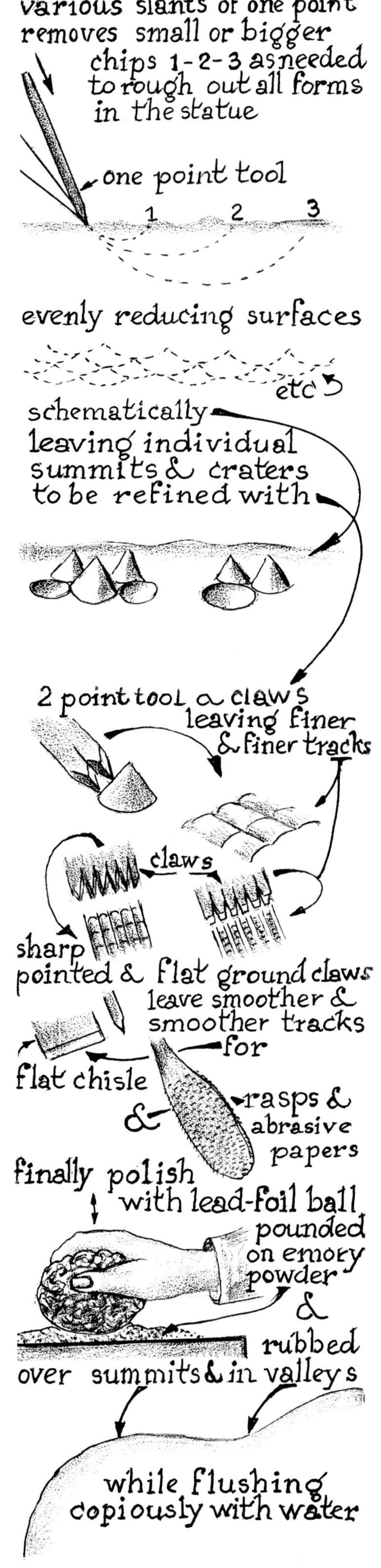

The job of attaining proper tool hardness is an unnecessary and avoidable headache for the artist. My admonition: Learn once and for all to make, temper, design and sharpen your own tools. Next to the important study of *form*, this should be your priority. Know all the ins and outs of your field. The making of your own tools is within arm's reach and makes you more independent and free of compromises. Every dexterous person will be able to acquire that skill by following strictly the step-by-step procedure shown in my book, ***THE COMPLETE MODERN BLACKSMITH***: Ten Speed Press, Publisher; Berkeley, CA.

Special Stone-Cutting Tools

Some are shown here with notations for their use. No doubt many sculptors may invent special tools to meet particular problems or needs. Be inventive at all times and end up becoming your own teacher.

The cleaving chisel. This is used for splitting stone. A groove is prepared in the block of stone, along which it is to be split. The one-point can somewhat deepen it; then it is refined further with a sturdy, sharp, flat chisel. The block itself should be heavy enough (200 pounds or over, depending on the size of the piece to be split off) to take heavy hammer blows without the remaining part becoming accidentally cracked. The slanted facet of the tool end directs the tool impact outwardly from the main block. If the cleavage runs parallel with the grain of the block, heavy hammer blows should start it cracking after a few blows. A little water in the beginning crack aids in deeper penetration and adds hydraulic side-force with each blow exerted.

Tapered drift-pins. A second method is to drill holes a few inches apart along the line where the stone is to break, deep enough to insert the steel tapered drift-pins. Each pin is successively and evenly hammered in, at first gently, one after the other. Repeated hammering, as a rule, will cause an even break.

The star drill. The crossed edges of the drill, hammered onto the stone, will crush it. The tool is turned a little for each hammer blow so that the stone, at the bottom of the hole, gradually pulverizes on impact. Using a tube, blow out the dust from time to time until the resulting hole meets the needed depth. This same system is still practiced with air power hammers. In the mines, some large-caliber star drills have full length, small diameter holes through which water, under power, flushes out the pulverized stone during hammering.

Modern carbide-tipped drills driven by electric, rotary motor power can be used on hard stones. They are less noisy than star drills and convenient when one is not equipped with air compressor outfits.

Bush hammers and bush-ended hand tools. The illustrations show how, on impact, the points *crush* the stone as did the star drill. The bush tool is the favorite tool for the sculptor who chooses a harder stone, such as granite, for his sculptures. Granite surfaces are often left with bush hammer textures. If a smooth polish is required,

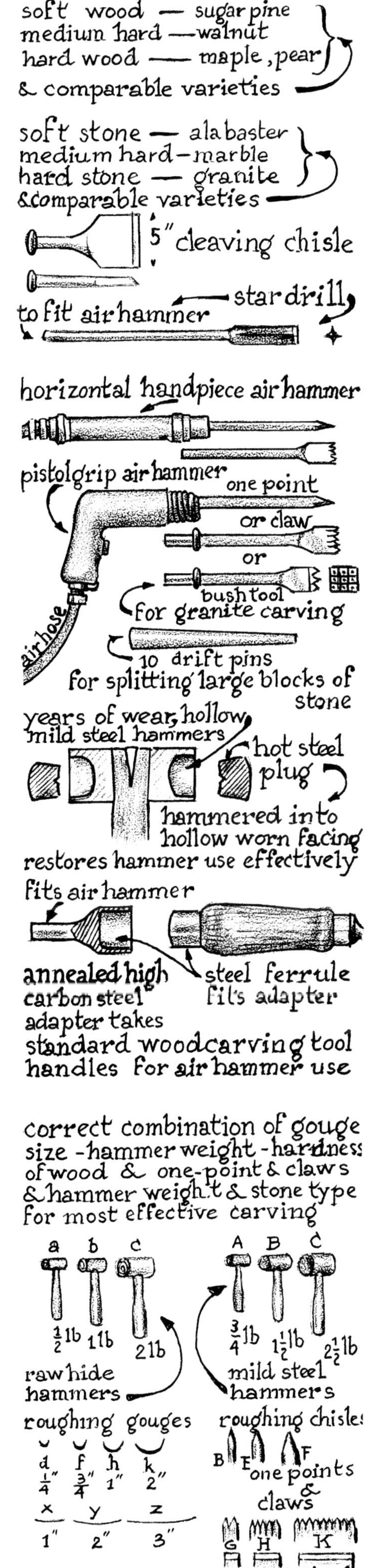

grinding and further refining is done with abrasive tools
and finally polishing buffers.

Bush tools are easily made if the studio has a little forge
to temper the waffle pattern a light bronze color after
brittle-quenching. (See *THE COMPLETE MODERN
BLACKSMITH*: Ten Speed Press, Publisher; Berkeley, CA.)

Rasps and abrasives. These remove the marks left by the
last claws but may be used after a straight-edged flat
chisel precedes them, in order to reduce wearing down
the rasps.

The *abrasive* could be any durable grit (garnet,
Carborundum, aluminum-oxide) glued onto paper or
cloth; patches can be stuck on wooden holders, as shown,
to act as little abrasive pads.

Sawing Stone

Although this is rarely practiced in a sculptor's studio,
knowing how it is done may prompt a stone carver to
apply the technique on a small scale.

Small semi-hard stones may be cut by power abrasive
wheels. Brick and marble slabs are cut in this way. Extra
hard stones, such as granite, jade, and rose quartz, are cut
with diamond wheels.

In Italy, at the Henraux marble works, I have watched the
cutting of large blocks of marble with an endless,
pulley-driven wire (spiral square) fed with water and
sand. Detailed information on this procedure can be
found in a good library.

A sculptor may sometimes wish to cut through softer
stones with a saw-type action resembling the wire, sand
and water method. Like a crosscut saw, the blade may
have a smooth or toothed edge, fed with sand and
constantly replenished with plenty of water while cutting.

Chemical "Etching"

Muriatic acid will dissolve limestone (marble is a form
of limestone). Wetting a smooth marble surface with this
acid takes the place of the more laborious emery
powder/lead ball technique (see page 62). The use of
muriatic acid, however, requires prolonged rinsing with
water afterward; you must make certain not a trace of
acid residue is left, since in time it would etch the surface
and dull the polish sheen, undoing the previous work.
This rinsing resembles the rinsing of photo prints in a
darkroom to make sure no hypo aftereffects will
gradually stain the prints.

Commercially, the acid system prevails as a shortcut to
meet public demand for highly polished material, often
bringing out the color and graining of specially veined
marble.

Beginning to Carve a Statue

How to Flatten and Smooth a Base of a Statue

This should be learned as a first assignment, to be used in preparation for any sculpture carving.

After chipping the unaligned bottom plane flat with the one-point, use the two-, three-, and six-point claws to refine the surface. A completely smooth surface for a base is not necessary since a statue, as a rule, is to stand on another flat surface. A steady contact between the two flat surfaces is what counts.

The illustrations are self-explanatory. In the end, a helper is needed to speed up the work; use constantly replenished sand and water to refine the surface flatness still further.

First Holding Method

The stone, on which you have just prepared a flattened surface may be held to a sturdy work table by mean of four tightly fitting cleats nailed to the work surface.

Alternately, the stone may be imbedded in hemp or sisal fiber, saturated with wet plaster covering nails driven into the top of a sturdy stand.

Second Holding Method

After preparing the stone with a flat base first, the most practical way to hold it fast for carving is by cradling it in sandbags. This is especially good for odd-shaped stones found in nature. Since the sandbags, being heavy themselves, will add to the mass of the stone, they will receive the hammer blows by supporting the stone, so that chips will crack off easier.

Choice of Stones

Very hard stones often make direct carving impossible. They may be *ground* into shapes which, when polished, often show a surface beauty of gem quality. Lapidarists, more than sculptors, enjoy arduous grinding and polishing when there is less interest in *form per se* as the sculptor knows it. The gemstone enthusiast's pleasure is more in the spellbinding glow, shine, sparkle and color of gem-quality stone than in sculptural products.

Soft stones, such as chalk rock, soft sandstone, alabaster, soapstone, tuffa, etc., can be cut with pocket knives and the like. Much work with soft stone is done in areas where such stone abounds and is cheap.

For instance, in Bali, Indonesia, most temple carvings are done in soft lava rock, but these deteriorate outdoors in twenty or more years through weathering. As a result, new temple carvings must replace the old from time to time. This explains why, for centuries and to the present day, the Balinese have kept the sculpture arts alive.

The modern Balinese, having seen many Western artists' works, are often inspired to do nontraditional carvings, which they happily and artistically incorporate. Sculptures made by the good artists reveal the widest

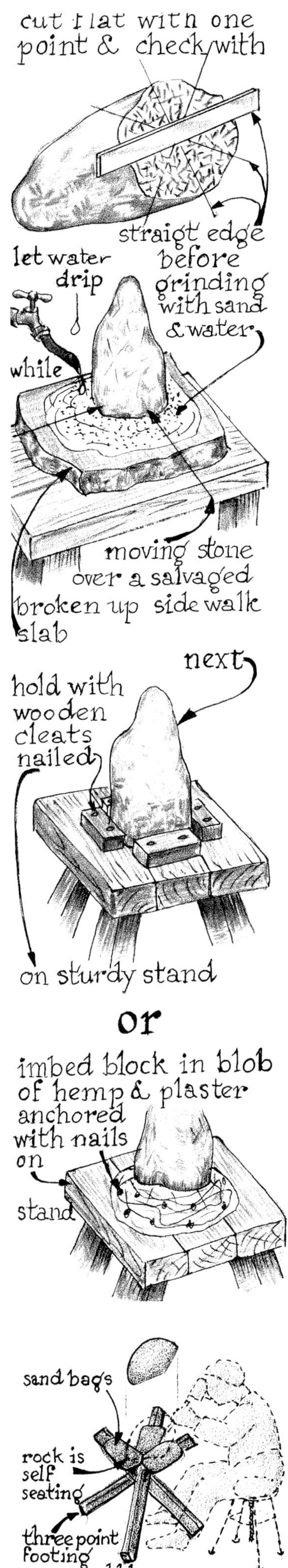

range of fantasies and are carved with extreme skill.
However, the poorly-carved tourist "junk" must be
forgiven considering the poverty among the populace
who, artists or not, will carve in order to make ends meet.

Medium-hard stones. In earliest historical times, the
talented among sculptors favored medium-hard
limestone and sandstone for their carvings. These stood
up quite well in the outdoors. Later, classical sculptors,
Greek, Italian and Roman, also carved in such
medium-hard stones.

I, too, have found the hard limestone and sandstone my
favorite material. One of the advantages of the *hard*
limestones is their nonabrasive quality, which helps the
tools maintain sharpness longer.

The abrasive *soft* sandstone wears the tool edges down
faster than nonabrasive *hard* limestones, so that the tools
require frequent resharpening. (Note: a steel knife blade
slashed through soft valve-grinding compounds
acquires a *dull* edge while shining at the same time.)

The resharpening job is made much easier by the
speedy, motor-driven dry-grinders which can resharpen
tool edges in a jiffy. (Always remember to cool the tool
in water frequently during grinding to keep the temper.)
Resharpening, no longer a time-comsuming chore,
becomes a pleasure.

Before quitting for the day, the sculptor can resharpen
a batch of tools in 10 or 15 minutes, making them ready
for the next day's round of work. That has been my
procedure all these years when working on a piece of
direct carving in limestone or sandstone. Hewing and
carving in a solid block of medium-hard stone is very
satisfying when a large batch of sharpened tools is
ready at hand for uninterrupted work.

Sculptors or artisans, when they let the chips fly, seem
to the observer to be spellbound, as those who have
visited studios or workshops will agree. Even the
non-artist or the hired stone carver making duplicates
can experience a vicarious pleasure in watching the
artist's work take shape under his own hands, even
though the creative part is not his.

When *prospecting for material in nature,* one must first
scale the stone for flaws, cracks, homogeneity or any
telltale signs that might threaten disaster if not
discovered before a piece of sculpture is under way.

First, with a heavy hammer, deliver a hard blow to the
stone. If it "rings," rather than sounding dull, chances
are all is well.

Second, with a hammer and one-point, probe all
suspicious spots (hard or soft) for cracks or rot. Cut
away all material around a crack until the bottom of it
has been reached. In time the remaining solid core of
the stone will be left and can be judged for its quality.
Only then should the serious carving of the visualized
composition begin.

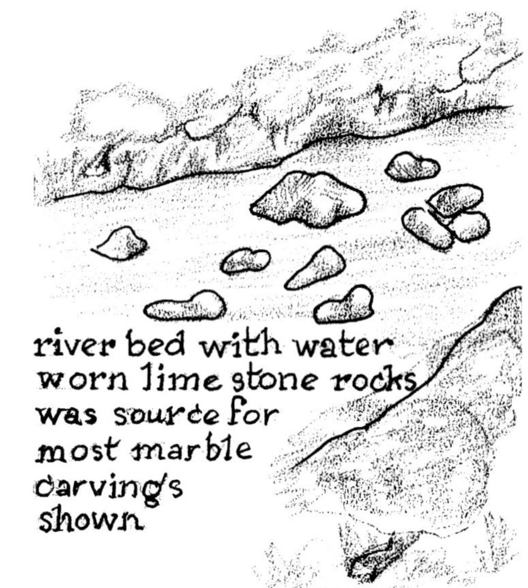

The Marble Hand

I chose to live in Florence, Italy where I could study marble carving techniques in the shops of the Frilli Brothers. I began my studies by making a plaster cast of the clay model I had made of my own hand. My Italian teachers felt they should not waste a bigger piece on me as a beginner, since they expected me to spoil such a difficult subject in a first try. After all, their tradition called for beginners to start with easy subjects like apples and pears, using waste pieces of marble, then gradually progress to more complicated carvings. The subject, which was my own hand, would barely fit within the piece they gave me.

My teacher, Mr. Ettore Masi, began instructing his first class in a soft gentle voice. But my "Non capisco" ("I don't understand"), one of my first Italian phrases, made him repeat what he said, only a little louder. Again, my "Non capisco" was followed by successively ever-louder answers. At last he threw up his hands in despair, believing me very slow-witted and perhaps a waste of time. Still, he was puzzled at seeing the fine model I made and cast.

But when, in the passing weeks, I learned more words, used their little forge to make and temper my own tools, and after two months finished *The Marble Hand,* (see page 124) without mishap, I established a reputation of such esteem that they began to refer to me as "Il professore."

Having thus progressed more and more, I had also become anxious to start working earlier in the morning, instead of waiting for my co-workers, who would show up later at odd hours. They gladly gave me the half pound key to the enormous ancient doors. The privilege had a price. Within a few minutes after I arrived and started work, I was attacked by vast numbers of fleas awakened from their night slumber in the pile of marble chips in the corner. Every five minutes I had to stop and rub them off my wrists, neck and ankles. But I was delivered from them with the first arrival of my co-workers, whose familiar blood they seemed to prefer. From then on the curses and scratchings were theirs.

With the warm summer days, the fleas had become unbearable, even to my friends, and Alphonso, the lowest in rank on the totem pole, wheeled out the chips, dumped all in the Lungaro, then doused the dusty corners with carbolic acid to discourage more flea breeding.

The walls of the workshop were lined with shelves that stored the stock of plaster casts from which marble duplicates were made for sale in their Florence shop windows. The floor space had a dividing wall, and large high windows lighted both work areas.

There was a little charcoal forge and a beat-up anvil where each worker could make his tools, a large foot-operated water-wheel grinder for tool sharpening, and a vise on a bench for filing teeth in claws. My own skills in tool making and maintenance sealed my acceptance into the group. Aware from the outset that I struggled financially, they refused to take any money for their guidance, knowing themselves what it meant to live from hand to mouth.

I wish they could have seen how, during all my following art career years, I applied their know-how of crafts and techniques in my work and teaching, thus carrying their torch in marble carving from past to present.

The Red Marble Torso
(See photo page 122)

Shown are the steps in enlarging this piece from the 1/3 size plaster model. Note that this little model was left in its clay pellet built-up state and that all critical points for measurements marked on its surface proved sufficient, leaving the smoothing of the surface for the larger marble.

Purposely, I chose a marble that was tricky (Rosso de' Verona). This type of marble is mainly used for decorative wall slabs in church altar lining, etc. Its beautiful veining and polished final surfacing make it choice material for veneering. I reasoned that knowing how to work ideal marble for delicate subjects, such as the hand, and tricky marble for more "chunky" subjects, such as the torso, would enable me to tackle most problems that such a range of stone varieties would present in the future.

The illustrations show the successive steps in the 3-caliper enlarging procedure. As with the pointing instrument, when all critical measurements have been transferred, the carver does the rest by eye-sighting only. My Italian teachers showed me the most effective way of smoothing final surfaces to their ultimate polish. A crumpled lead foil ball is pounded into fine emery powder spread over a board. The emery granules become halfway embedded into the lead. The valleys as well as the summits of the marble surface then can be reached with the "give" of the lead so that protruding parts of the surface will not wear down more than the valleys. Large amounts of water should be used to flush away the collected stone pulp from the lead ball. (See also the chemical method described on page 64).

Unavoidable injuries to the stone sometimes happen during the chipping. The one-point tool, at its deepest penetration, crushes the stone and pulverizes it to a depth of 1/16" at its point. This leaves chalk-white spots on the surface, sometimes referred to as *rotten* spots. Skin-deep carving over those white-spotted surfaces with razor-sharp fine teeth claws will reach the bottom of the spots, leaving a uniform uninjured surface. The white spots should not worry the sculptor doing direct carving, if he leaves enough reserve material for the follow-up claw carving.

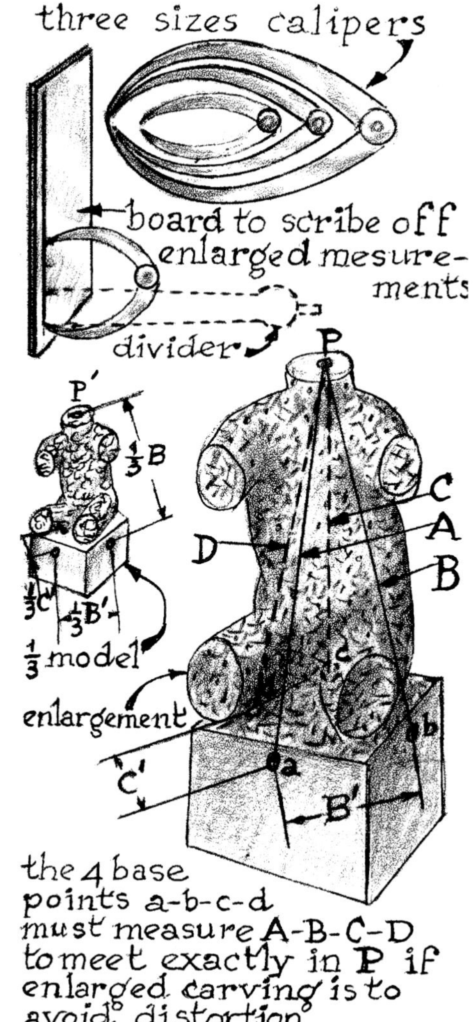

Chapter 9

Direct Carving in Stone or Wood

Direct carving means cutting directly into a block of stone or wood without the use of measuring devices, models, pre-studies, sketches or anatomy books . . . all of which are like crutches needed initially during studies.

Such freedom in sculpting comes about if the student practices and follows diligently the assignments and theory studies until he feels he can throw away those crutches.

By using the techniques of stone and wood carving, the student learns to work from the outside, inwardly directed, until he reaches the final form surfaces he visualizes. This is the opposite approach from the modeler, who builds with clay from the inside, outwardly directed.

In carving, the principle is to cut from the block chip after chip, round and round, as a beaver does. But the sculptor must remove only the minimum of material, so that what remains is the *largest* composition within the block, unlike the beaver, who cuts toward zero to fell his tree.

A First Carving in Stone or Wood

The illustrations on the following page simulate the live demonstration: the progressive sequence when cutting chip after chip, carving toward one's *visualization* of the composition. Keep always in mind that *form per se* is the rule, regardless of subject matter or size.

When carving small or medium-size pieces, there is no need for a studio or elaborate equipment. I did the 15″ and 20″ carvings (shown in Chapter 15, **Sculptures Analyzed**) while sitting or standing in a small space under proper light. For these small carvings, the tools used were made like those shown in my book, **THE COMPLETE MODERN BLACKSMITH**: Ten Speed Press, Publisher; Berkeley, CA, their design based on the manipulation of wood engraver's burins adapted to small gouges. (See pages 119-120)

If a skilled clay modeler attempts *direct carving* for the first time, he will find it useful to remember the definition of *form* demonstrated by the pudding and the pudding mold, the cast and its mold. With his already accomplished skill in clay modeling, he is ready to apply that ability to the carving of solid material. He may become an instant convert from clay modeling to stone or wood carving. I have seen this happen again and again.

At first a variety of material, such as plastics, ceramic, bronze, etc. may hold the modeler fascinated by the craft of casting work rather than carving *form*. Another factor may hold him back from carving stone or wood: the higher earnings with less arduous labors in casts of bronze and other materials.

Many artists postpone doing art for the love of it until they think they can afford to do so. Who is to say what should or should not be done when each of us does the best he can under his own circumstances? After all, philosophical implications must be digested before becoming meaningful, to be applied by those who are able to *live* them, besides be conversant with them.

How to Begin

The student will need to make a small clay sketch of his composition first. From it his teacher can pinpoint problems and demonstrate corrections. (The advanced artist may not need a model.)

The small sketch then can be cast in plaster. The most critical spots, where it is judged that the final carving is to touch the outside of the original block, can be marked with a felt-tip pen. These markings are *tangent points* which must not be lost during carving. *From* those points material is carved *away* toward the visualized local forms to which they pertain.

Stance, proportion and form approximation are of major importance throughout the carving procedure. *The stance must not get lost*, especially as we work around the 360 degree viewing, or it may end up as straight as a ramrod.

To sharpen one's visualization, think of the composition as enveloped by a membrane which stretches over individual protruding forms at *tangent points.*

Now all spaces in-between are carved away step by step. Start carving from the tangent points, where the "membrane" touches the forms; the marked points simply show the "lay of the land."

As soon as the forms around the tangent points become recognizable approximations, *stop carving*. Review all that has been done so far, turning the work round and round, before resorting to corrective carving here and there. Gradually the emerging composition is revealed, bringing about an exhilarating sensation, as if the figure looms out of the mist. In this manner, danger spots are surrounded with reserve material; you can maintain control, and the beginnner is released from the fear of carving too deep anywhere.

At one time, my stone-carving master in Lorado Taft's studios in Chicago was asked by a visiting lady, "Mr. Zimmerman, what do you do when you go too deep?" The thin old man stopped his carving, looked over his steel-rimmed working glasses, answered in his thick, German Swiss accent, "I djoomp in de lake," and continued carving where he had left off.

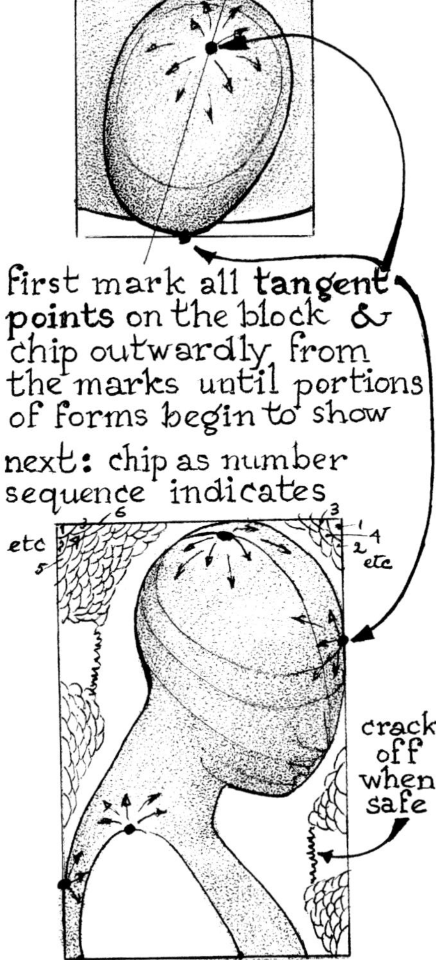

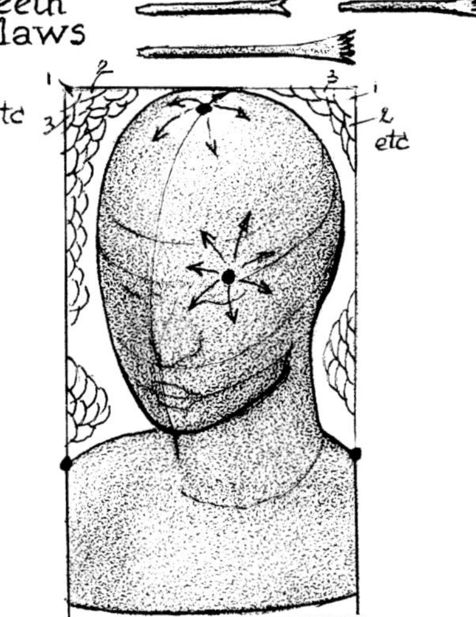

on non abrasive stones use rasps
after claw finished surfacing

Let it be said again that, during sculpting, perfect control can always be assured when a little material is kept in reserve to allow for corrective carving. In crafts that rely on a *direct* approach through *sighting* instead of use of instruments, the artist's creative flow is least impeded, his verve unhampered.

In all direct carving, *the moment when the artist stops carving* is a critical one; *he must know when enough is enough.* Has the final surface been truly reached? Should we take off one more chip here, another one there?

A cartoon in a humor magazine shows a sculptor with hammer and chisel in hand, standing on a scaffold above the head of a heroic-sized figure. He has given it "just one last tap"—splitting the piece full length in half.

When is a piece finished? Be reminded of a bullet shot vertically up into the sky. Its velocity diminishes up to its culmination point, then it falls back. Ours is the critical moment when we *feel* that we are as near as we can come to our own culmination point, and we must stop just before reaching it if we are to avoid falling down or undoing what we accomplished before. It is a philosophical cliff-hanger . . . shall I stop or shall I not? Self-discipline must enter to save the day.

Beginners sometimes feel that each study should end up as a masterpiece. When they reach the limits of their ability they are likely to overwork a piece. Then fear, born of inexperience, slows down their pace until they stare themselves blind, and there is no more progress; they bog down. At this point it is time to stop work, seek some diversion, or rest.

With a fresh start, carve from one location to the other, crisscross all over the piece. Stop again and again to review the work done thus far, in order to sharpen judgment.

If, at this time, there is a feeling of helplessness, lay the piece aside and start carving another composition until with it too you reach your limits. After carving more pieces, return to the first one. Examine it carefully and you will then discover that you have gained experience while doing the successive pieces, so that you can carve to correct mistakes in the original that you had not noticed before. In this way you will get closer and closer to your visualization with less danger of spoiling the piece. In time, improved skill and insight enable you to see further ahead as to just what material must be removed from the block. What once was confusing about the uncarved areas between unfolding forms, now becomes simply a chore to attend to in due time.

Early fear now becomes boldness. In time, rapid carving becomes a real pleasure of certainty and daring, of working on separated areas and knowing the piece will come out right. This is the ultimate reward of self-discipline and restraint when needed, with control and constant reviewing of every phase of the work. The meaning of form becomes clearer and more manageable; everything seems to "unfold" fluently.

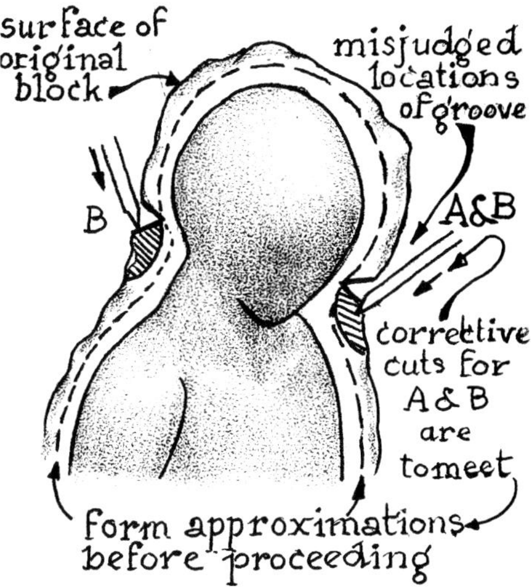

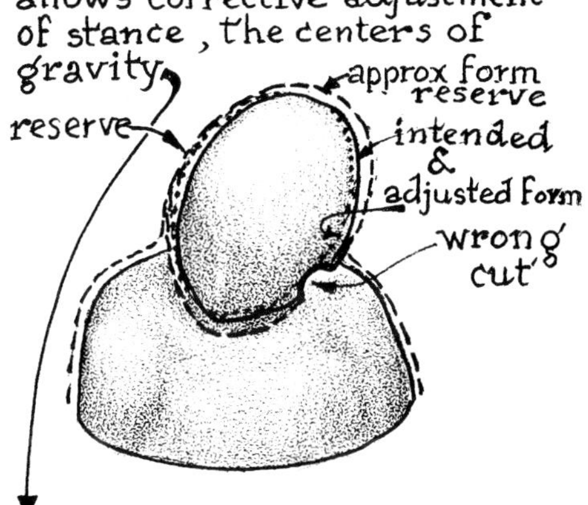

the new stance adjustment after corrective carving is acceptable if close enough to original articulation of body parts for the composition

It is only now, in our process of learning, that the unfinished, as well as the finished works of the old masters can be appreciated. When we are over the worst hurdles, we become our own teachers, and in time, instead of *reading* books, we may possibly end up *writing* them, adding our own contributions to what has already been written.

The Importance of Articulation during Direct Carving

The *stance* of a figure requires that the centers of gravity of the large, separate form approximations have been correctly placed.

Warning: The gradual cutting here and there, round and round, tends to shift form relationships without our noticing. A *straightening* of the previously more angular *stance* occurs. Sometimes we discover this too late to carry out corrective carving. Exasperated, we admit that if the carving had been done with measuring tools from a precise plaster model, for instance, such error might have been avoided.

However, being forewarned of the dangers of misjudgment in direct carving is half the battle. Often, using a little exaggeration in the *stance angle* during the roughing-out will allow for some of its loss during progressive carving. In the end, the exaggerations will have been softened to the final form approximations, well before detailing starts. After the novice has had a few close calls with mistakes while carving, he becomes well prepared not to fall into the same trap again.

Another danger is that we may be tempted to "fix" angles in a needed stance by cutting grooves between forms where we believe the form intersections ought to be. Should it be necessary to relocate the forms, those deep grooves will eat into adjacent forms, leaving insufficient reserve material for corrective carving. It is very important that the *stance* of the human figure in sculpture look logical to the viewer. Therefore, cutting incorrect grooves often spells failure.

Once more then, go over your correct clay studies, never underestimating the importance of them. Clay modeling remains the most time-saving and effective way to learn what can and cannot be done in shaping and grouping forms. It also is the simplest way for the beginner student to be guided toward the skill of *direct carving* later on.

Important things to remember:

1. When beginning a carving, *never dwell on favorite spots* in the early stages. For instance, if a figure's face in a composition plays the most important part, it tends to become too small or too big if carved before the other parts of the composition have been carved. Check on the correctness of proportions, stance and articulation when practicing clay modeling. Be aware of the danger of losing track of the rest of the body when a favored part grows out of proportion.

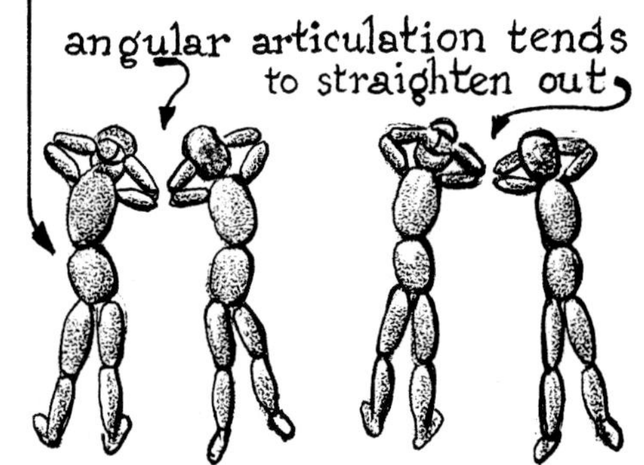

2. Never use the term "blocking-out" in regard to a composition. Instead, use the term "form approximations" when composing groups of forms to be shaped. It is best to stick to imageries nearest to what we mean to portray in three-dimensional form. To "block" suggests cubical forms which cancel out *positive* and *dynamic* forms.

3. When two *positive* forms intersect one another, refer to lines of *intersection*, not to lines as in a drawing or of a silhouette. *Talking about lines in sculpture undermines correct thinking in terms of form. Think always of FORMS: lines are only the result of form meetings* (lines of intersection). Learn to think three-dimensionally *directly*, instead of in a roundabout way.

4. Consider at the very outset which is to be more important to you: form for the sake of form or material for the sake of its polished color, veining, texture, etc.

5. Always carve *outwardly* from the tangent marks of forms; never carve from the deeper areas between forms toward those tangent marks.

6. Do not draw silhouette lines on a beam to be hand-sawed for later sculpture carving. This works against three-dimensional thinking. Learn to visualize three-dimensional form directly, from every viewing angle; do not just think of seeing outlines from one direction at a time. Recognize that if a piece is band-sawed first from one silhouette, then from a second silhouette under ninety degrees, the result will be a bastardized configuration unrecognizable as the originally visualized composition. Therefore, erase from your mind the whole attempt at shortcuts using silhouette carving or sawing. Direct carving has no room for line substitutes.

How to Proceed without a Pre-Study or a Teacher's Help

When working in *wood*, clamp pieces that are larger than 12" in length in a vise (See page 82), so the composition can be roughed-out with hammer and chisel before detailed carving with small hand-pushed tools begins.

When carving in a large block of *stone*, weighing 50 pounds or over, *work only with the one-point tool, until all form approximations have been carved. Only then is detailing done with the claws* (followed by sanding, rasping and polishing for a final smooth surface, if desired).

Stand in front of the untouched beam or block, all the while *visualizing* the composition you aim for. Next, judge as best you can all the *tangent points* where the figure in its stance is to touch the surface of the beam or block as if it were leaning inside against it. Mark these points with chalk, from every angle all around the beam. Check the accuracy of your judgment for a second time,

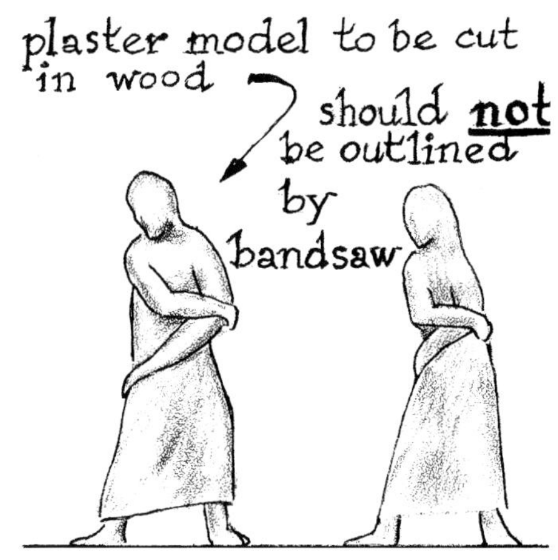

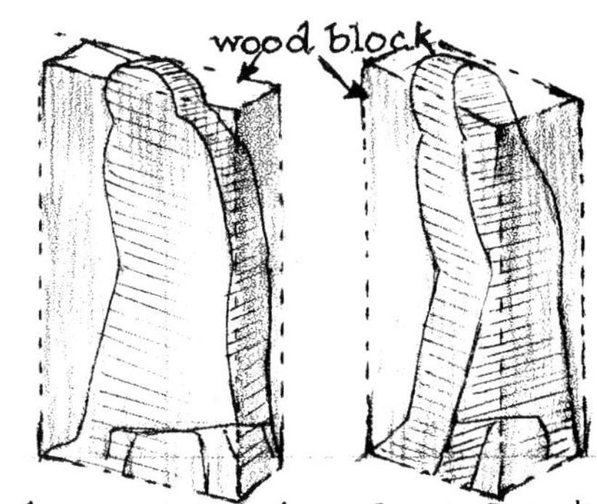

schematic showing of cuts by band saw along 180° silhouets of model harms visualizasion of model

making little corrections here and there; finally, use a black felt-tip marker. Your visualization by this time has become sharper and sharper as you prepare to start carving. (See also page 109, *The Future* analyzed.)

Begin carving (as illustrated on page 110).

Final steps. First make certain that the *lighting* is perfect to show all the subtleties on the final surfaces of the forms at their best. The finest-tooth claw may be the only tool we need for evening surfaces on stone. But, if desired, further smoothing by sanding or rasping, followed by polishing, may be your choice for the final step.

Once we are able to carve *directly,* we can understand why and how sculptors of note in the past became such experts. They *thought* three-dimensionally, working without necessarily making drawings or preliminary studies.

Examine the roughing out steps of Michaelangelo in his unfinished *Slaves.* When we look at them closely, we see that the rough two-pointed claws barely reveal the faces. He did this only *after* the other parts of the whole body, as well as the body stance, had been taken care of fairly well, thus reassuring himself of overall correctness. In many pieces the *mood* comes not necessarily through facial expressions alone, but as much, and sometimes more, through the *stance* and *grouping of the bodies.*

The Claw as a Finishing Tool in Stone Carving

Only after the one-point stone-carving tool has roughed out and approximated all forms in the composition, do the finishing tools take over. The novice often yields to the temptation to start using the various fine-toothed claws too soon, generally through fear of going too far with the one-point. He is also impatient to see the final form shapes and surfaces before all excess material is carved away by the one-point. A common problem for the beginnner when working with the claws too soon is that the work is slowed down unnecessarily.

If one desires to smooth surfaces further, this can be done with flat chisels, rasps, abrasive papers, and ultimately with water and balls of lead foil and emery powder, as shown in the illustrations in Chapter 8, page 62.

Using Mechanical Hammers in Direct Carving

WARNING: ALL HAND-HELD, MOTOR-DRIVEN CUTTERS CALL FOR ADDED SKILLS AND PROTECTIVE GEAR TO AVOID DANGER OF ACCIDENTS. WEAR GOGGLES AND EAR PROTECTION!

Although the cutting of stones with mechanical hammers has been practiced for generations, the use of *air hammers for wood carving,* at least to my knowledge, was not practiced until I decided to try making woodcarving gouges and adapters to be used with air hammers.

In *stone carving,* heavy air hammers saved energy and speeded up work in quarries. Small air hammers were

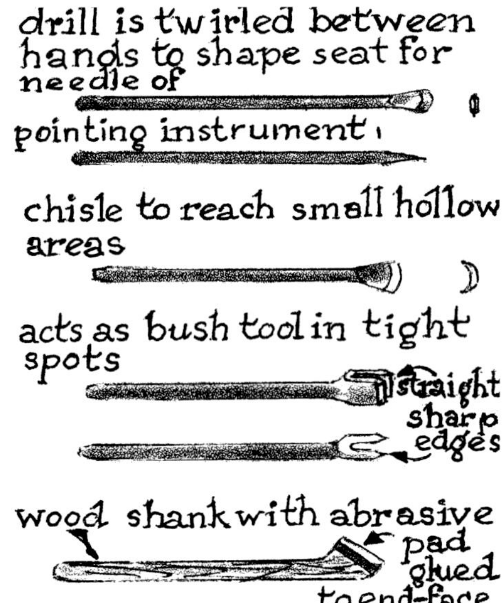

used by sculptors to carve statuary in mass production. This I observed in Pietra Santa, Italy, where miniature air hammers were used for quantity production for the tourist trade.

In the shop where they carved, rows of workers sat at benches, using very small air hammers that buzzed like barbers clippers. Each worker had a small statue in front of him, carving the part he was assigned to do. One did only feet, another only arms and legs, and still another only faces and hair. It was a well-planned mass production method. Inserted tool bits could quickly be changed for others: one-points, claws, and any tool tip needed. The small statue surfaces were hand-rasped, sanded, and polished with acids instead of buffers. The models were followed closely so that their duplicates would be acceptable to the artist. If public taste called for saccharine expressions on the faces, they appeared in all the duplicates.

My visits to these shops impressed me with the fact that air hammers for direct sculpting could work well. Back in the United States I tried out mechanical hammers but found them to be too fast in the final surfacing of forms. In direct carving, therefore, the slower hand-hammering method had to be used for the delicate finishing work. It is easy to see that during final phases of direct carving one must stop frequently to contemplate the next and more careful moves. Fast mechanical cutting is too dangerous during detail work because of the possibility of overshooting one's aim. The noncommercial artist can do without speed.

Although I have never possessed one of those miniature Italian air hammers, I believe it quite possible that those with greater skill and talents than mine could successfully use them, even in direct carving.

Power hammers save a great amount of energy when used in roughing out large sculpture. Larger pieces of wood sculpture lead me to use mechanically hammered wood gouges. It was a revealing discovery that the use of mechanical hammers allowed the dynamic flow of positive forms to come about more readily than it would have with the use of hand hammers. Bush hammers are used extensively by sculptors working in granite.

Adapting Wood-Carving Tools to Mechanical Hammers

At first I looked for motor-driven, reciprocal hammers that could be plugged into a regular electrical outlet. I found a compact one manufactured by the Milwaukee Electrical Tool Equipment Company. It worked satisfactorily, but I regret that the company stopped its manufacture, claiming there was not enough demand for them by sculptors. I ended up designing *adapters* for both systems, air and electric motor-driven, to take my regular wood-handled wood-carving gouges. It has remained a puzzle to me that other sculptors visiting me were amazed that air hammers could be used with wood-carving gouges (The illustration on page 63 shows this setup).

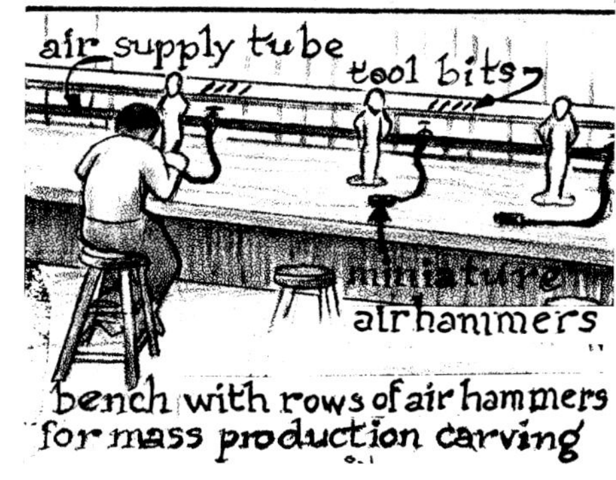

bench with rows of air hammers for mass production carving

I was fortunate that I could design, forge and temper all tools I needed and also share the know-how through my teaching and in my books on the subject of toolmaking. I strongly advocate that all sculptors learn how to make their own tools.

A word of caution: Electrical motor-driven hammers are more vulnerable to wear and tear than air hammers.

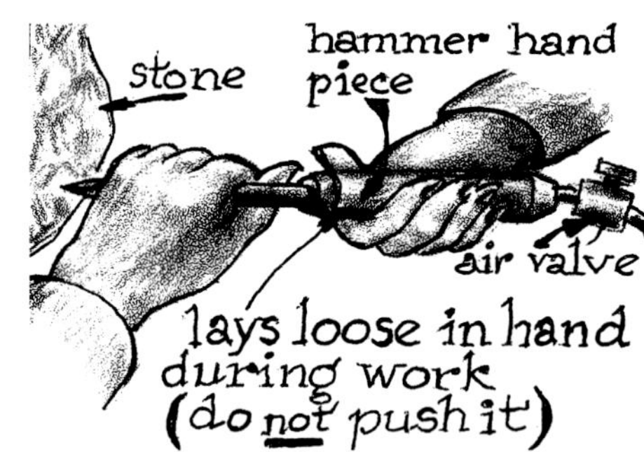

Getting the Most out of Power Hammers

The oldest air hammer design calls for holding the hand-piece *horizontally*, letting it lie in the hand loosely, and not pushing it during use (only *guiding* it). The hand-piece should merely *follow* the guided gouge, then there will be the least hand vibration.

In all *hand hammering*, never look at the point where the hammer strikes the gouge handle but only at the gouge cutting-end, and let the hammer follow the hand-guided gouge. *Pushing* a mechanical hammer hand-piece increases hand and arm vibration and can eventually cause an occupational handicap. One unexpected air hammer advantage is that the air exhaust cools the hand while you are working. (There is no overheating of hand-pieces.)

STANDARD INDUSTRIAL EAR MUFFLERS SHOULD BE WORN TO PROTECT THE EARS FROM NOISE. WEAR GOGGLES TO PROTECT THE EYES.

Selecting an Air Hammer

Library catalogues show the widest choice of air hammers designed for industrial use. Among them, those with the greater frequency stroke will work best for sculptors.

Repeat: If the hand-piece is of a design that lies horizontally in the hand, its mass counters the force of the blows that do the cutting and thus reduces vibrations. Remember that low-frequency heavier blows are *driving* blows which make the carving or tool give way. This necessitates holding the hammer tightly or even *pushing* the hand-piece, which strains the hand and arm. Hand-pieces designed with a *pistol grip* for convenience of holding may be improved by being wound with sponge rubber around the grip to muffle vibration.

The Relationship between Hammer Weight, Tool Cutting-Size, and the Hardness of Material To Be Cut

Only practice will sharpen one's judgment as to which hammer goes with which tool and which combination is best for wood or stone. Making the correct tool selection results in the most effective carving. High frequency, lighter hammer blows, cutting smaller or thinner chips, result in smooth cutting and easy guiding of the tool in any direction. This is the answer for *direct carving in wood*, provided the tool edge is *razor-sharp* and *polished*.

In *stone carving*, because the air hammer blows are light and of a high frequency in order to cut smaller chips, the razor-sharp tool edges can be *almost* brittle-hard, without danger of breaking.

Limits of Mechanical Hammers

Large caliber and slow-frequency air hammers call for a two-cylinder, five horespower compressor to keep up with the volume and pressure (about 90 psi) of air required by these tools.

If only a one-cylinder compressor (two horsepower) is available, its usefulness can be extended considerably if it is equipped with an automatic pressure switch and a 100-gallon storage tank. This lower capacity system should work well with light caliber, high-frequency hammers.

If *noise pollution* is a neighborhood concern, the sound must be muffled in some way. Insulation boards around the compressor areas as well as wall soundproofing in the studio room in which hammering takes place will be necessary to make doubly certain neighbors will not be disturbed. Remember that sound travels mostly *upward.*

Ideally, the compressor unit would be placed in an earth pit. The sides of the pit then absorb all sound that travels sideways. But the sound of the hammer still remains.

Air hoses. Those of smaller diameter create some loss of air pressure through friction if hoses are long. The larger diameter air hose is not only free from this but also allows for a higher volume of tank quantity storage, thus helping to hold the pressure up longer during use.

Other Power Tools

In wood carving, rotary rasps and cutters on flexible shafts driven by electric motors can be useful, but the *sideways grabbing* of the tool when it catches the wood and yanks the guiding hand sideways *endangers the forms being shaped.* Sufficient practice is necessary to overcome this annoying reaction of handheld rotary cutters. A disc sander also has the same handicap. But when it has a rubber-backed or flexible pad, it may be somewhat easier to manipulate than solid steel cutter inserts.

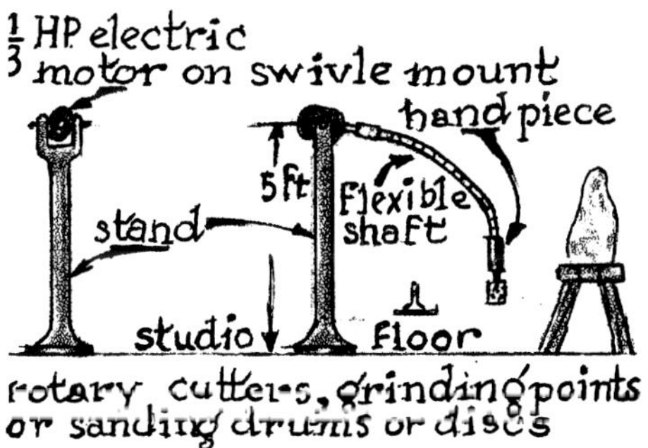

Making Rigs for Heavy Air Hammers

Heavy-blow air hammers are, as a rule, of *low* frequency strokes. The single heavy blow on a large roughing-out gouge or stone one-point chisel makes the hammer hand-piece rebound in mid-air. This action severely strains the hand when the hammer is used for a long period of time. The fact that one has to hold up the heavier hammer as well as hold its rebound to make the cuts more effective, calls for *pushing* the hammer. To meet that problem halfway, I simply use counteracting hammer weights clamped on the hand piece while also using a combination counterweight hinging rig which allows for easier tool guidance. Depending on one's work area, a rig may be improved inventively over what I have shown. Do not hesitate to consider ideas that may use pulleys with clothesline cords with counterweights, etc., as you may require; the main thing is to not let the rigging get in the way of easy tool operations.

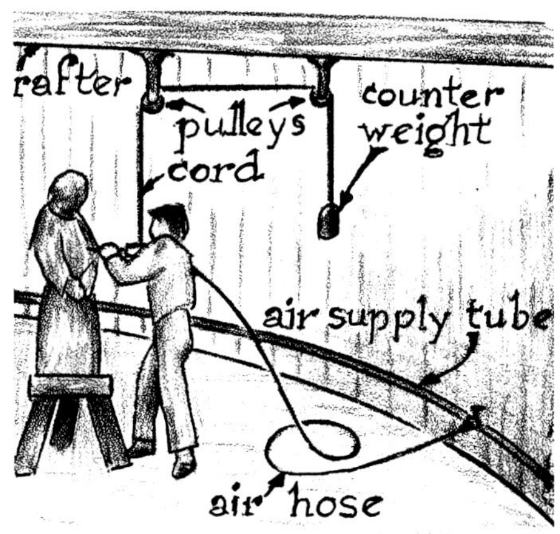

It is surprising how often you can find sections of
machinery, on scrap piles of dealers in scrap steel, that
lend themselves to being assembled as such rigging.
Many a discarded dental chair and outmoded hospital
operating table accessories, with hinging riggings can be
adapted to a sculptor's mechanical equipment.

Air Hammer Accessories

Every hand piece should have an easy finger-control air
valve that can regulate air flow and cut it off instantly.
The old-fashioned hand-piece that lies horizontally in the
hand requires an accessory control valve in the air hose
next to the hand-piece. This equipment can be found in
catalogues, which may be available in larger city libraries.

At the time of this writing, manufacturers do not offer
adapters for wood-handled carving gouges. You could
have them made by a machinist if you have no way of
making them yourself. An adapter should be *light* in
weight, but tough enough to withstand metal fatigue
under sustained day-to-day heavy hammering. Should
an adapter be heavy, it will reduce hammer effectiveness
that much more. Regard a light adapter as an extension
of the carving tool handle itself. A rule of thumb: The
lighter the tool, the more effectively the wood is cut.

The Hardness of Tool Cutting-Edges

When considering wear on tool cutting-edges, keep in
mind that a given amount of energy may be divided over
many light blows, or a *few* heavy ones. This means that
the stroke of a high frequency air hammer will result in
lighter tool edge-loads since the transferred energy is
divided over *many* blows. This is opposed to the heavy
tool edge-loads that result from using low frequencies,
since the same amount of energy must be transferred
over a *few* blows. Therefore, the higher frequency, harder
tool-edges generally stand up longer before resharpening
is needed.

Advantages of High-Frequency Air Hammers
for Wood Carving

*WARNING: BE AWARE OF THE INHERENT DANGER
OF ALL HANDHELD CUTTING TOOLS. WEAR
GOGGLES AND HEARING PROTECTORS.*

As with stone-carving tools, wood-carving tools also
undergo less strain with high frequency air hammers.
Instead of choosing a much heavier and blunter-angled
cutting edge, it is best to choose a thinner, correctly
tempered gouge blade with a less steep beveled edge.

In wood carving, such thin-bladed gouges require less
hard hammer blows than a thicker-bladed gouge to cut
the same wood volume.

Thus, stone carving with high frequency air hammers
and lightweight *harder* tools is comparable with wood
carving using *thinner* gouges. With both, these tools can
be guided easier and will need less frequent
resharpening.

Carbon-Tipped Stone-Carving Tools

Commercially available, these tools will stand up under heavy cutting, provided their manufacturers have succeeded in perfect bonding of the carbon tips on annealed, high carbon (or alloy) tool shanks.

The one-point and flat chisel-end tools are offered mostly in carbon tips for stone carving. One possible handicap: Carbon tips may be too brittle under very heavy hammer blows and may break.

The Gasoline Chain Saw

CHAIN SAWS: FOLLOW SAFETY DIRECTIONS GIVEN WITH THE TOOL.

When this tool was first introduced, I saw immediately a good use for it in direct carving of wood sculpture, wood bowls, benches, furniture, etc. In roughing out, one can use the chain saw to easily remove big chunks of material, then follow-up with large wood gouges using hand or air hammering.

Electric Chain Saws

These should be powerful enough (one horsepower or over) for sculpture purposes. They are somewhat less dangerous and less noisy than gasoline chain saws, and they are free from air pollution. Pulling the trigger for starting and stopping is similar to turning a lightbulb switch on and off. When chain saws were first introduced, I immediately advised many of my sculptor friends to try them out, and they have used them ever since as a very useful tool in the studio.

Chain saws, when razor sharp, can be used like a rasp. To use the saw effectively, make sure to steady the tool, if it is light in weight, so that the chain and bar do not dance up and down. You may be tempted to clamp a weight on the bar to counter such movement. In all inventive improvements made upon a tool in order to adapt it to a use for which it was not designed, careful testing should be done before settling on the improvements.

Never hesitate to introduce new uses for promising tools, *being sure at the same time that they are safe.*

Again, it is here that the sculptor ought to learn enough about blacksmithing and machine shop work to make his own tool to meet his special needs. In the United States it is possible in adult evening classes to use a wide range of shop equipment for individual projects with a teacher's help and supervision. Most good teachers encourage pupil input, inventiveness and initiative.

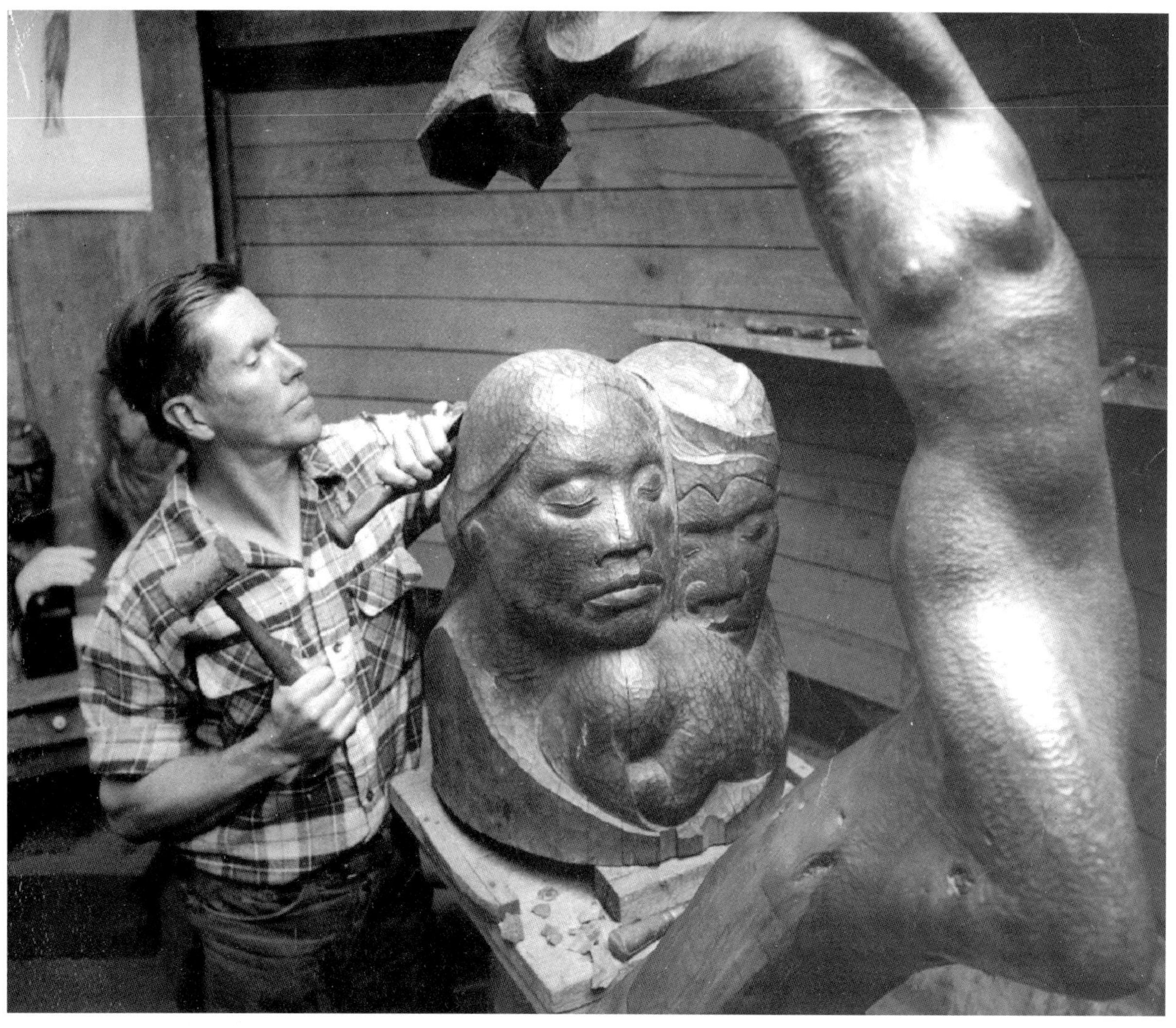

Alex Weygers puts the final touches on "Balanese Family", a gift to The Monterey Institute of International Studies. The wood block for this work was imported from Java.

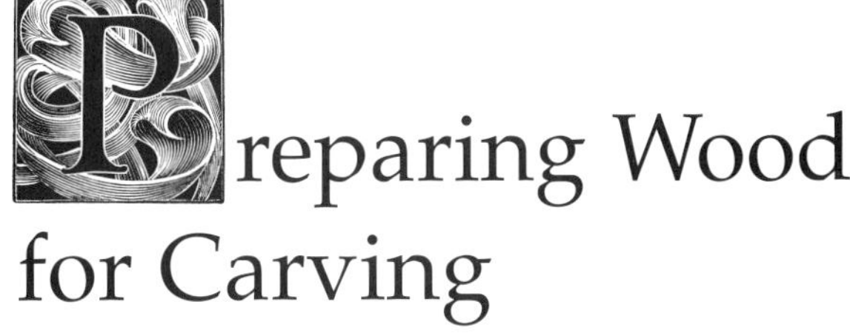reparing Wood for Carving

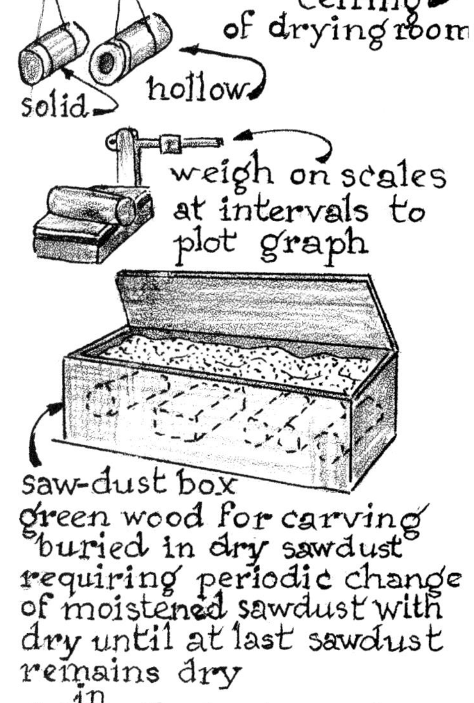

green wood for carving
buried in dry sawdust
requiring periodic change
of moistened sawdust with
dry until at last sawdust
remains dry
this method wetness of core
travels outward more evenly

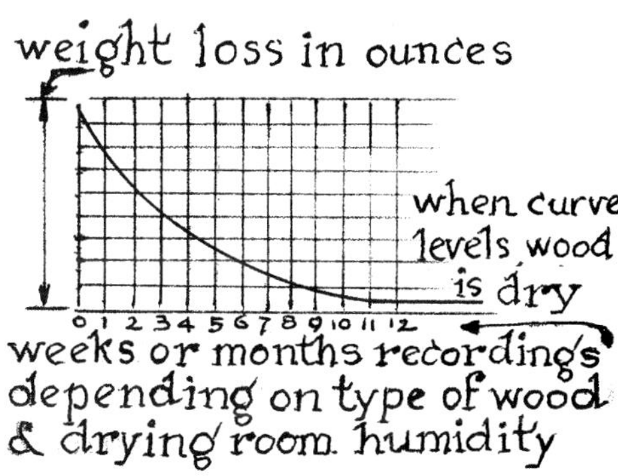

weeks or months recordings
depending on type of wood
& drying room. humidity

Wood curing is the process used for keeping wet wood from checking, cracking or warping during drying. Wet wood shrinks when it is dried. Dry wood swells up when it is made wet. While in the process of drying, wood must be compressed *very slowly* to keep opposite strains below the breaking point of that material.

Compressibility of Material

The famous bent stone lintel, which rests on columns in Egypt, has bent deeper and deeper, over the centuries, without breaking. Because upper grains are compressing and lower ones are stretching, simply under the force of gravity, this bending is possible.

Heated wood becomes limp as cheese and can be bent for the making of curved furniture, ship's ribs, etc. Once the wood is dry, it is heated for bending purposes, and when it is cooled in the desired bent position, it will stay bent.

Kiln drying is the process of "cooking" wet wood to drive out most of the moisture. After drying is complete, the kiln is then cooled slowly to allow the wood to compress in the limp state. Each particular variety of wood dries at its own rate, without checking when allowed to cool slowly.

Variations in Curing Methods

When a tree is uprooted and left to dry with its roots and leaves intact, the core moisture is able to escape a bit faster through the leaves and bark; this creates less shrinking strains that might cause the danger of checking.

Sometimes a whole stand of trees to be harvested is *ringed* so that, left standing, the trees dry gradually during several months and emit moisture through the leaves, which speeds the drying process and prevents checking.

Drying Sections of Wood Selected for Sculpture Carving

First seal the ends of the wood with shellac, or paint with roofing lap cement or wax. Leave the wood in an unventilated, dry, shaded room (without sun shining on the wood) or hang it from a basement ceiling. As it dries, weigh the piece every week and plot the weight on a graph. The curve, week after week, will be seen to level off. In an even-temperature room the line will, in time, become horizontal, indicating that the wood is dry and ready for carving.

Carving in Wet (Green) Uncured Wood

This is possible and often desirable. The sculpture *Malaya* (page 121) was carved in this way. First it was roughed-out within three days and kept wet each night with a damp cloth. The over life-size composition lent itself to being hollowed out at the core to within three inches of the outer carved surface. Augers and a curved sturdy wood gouge were used for hollowing. Careful repeated examination by sighting as well as with calipers, secured a fairly even three-inch thickness.

The piece was set up on a few blocks to let the air (by osmosis) reach the inside easily. It was placed in a shady dry room with no sun to shine on it and no air currents, and the drying went evenly. Weighing the piece from time to time over a month showed the loss of weight and then a leveling off, indicating that it had dried enough for me to commence surface carving. During the carving, the drying continued from the inside as well. At the first sign of tiny cracks on the surface, I would wet it a little at the end of the day to prepare it for the next day's carving. The cross section of the piece, which looked like a doughnut, reacted like a rubber band, freely releasing its stress to a smaller shrunken diameter; the empty insides allowed the "doughnut" to contract without strains.

Advantages of Carving in Wet Wood

There is no need to wait for drying. The gouge cuts through the wet wood like cheese, and the oozing sap lubricates the gouge edge, easing the cutting. Many a sculptor, having once experienced this, quickly develops a taste for working in wet wood, especially when he has discovered varieties of wood growing all around him that never reach the commercial market. Once he learns what and what not to do in the drying and curing process, he can become quite proficient in effectively meeting his wood problems.

The small sculpture *Embrace* (page 121) was wet when carved. It was cut in half lengthwise and hollowed out to dry, with enough thickness left for the carving of the outside. After quick drying, each half was sanded down precisely flat and glued to its opposite half, then carved as shown. It so happened that the lemon wood could have dried without these precautions if I had simply drilled a hole in the center to speed drying from inside as well as outside. I have found that the citrus woods are less subject to checking than many other woods.

My own experience remains limited to the types of wood growing in my area. Among the softer and medium hard woods that dry with little or no danger of checking are poplar, cottonwood, alder, willow, juniper, cypress, pine, buckeye and cascara. Next come most of the fruit woods: pear, cherry, apricot. . . . The sculptor prepares these by painting or shellacking the ends of the wood in order to retard drying and prevent checking. The wood has a chance to compress while stored in even-temperature, shaded, dry rooms without strong air circulation or sunlight.

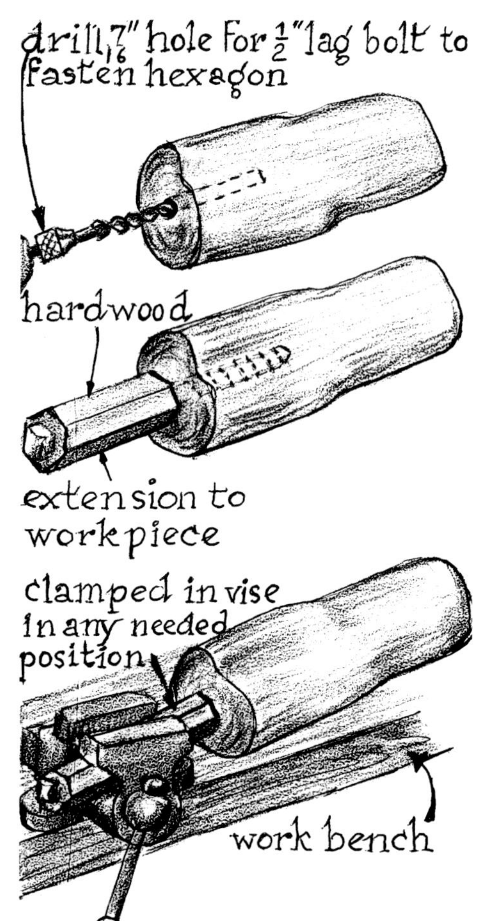

Only if in a hurry do we need to resort to drilling a hole in the center to speed the drying somewhat; or inventively, you can apply other methods based on your understanding of all the factors involved, as explained above.

Harder Woods with Less Compressibility

Madrone, manzanita, desert "iron" wood, mountain mahogany, and others no doubt growing elsewhere and so unknown to me, all fall into this category. The safest way to deal with these varieties is to find them dead on the stump. Examine them for beetles or worm infestation, and salvage those portions that seem to have enough volume for the composition you have in mind. Remember that expansion and shrinkage, which occur from weather, temperature and moisture changes, break up harder woods much faster than softer ones.

Note: Each sculptor who is fond of wood carving owes it to himself to try woods other than the usual walnut, etc., available commercially. Each one in his own area is bound to find many unfamiliar varieties. Test them with a sharp gouge, whether they are wet or dry, for use as a possible carving material. Get acquainted with them. I have snatched many a piece out of friends' fireplaces, that turned out perfect for my purpose.

Warning: It is important to watch out for wood beetles and worm infestations. (See illustration.) One's judgment sharpens after many trial and error experiences that blend disappointments with the finding of treasures. What could be called a waste of time in some instances, is compensated for by the pleasures of outdoor treasure-hunting.

Telltale Signs of Infestation

A tree found dead in the forest may be naturally cured and seasoned, but often becomes food for wood grubs or beetles. As a rule, wood beetles leave a ring of fine dusty wood pulp around the tree's base.

Testing a tree by cutting into the wood may show that . . .

> 1. Only the outer sap ring of the tree was the beetle's food, and the core of the tree has remained unaffected.

> 2. Worms have left holes filled with the wood residue. These "paths" may be followed by cutting with a wood gouge until the grub is located, thus making certain that the remaining wood is free of any future damage. Some variations may be experienced, but all should end with freeing the wood from insects before carving starts.

The illustrations show the best method to rid the carving of wood beetles.

The action is based on the insect's instinctive fear of a woodpecker's drumming sound and vibration of the wood. The orchardists strap onto the tree trunks a powerful motor shaker and spread a drop cloth beneath

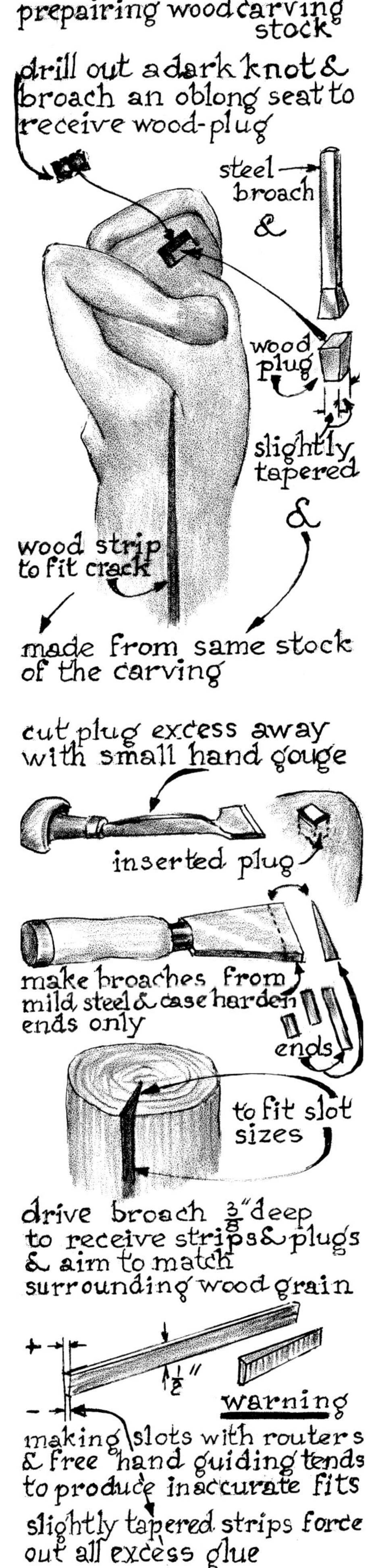

the whole tree. The vigorous vibrations of the eccentric flywheel-type motors cause the insects to escape and fall onto the cloth, where they are gathered and destroyed.

If a carving in an untried wood shows telltale signs of wood beetle infestations (fine wood powder at base of carving), take care of it immediately. The illustrations show a practical method, similar to the orchardists, applied to a wood carving. In this method, we improve on the woodpecker by striking the bottom of the carving with repeated vicious hammer blows. If the carving is not too heavy, there is double harm to the beetles inside, who receive, besides the vibration, the remaining force of the blows and are more than eager to get out to avoid death.

This method is better than soaking the carving in poison liquids, because in the latter method, the liquid will be absorbed by the pulp in the boring channels, which will shut off deeper penetration and not allow the liquid to reach the insects. Encouraging the live insects to "back out" is the most effective way to rid the wood of them.

I hung my carving, *Windswept*, from the ceiling over the table with newspapers spread below. With repeated vicious hammering, the beetles dropped out. When at last no more appeared, I injected insect poison in all the little holes, brushing the carved surface with it as well. Later I shellacked it overall, and the treatment proved successful.

Other methods of preparing wood for carving are illustrated and self-explanatory. Once the curing principles have been understood, the reader is bound to extend, with his own ideas and experiments, his ability to prepare wood for carving.

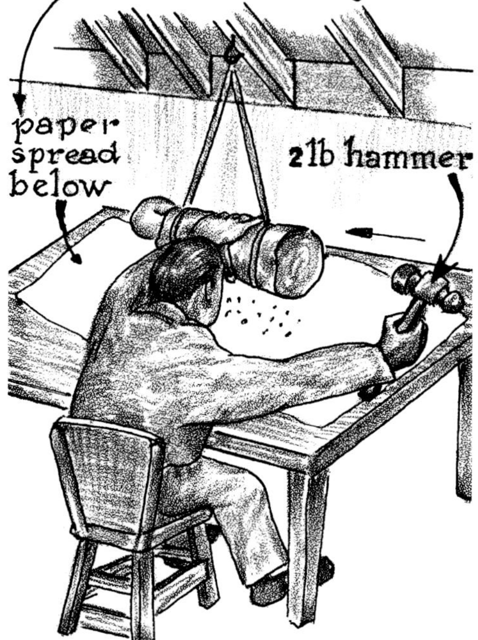

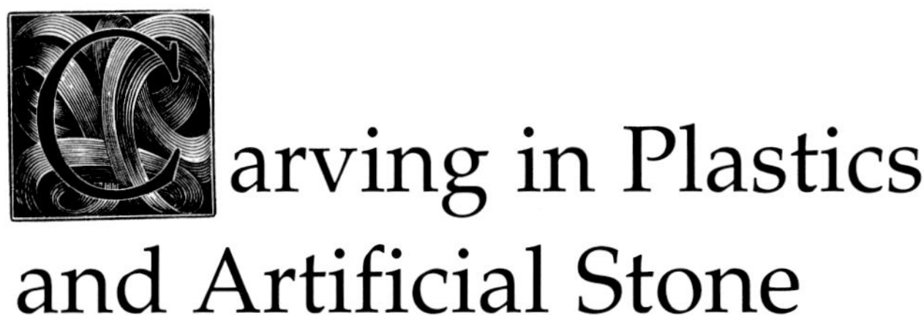

Chapter 11

Carving in Plastics and Artificial Stone

Plastics

When plastics are cast in blocks, large or small, they can be carved with wood-carving gouges and afterward sanded down and polished. Many sculptors find this type of material desirable for its translucency, which gives the impression of a *blending* of form and material; this is especially true when the subject matter stresses abstractions, which tend to lead the eye from *positive* to *negative* form character.

A mold from a clay model can be used to cast a plastic mix. The casts may be further finished by carving (if oversize), or finished by sanding and polishing, if these alone are desired.

Styrofoam can be cut with a knife and similar tools. Since it indents easily, it must be coated with hardening plastics as a finish, which can be sanded down in order to refine details. Styrofoam can be used for temporary displays in store windows and at fairs, carnivals and such. It is useful when labor-saving and time-saving material is needed.

When using modern plastics, follow manufacturer's instructions, including warnings of toxic dangers; use plenty of ventilation and a protective mask.

Plastics are known to be long lasting in the outdoor weather, but like wood, they still burn in a fire.

Artificial Stones

These are cement mixes with crushed marble, granite, limestone or sand, etc. blended according to the artist's choice. Correctly proportioned mixes can be cast into blocks which can be carved with regular stone-carving tools in the same way as natural stone.

Adobe as Modeling and Carving Material

Adobe, a mixture of earth and water, must be "stabilized" (waterproofed with emulsified asphalt). One adobe brick 4"x12"x24" requires one pint of emulsified asphalt.

If modeled oversize, the hardened dry piece may be roughed out, then carved with regular stone-carving tools. It can be painted when dry with latex paints which will not let the asphalt *bleed* through the paint, as will oil-base paint.

Carving Letters

Stone sculpture of monuments, tablets, gravestones, etc. sometimes requires *intaglio* letters to be cut.

The artist can transfer letter outlines from paper, with stylus and carbon paper, onto the flat material to be carved. If the paper is thin, it can be glued onto the stone or wood and the carving done directly through it, as if the paper were not there. Hand-forged tools can be used to cut letters in *soft splintery wood;* they are designed to cut through wood without danger of splintering.

Sandblasted Letters

A rubber template is used, in which the letters have been cut as a stencil. Cemetery gravestone cutters have instruments that can cut such templates. The template is stuck onto the stone and the sand blown onto the stone surface. The letters, in their rough state, show in contrast with the polished surface of the slab.

Cutting Raised Letters

This is more difficult than intaglio cutting. The background needs to be recessed around the letters, but there is a danger that carving around them may cause damage. When there are many letters, a mechanical router can speed up the work. After routing, a hand tool may be used to go over the whole recessed surface in order to eliminate the machined appearance caused by the use of a mechanical tool. The sign carver often prefers intaglio work, because it requires less time spent on carving.

Intaglio Sculpture Carving

A hollow matrix can be carved or scraped into stone or plaster, to a very shallow depth as with coins and medals, or deeper for cast relief work. Light, sheering by the plane into which the carving is done, creates the illusion of positive, instead of negative forms.

Looking into the hollow molds made from sculptures or clay models, one sees the illusion that is created. (See page 18) It is as if every recession has become a protrusion and as if the light strikes the forms from below instead of from above.

Clay modeling tools, used in scooping movements, tend to dig and scrape hollow tracks. If we use them in this way on a flat piece of plaster, such hollows become protrusions when a cast is made of the plaster. Such casts show surprisingly clear and sharp positive forms, tempting the beginner to apply this *intaglio* carving to the making of other artifacts: pastry molds, stone insets for rings, or stamps for sealing-wax.

To aid one's judgment, one can test the hollow matrix at various stages by pressing a bit of fairly stiff clay into it, as a "proof" impression, until the master mold yields the desired result.

The beginning student is advised to try some of this work so that he may add to his various ways of getting clear, positive forms in a sculpture cast. He may be tempted to become proficient in this relatively easy method of obtaining positive, dynamic forms, especially when casting in artificial stone.

With modern electric vibrator-needle cutters, *glass* is easily etched to the needed depth in low relief. Worked from the back, the etching is seen *through* the glass, giving a positive effect. These compositions can include body forms of human figures as well as many striking design arrangements.

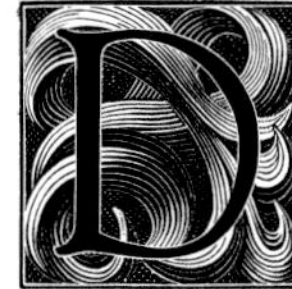rapery over Forms

The illustrations show what happens to a sheet of flexible material that falls in folds over a flat background or a human body. It will seek to match the planes, revealing the forms behind it.

If, instead of a flat plane, the rounded parts of a body control the positioning of the drapery, the student has the opportunity to be inventive and extend his skill in   handling drapery. For example, deep undercuts often prove unnecessary. Instead, careful softening of the drapery folds makes the composition more sculptural, yet acceptable as realism.

Drapery that hangs curving downward from a body tends to flow like the free-hanging curves of a chain, or forms approximating *parabolas.* As young students in a mathematics class, we were confused about types of curves. One question was, "How do you distinguish a parabola from other curves?" Our very earthy teacher clarified the matter by telling us to observe little boys urinating as far as they could over the edge of the bridge. That downward curve, he said, was the curve of a *parabola.* Naturally, this was forever fixed in our memories.

The illustrations show modifications of curves, which sharpen the closer we get to their focal points. Many artists have become fascinated by the flow of drapery, and their treatment of the subject can be examined in paintings and sculpture throughout art history.

The beginner can experiment with stiff cloth, observing the strategic *breaks* in the curve on its downward path. When paper is used, it folds similarly to cloth. Compare many different materials, such as foil and sheet metals. Examine pictures showing the accidental buckling of plates of steel.

The Greek sculptors often exaggerated drapery by scraping deep hollow slots between the folds to imitate real cloth. Viewed from the front, one could see no more than the beginning of these folds, slots showing the beginning shadows of the deep cuts. Deep slots did not increase the illusions of the folds. A 1/4" depth would have had the same effect as the 3" slots. (See illustration.)

In drapery, as well as in all sculptural detail, simply suggesting reality, as a rule, suffices. With all optical illusions, we make use of the viewer's acquaintance with the familiar things that surround him in daily life and his willingness to accept in his mind's eye the *direction* of forms going beyond his field of vision.

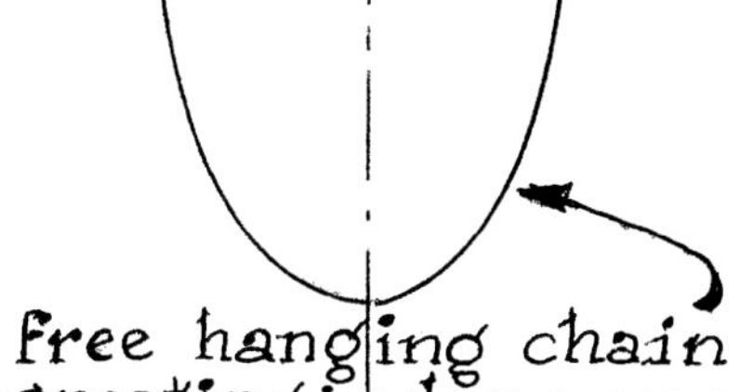

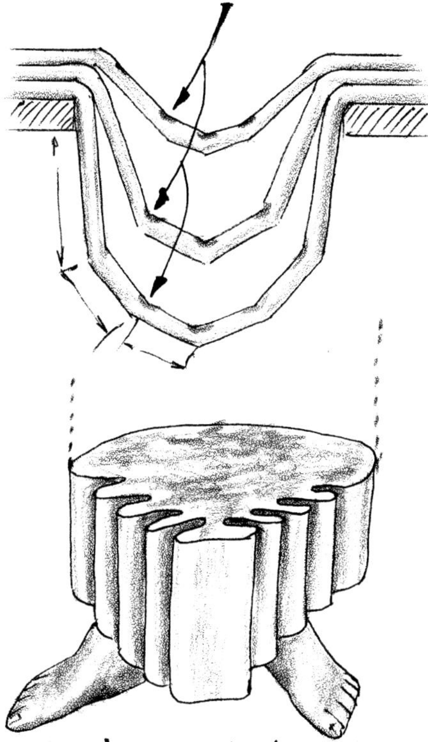

a broken old Greek marble statue shows 3 inch deep slots cut in drapery folds to create realism of model

Drapery and Optical Illusion

The illustrations show cross sections of drapery folds on a flat plane. If the folded clay layer is lifted off intact and gently pushed flush with the plane, the result shows a workable method of keeping drapery close to the body while assuring the viewer that nothing is missing of the body forms below it.

The same can be done with modeling a beading to decorate a clay pot, by bending it along the rim. Thus seemingly complicated detail is simplified. Endless other applications are open for the inventive artist.

Study Exercises

Crumple a handkerchief or sheet of newspaper. Closely observe how various materials show their random fold patterns and critical breaks differently. Heavy blankets hung over furniture, this way and that, have softened folds. Each type of material responds uniquely to gravity, to the push and pull of the forms below it, and due to its characteristic weave.

Once the artist has become familiar with the recurring fold behavior of all drapery, he can be inventive in its use. No longer dependent on models, he will find that simple approximations are most suitable for sculpture subjects.

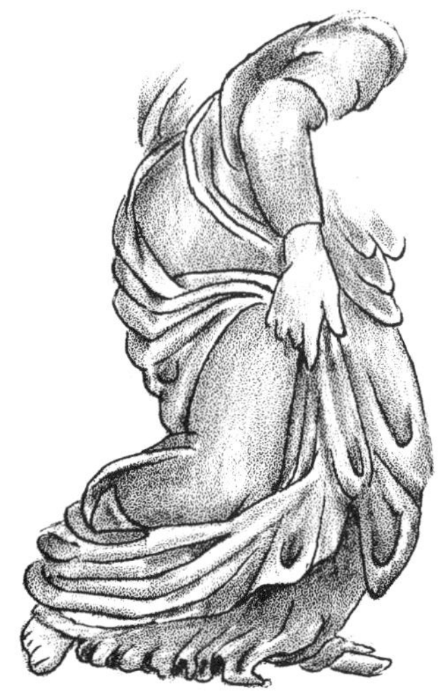

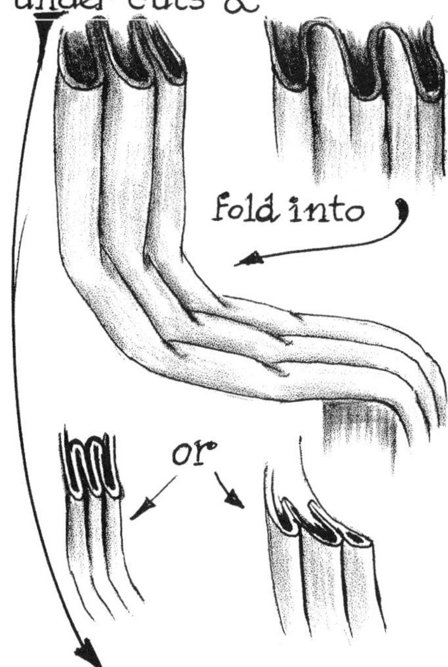

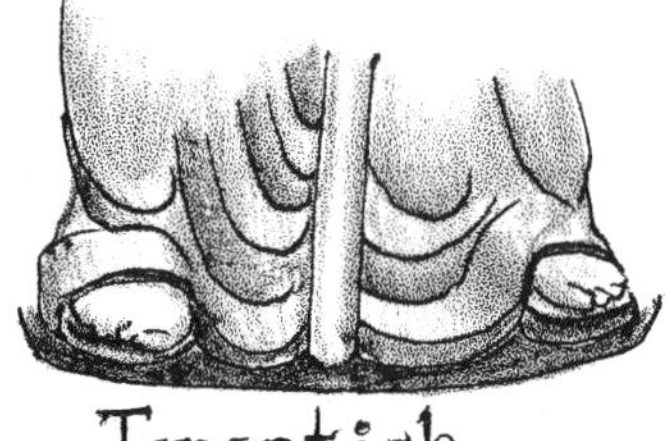

Tryptich

Chapter 13

Collecting Heavy Stones and Logs for Carving

One time, as I drove my pickup along a mountain road, I spotted a 200-pound rock of fine sandstone lying where a road crew had bulldozed it to one side. As I stood there figuring how to get it on the truck bed, I heard footsteps behind me. Turning around, I saw a giant of a man, one of the road crew, who asked me somewhat gruffly, "What are you trying to do?"

"Figuring how to get the thing on the truck," I said.

"What you gonna do with it?"

I told him I was a sculptor and said, "Carve a beautiful woman out of it."

Before I could gather my wits, he brushed me aside and stood, legs wide apart, over the rock. He picked it up, his neck veins to the bursting point, said, "I'll do anything for a beautiful woman" and placed the rock gently on the truck bed.

However, this providential and enthusiastic help is a once-in-a-lifetime happening, and we are usually left to do a job with our own skills, a few tools and our own common sense. How to meet the problem of hauling treasures from the field to the studio is many a sculptor's task.

Moving Heavy Material and Equipment

WARNING: WHEN MOVING HEAVY MATERIAL AND EQUIPMENT, BE CAUTIOUS AND TAKE CARE NOT TO TAKE UNDUE CHANCES; THERE IS ALWAYS A DANGER OF INJURY.

In modern times the pickup truck is our most useful and needed tool for hauling carving material and for many other tasks that would otherwise overstrain our backs. (See Chapter 14.)

Naturally, a four-wheel drive with winch fore and aft is a sculptor's dream. I made do with a 1932 Chevy jump-seat coupe converted into a pickup with overload springs, and for several years it served me well. If the beginning sculptor today is in the same position I was then, and considered "poor," he must meet the same basic hauling problems I did. It is possible, with limited equipment *and taking care not to take undue chances*, to move and haul heavy materials as needed for large carvings outdoors or in the studio.

In the Orient, I witnessed a dozen or more men in a "group-for-hire" crew carry out the raising of a 2,000-pound piece of machinery in this fashion.

Each man had an eight-foot long, strong, bamboo pole. The root-end had been fire-charred for hardness and, using that blunt-pointed end for a "purchase" point, they used their body weight and muscle at the other end to jockey-up one corner after the other, while someone slipped propping beams underneath the raised spots. Thus, within a few hours the machine was brought to rest on a pile of crossing beams, high enough to be jockeyed onto a heavy flatbed truck.

The old adage, "Give me a long enough lever and time and I can lift the world" applies to our field problems in the transporting of sculpture material.

Moving heavy stones and logs with limited means always invites the danger of breaking ropes, chains and cables and losing control of heavy loads in suspension. Once it is understood what is involved mechanically, each individual has to stand or fall by his own judgment. Many accidents in my lifetime caught me by surprise. That I survived is still amazing to me!

Chapter 14

The Studio, Shops and House

Setup of Studio Equipment

Some sculptor's studios I have visited seem overly large and ambitious. Others look cramped and handicapped by awkward arrangements.

However, all sculptors ultimately recognize just what will be most needed to help them do their work efficiently, saving their backs and time. All face problems of lifting and transporting heavy weights: rocks, logs, machine tools, construction and building materials. In that regard, their needs are very different from other artists such as painters, draftsmen, potters, printmakers, etc.

The sculptor's studio should be on level ground, if possible, to ease the moving of tons of weight on dollies and rollers. A perfectly level, smooth, reinforced concrete floor is practical and can be easily hosed off for cleaning.

If inside space is limited, an outdoor sculptor's "yard" is especially good for doing large sculpture work, plaster casting and mold making.

Sometimes extreme ambition drives the sculptor to do heroic work of truly mountainous proportion, like the Rushmore Memorial or the Crazy Horse mountain sculpture in the Dakotas. Such enterprises become engineering projects requiring machine tools, dynamite, bulldozers, scaffolding, and cable transportation.

My own work, in addition to sculpture carving, includes clay modeling, casting and mold making, end-grain wood engraving and printing, blacksmithing, tool making, machinist work, and some photography and teaching. All of these subjects required variety in the planning of studio and shops. I built to meet all of those needs. At the same time, I felt that the *esthetics* of the place had to be considered, and this influenced the placing of the various work areas, the materials used and the architectural design; and all this had to be accomplished within a very limited budget.

Inevitably one finds one needs a little more room here, a little less there.

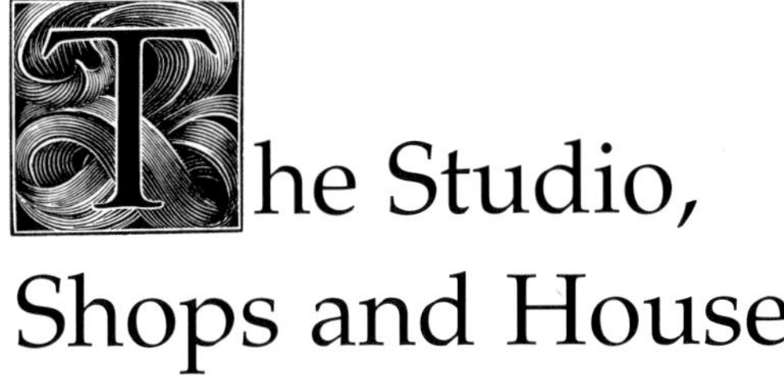

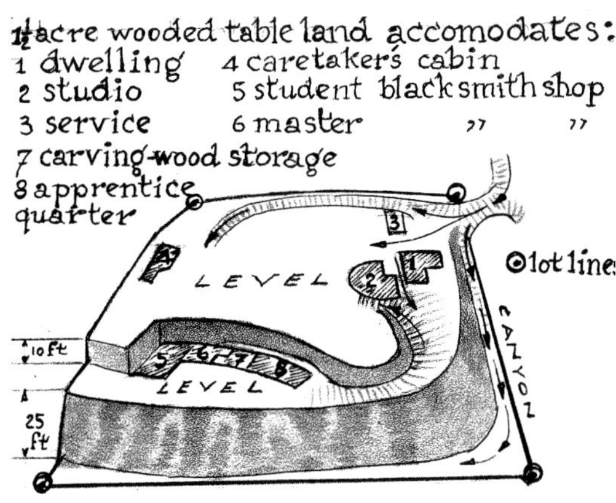

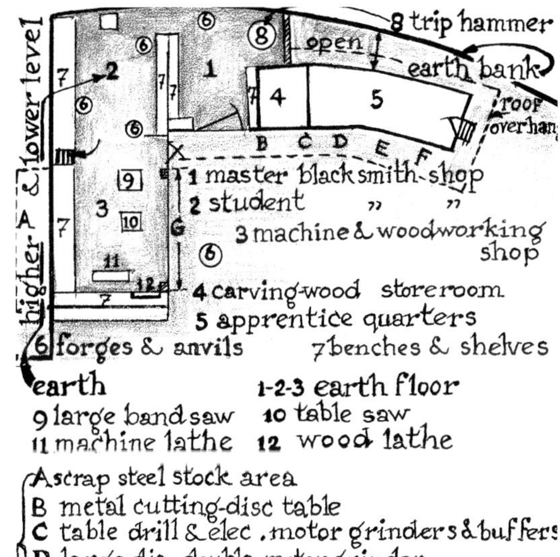

A Studio for Stone and Wood Carving and Plaster Casting

A practical studio should have some essentials:

1. A large, sturdy workbench with drawers to hold the necessary tools, such as motor grinders and buffers for quick tool-sharpening. There should be storage space above and below the workbench.

2. Good lighting over the bench for good visibility while working and to avoid accidents.

3. Several strategically placed electrical outlet boxes for power carving tools, drills, etc., as well as air compressor outlets for connecting air hammer hoses. All should be installed along the wall at bench level.

4. A steel-reinforced concrete floor, which is valuable for any studio that needs to take blocks of stone weighing several tons. By simply placing a large thrust-bearing under the center of gravity of the block, the block can be turned around with fingertip control. The mass of the block can take moderate hammer blows, with little or no "wedging-up" from below.

5. If possible, an overhead chain hoist, a most useful and important item, to lift heavy weights onto sturdy stands. (See illustration.)

6. A hose. Since it is the sculptor's chore to clean the floor each day, it is an advantage to be able to hose down the chips and spillings of stone, wood, plaster and dust. Too often, sculptors' studios show signs of frustration with the unwieldy accumulations of debris.

7. A practical work-space. Often, more time and energy are wasted in very large shops than in smaller compact ones. If we need to work in one location and must reach for tools, water, brooms or other articles, they should be close at hand in order for our work to continue without interruption. A small shop has that advantage. It compares with a photographer's darkroom plan, which is ideal when everything needed is within arm's reach.

A Studio for Clay Modeling

There should be a large north skylight giving diffused light over a central platform on which the model or workpieces can be placed. If clay modeling is taught in the studio, there must be room around that central location for a few student work stands with enough elbow room between them.

This area should be separate from the stone and wood carving location since clay modeling can make a floor messy. When oil-base clay is dropped, it picks up all kinds of litter and takes a lot of time to clean up.

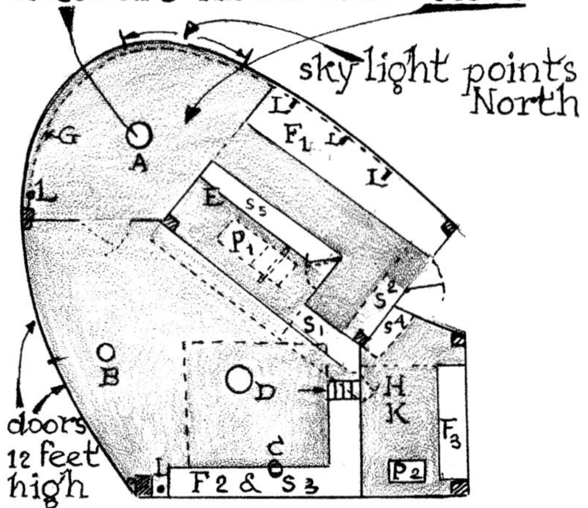

A 1½ ton hoist above work stand
B 2 ton " " " "
C ¼ ton " " work bench
D work stand below high skylight
E glass enclosed printing room
F work benches 1-2-3 & shelves 1-2-3-4
G ½" standard pipe air suply
H small printing press room
K dark-room below "
L compressed air outlets
M main building columns
S shelves & cupboards

Weight-Lifting Tools and Moving Equipment

Modern equipment is offered in such a wide variety that a sculptor with moderate financial means can acquire some of it, to his great advantage. Among these are hydraulic, mechanical or air pressure lifts, winches and hoists. Slower, hand-operated chain hoists are just as effective as faster electrically driven ones, and their operation is well within the muscular limits of the average person. Steel bars for leverage, chains, ropes, pipe rollers, block and tackle, wedges of wood or steel, strong wooden boxes, large blocks of wood, and all simple implements aimed at facilitating the handling of heavy weights become a sculptor's standbys.

The Pickup Truck—A Power Source

A pickup truck is the sculptor's best friend for all hauling and prospecting activities and for getting the material to the studio. Never underestimate its usefulness. Besides transporting heavy stone blocks, logs and machinery, it can pull, drag, push, lift, tumble, drive mixers with its rear wheel jacked up . . . so many uses based on the engine power underneath the hood. Even the lightest weight car packs a monstrous power compared with household utility motors. We can make use of it whenever muscle force would otherwise be strained to its limit.

Even indoors, when weights must be lifted without a chain hoist, cable or rope can be snaked through a hole in the studio wall to a pulley-block suspended overhead from the ceiling joist, making a simple lifting rig. The pickup, standing outdoors, then pulls the weight up as a helper signals. Such practical applications, enhanced by your own inventiveness, can lead to endless other riggings.

If the truck has no provision for lifting a heavy rock or log onto the truck, bolt a hand-cranked winch onto the truck bed just behind the cab and pull heavy loads along sturdy planks onto the bed, as shown.

Whatever final rigging you decide upon, weight hauling should not worry you, now that in our machine age, equipment is within reach of most of us. This labor-saving machinery frees us to pack ten lifetimes into one. Learn to cash in on it, just so long as you have learned to AVOID ACCIDENTS CAUSED BY IGNORANCE OR TAKING UNDUE CHANCES.

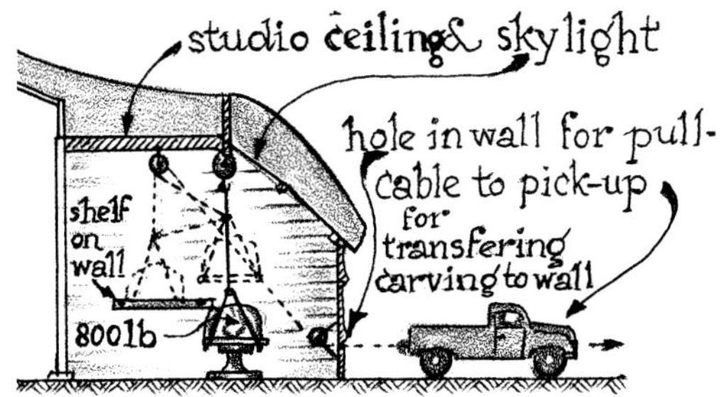

rigging as in double winch maneuvering for loading of cargo in ships
floors are reinforced concrete, level with outdoors

p_1 & p_2 hand printing presses

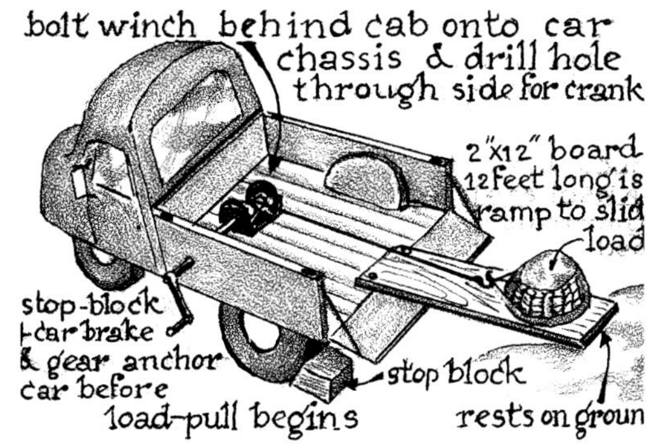

Stands for Workpieces

I have found that a converted, secondhand dental or barber chair is one of the most useful tools in the studio. The oldest models, that can be raised about 18″ and have means of locking and turning, are the best. It is advisable to have, close at hand, several sturdy stepping boxes and one or more adjustable wooden stands.

Tool Making

I believe that part of the sculptor's studio setup should include equipment for making and sharpening tools. My book, *THE COMPLETE MODERN BLACKSMITH:* Ten Speed Press, Publisher; Berkeley, CA, covers this subject thoroughly. There is no doubt in my mind that all who read it will come away with the conviction that any dexterous person, which most sculptors naturally are, can learn how to make his own tools, and it is a pleasure as well. The artist can use my books as guides to being self-taught in this craft, which simply requires practice and a minimum of equipment. The sculptor thus becomes independent for life in providing himself with his needed tools.

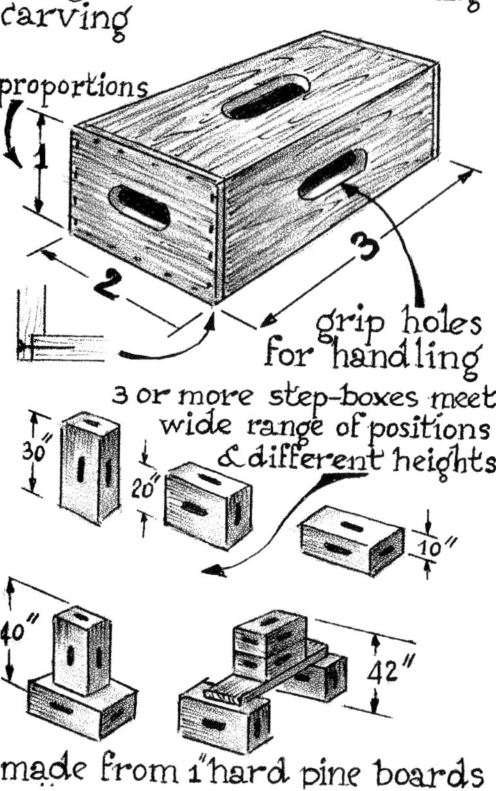

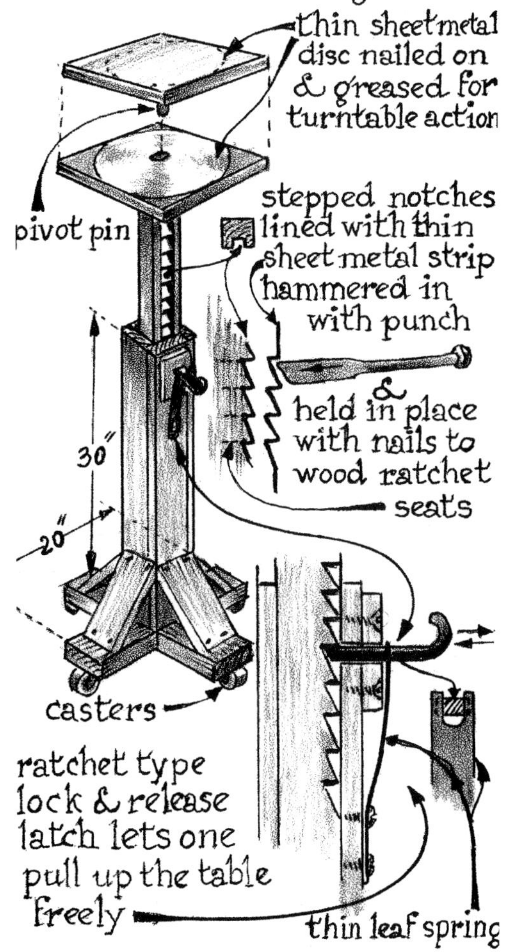

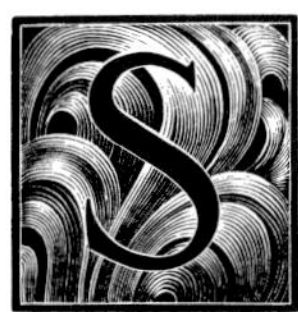

Chapter 15

Sculptures Analyzed

Malaya

The original section of a tree from which this carving was made reached me at my parent's home in Java, Indonesia, and had been freshly cut in a nearby jungle. The government's forestry department, which furnished it for me, warned that this wood (podocarpus) was subject to much checking.

In the village blacksmith shop I quickly forged a few needed gouges from discarded files. I roughed out the composition in its approximate form, while keeping the wood constantly wet. I next hollowed it out, leaving about three inches thickness of wood below the outer surface. (See illustration.) Thus, drying took place from the outside and inside simultaneously, which reduced the shrinkage tensions to a minimum. With the wood secured in this way against checking, I could then leisurely carve the details.

The advantages of working in wet (green) wood are that the tool is lubricated by the wood sap, harder wood is easier to cut when wet, there is no long wait for the wood to be cured (dried without checking) when hollowed, and all excess wood is carved off quickly.

In the case of this carving, the original ivory color of the wood unfortunately became stained and streaked, obstructing the subtlety of facial expressions. A light-colored paint patina was required to reveal these expressions best. The student should note that all form approximations in this composition compare with the assignments for compositions in abstract forms.

To portray symbolically the life of the Malayan family, I carved, at their back, the caribou (water buffalo). This farmer's beast of burden, which works the plow, the water wheel and the primitive sugar mill, is comparable to the tractor used in America. Showing only its head and a portion of its massive body proved enough to round out the spirit, meant to shine through this sculpture, of man and beast together meeting life's hardships.

The student should examine closely the soft treatment of the eyes, nose and mouth of the man and woman. To have carved razor sharp depressions would have destroyed the work's sensitive quality. However, once the desired facial expression has been attained, the sculptor may then apply locally, here and there, sharp form intersections which, if far enough from those subtle areas, may enhance them by contrasts: the mother's hair, the father's headgear, the buffalo's horns. Deliberate but sparsely spaced touches of sharp form intersections always help to offset or compliment refined form treatment elsewhere.

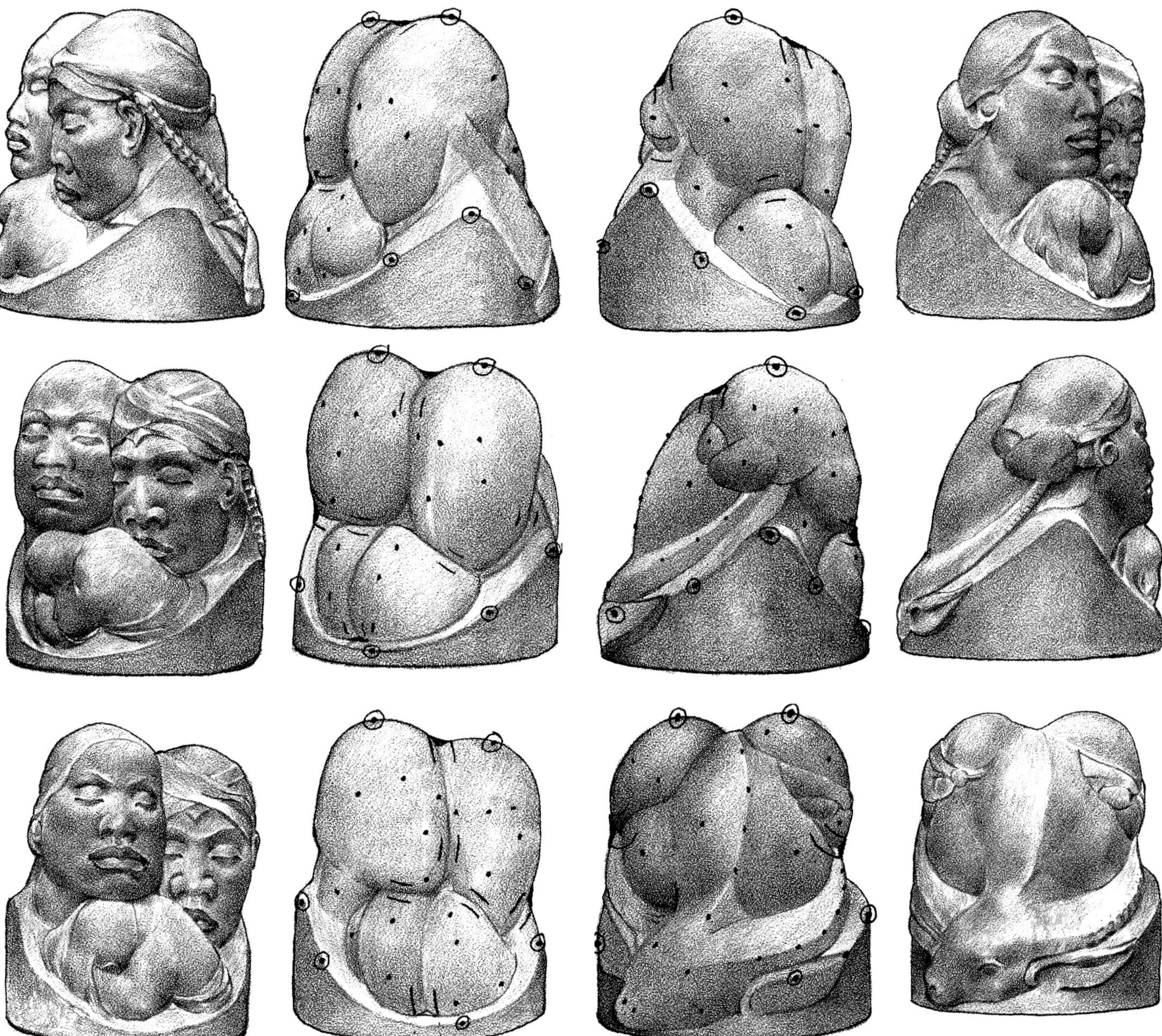

the six views of the
visualization of the
carving-to-be lead to
the form approximations
shown before detailing
in carving ought to start
(see photographs of the
finished product)

leave reserve material
between all adjacent
forms for corrective
carving & final form
intersections in the
phase of detailing all
recognizable subject matter
(faces, child, water buffalo)
⊙ tangent points on block
• critical points guide detail

form approximations
are to suggest compositions
in abstract forms into
which the realistic subject
forms fit tangentially

this procedure assures
sculptural quality in
a carving

avoid razor sharp
meeting grooves
between all form detail
when subtlety in mood
is aimed for

the illustrations show
exagerated lines of form
intersections for student
benefit to locate all
form placements

Descent from the Cross

(See photo page 125)

Carved in manzanita wood 11″ high, four figures are grouped around the central cross. Nicodemus, Joseph and a helper lower the Christ figure. Some drapery and fill-space forms create the illusion that all the bodies fit together in snug positioning, even if such closeness would prove impossible in reality.

The student can recognize in this piece the value of skills he has learned in the assignments requiring studies of four abstract forms set off by a base, which have the aim that not one form be hidden completely when the composition is viewed from all angles.

The storytelling aspect of this type of presentation lets the spiritual whole emerge even though only portions of the bodies are shown. Thus, the viewer can visualize all body extensions fitting together naturally, which aids his receptiveness to the "story" as it is told.

The detail photographs of the faces of Nicodemus and Joseph demonstrate that the quality of the final small carving is viewed more conveniently when enlarged, even if the tool marks become more noticeable. The factor of "size" remains relative to a viewer's opportunity to see form easily.

Small carvings benefit from close-grained hard woods, preferably of light color and without distracting stripes of the grain.

Should your eyesight require glasses for close-up work, by all means extend your skills with the use of magnifiers. The eyes of engravers are aided by a strong engraver's glass, which does not harm their vision.

Embrace

The piece of lemon wood was given to me in 1937 by my friend George Hensley, a woodworker practicing in his shop near my Berkeley studio. He repaired furniture and made all sorts of wood artifacts, using strictly machine tools. He had a wealth of experience in many different fields and was a walking encyclopedia of information about a seemingly endless variety of occupations. Its range covered gold prospecting, sharpshooting demonstrations for rifle manufacturers, survival techniques in the wilderness forests and deserts, embalming for undertakers (in which he was expert), methods for curing wood (also expert), finishing techniques for wood surfaces. . . .

It was he who taught me the most about wood-curing methods, and in time we would compare notes on inventive ways of doing it still better. (See Chapter 10, which discusses wood curing.)

The lemon wood he gave me was green, and this was my first experience with this material. I reasoned that his problems were different from mine; warping of wood during curing/drying was unacceptable to him, but less important to me. The possible infestation of beetles, worms and termites after carving, however, was not welcome to either of us.

The illustrations show the composition I had in mind. I began by cutting the piece lengthwise in half, then hollowing the core but leaving enough thickness for the figure carving. I let the two parts dry rapidly, hanging them from the ceiling in a dry room with some ventilation. I adjusted a resulting slight warping of the pieces by sanding each half on the saw-cut side using a coarse garnet sheet stuck on a piece of plate glass that acted as a surface gauge. New sheets of flat abrasive paper do not need to be glued to the plate glass. By simply rubbing a little bee's wax on the back of the paper, one can sand with it and it will not slip during sanding.

Once the halves were accurate, a casein glue was used to bond them together. All bonding of materials is strongest when the fit is perfect and the amount of adhesive used is a minimum. The carving has stood up well in all these years. Strong rubber bands cut from a salvaged inner tube were stretched around the assembly. The pressure of each of the five bands, pulling about 30 pounds, squeezed out all excess glue. Later, the carving showed no seam, the wood grain blended well on both sides, and there was no glue stain.

As the illustrations show, the form approximations were done first. Then the detail was carved with small engraver-type gouges. The final surface on this light-colored wood was to be smooth but not "commercially" shiny. To attain this, small pieces of fine grit garnet paper, stuck onto rubber pads at the ends of faceted wooden sticks, were used to refine the surfaces.

Next came the moistening of the finished surfaces to raise
the softer fibers. When dry, the surface was re-sanded with
new, razor-sharp, fine-grit sections of garnet paper.
A clear shellac filler was used to finally close the minute
pores in the wood. When it was dry, all excess shellac
was removed with new, razor-sharp fine grit, causing the
shellac to be flush with the wood. With a little wax and
cloth rubbing, I finished the work.

Hand-rubbing, claimed as a practice by many old cultures
(often tied in with "spiritual" aspects), actually does the
following: raises the softer grain of the wood because of
the natural moisture of the skin, eventually wears down
those protrusions because of the length of time spent
rubbing, and seals the wood by way of skin oil.

It can easily be understood that the exact same results
can be achieved in a fraction of the time with the aid of
more modern means. In addition, various attachments to
the rotary tools (fiber brushes, cloth buffers, etc.) will
prove to be a great boon to wood carvers, making
hand-rubbing outmoded.

Zephyr's Embrace

The lemon wood for this piece was salvaged from a pile
of orchard prunings. I could see why they had removed
this section since it showed several dead or rotten spots.
After I cut out the bad portions, enough sound wood
remained to carve the flow of forms, and within it I
visualized the composition shown here.

But my untrained eye could not see the worm that had
bored into this piece. Luckily, I had begun carving in an
area that soon revealed its path of entry and, following
deeper, I found that it ended at the bottom of the foot of
the woman. It was a fat worm, a beetle larva. Fortunately,
no other insect infestation remained, and the carving
gradually emerged with just enough wood to spare for
relief treatment of sections subtly blended with abstract
forms, leaving much leeway for the viewer to interpret
the subject matter.

I found it remarkable that the lack of material for the full
third dimension around the man's head and the woman's
breast still allowed the carved lower relief to be easily
acceptable by the viewer once the esthetics of the whole
composition had the chance to sink in. In fact, more
realistic dimensions would actually have been less effective
than the more subtle treatment. Slower, more spiritual
realizations weigh more than obvious instant readings.
This is a lesson for the beginner, who may be inclined to
neglect the value of subtlety to emphasize spirituality.

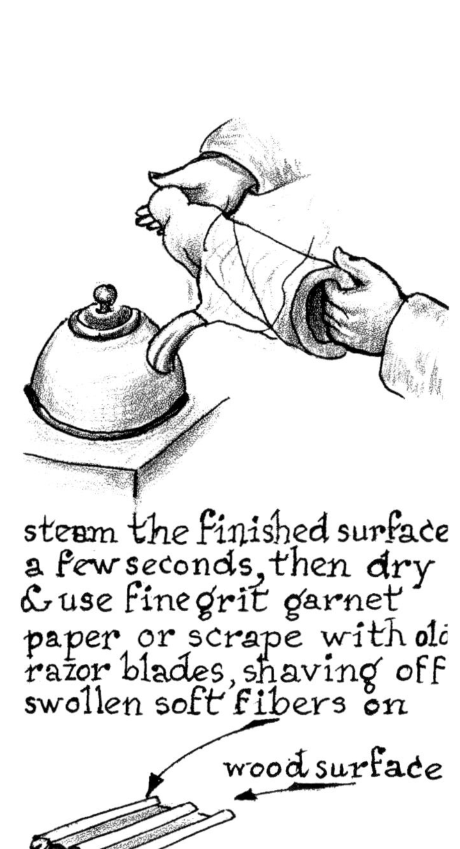

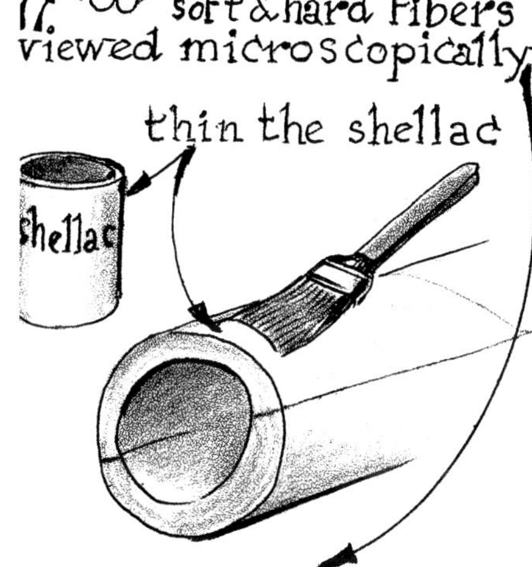

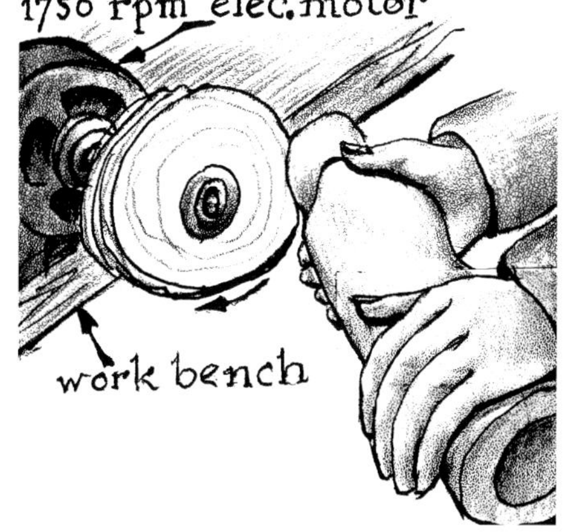

Drapery

In sculpture, the use of drapery is most effective when we want to show fine body forms through or under its covering. Over the bare body, drapery will "hang-up" on the protruding parts. This allows the viewer to visualize further the extensions of the covered body forms. Even thick drapery, such as a blanket, may reveal enough of the anatomy to complete the impressions so subtly presented. (See Chapter 12.)

Specific Detail

In *Zephyrs Embrace*, the man's hair, blown over the woman's arm, follows its form. As we follow the arm's extension we can clearly recognize the woman's hand halfway covered by the drapery. Behind her head the left arm is partly covered by her flowing hair.

The positions of the bodies behind the drapery may be imagined, however faintly, even if there remains doubt about the artist's intent. But the artist has provided enough volume of wood for this part of the carving to contain the pertinent sections of both bodies. Thus, the viewer is not adversely struck by an impossibility of the body being contained within the piece, because of the logic behind the optical illusions. These optical illusions in time lead him to visualize what is "hidden."

It is a very important point to remember that the artist must never have the bodies look chopped off when full or partial bodies are intended. Examples can be seen in the sculptures called "herms" in old Roman gardens, which show only the upper parts of bodies emerging from tall, sturdy geometric bases that allow the eye of the viewer to perceive the extensions of the bodies hidden within them. This allows room for the lower part of the body, even if it is not carved.

Some compositions are made to be viewed from in front only, while others are made to be viewed only from a 3/4 view. They may be located in gardens or angles of buildings and must be tailored to the consequent restrictions. The sculptor must make the best use of the situation within those limitations.

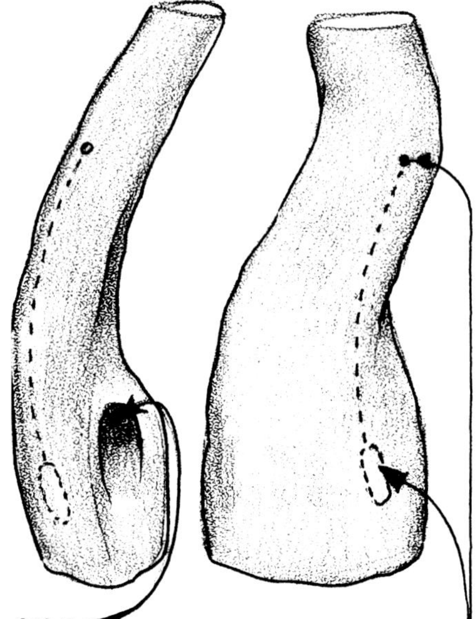

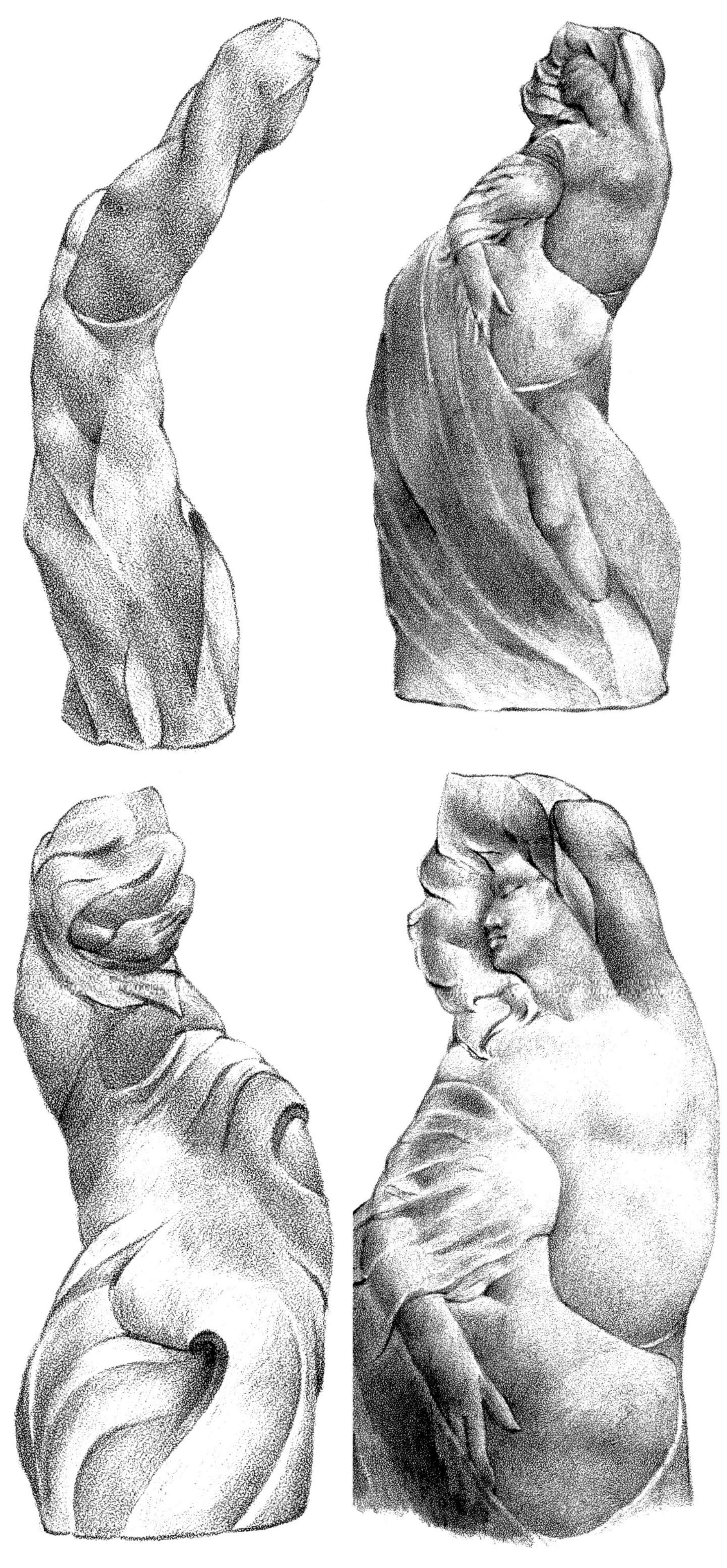

Family 1

This was carved in a piece of olive wood. First a wide check had to be filled with a strip salvaged from a similar piece of wood.

The illustrations on the following pages show the logical steps the student can follow in projects of his own.

Step 1. After repeated, round and round viewing of the piece, begin your visualization by marking the *tangent points* where the separate bodies "lean" inside against the outer surface of the piece, as if it were a thin hollow shell. The first form approximations that are carved help to sharpen our visualization for the second step.

Step 2. The first tangent points, having been left intact, will remain our "landmarks," as it were, but allow for the beginning of some body detail. However, it is important that the *material reserved* between the single forms be kept for later corrective carving. (Avoid using all grooving tools. Illustrations show black areas between single forms where reserve material is left.)

Step 3. It is now safe to begin the final details: faces, hands, drapery, etc.

However, *be cautious* never to overshoot your aim. Hold back any time the slightest apprehension is "sensed." Simple reorientation and successively shallower gouges will maintain the needed control.

Smaller pieces are easily held by hand, while being carved as one sits comfortably in a chair under a diffused, overhead light source (or with the north light in the studio). By manipulating little hand gouges with the skill of an engraver, the sculptor can carve the minutest detail with absolute control.

The illustrations showing the carving of the *pipe* should be followed exactly, in order for the student to practice tool manipulation. (See page120)

Family 2

This was carved in toyon wood and is 12″ high. As in the carving of *Family 1,* the figures at first are only approximated, with use being made of optical illusions wherever a viewing angle allows local form directions to disappear into the center of the piece. (See illustrations on page 105)

Since the figures of the parents are behind the sitting boy, the viewer is not disturbed that there may not be enough material for them.

The form approximations allow for corrective carving before detailed carving is begun.

The student is advised to analyze the illustrations of the three small *"Family"* carvings extensively, in order to test his ability to judge depth measurements of final forms related to marked tangent points, before he starts carving.

All his efforts in learning to carve *directly* without the use of measuring tools (calipers and pointing instruments) are aided by such exercises in analysis.

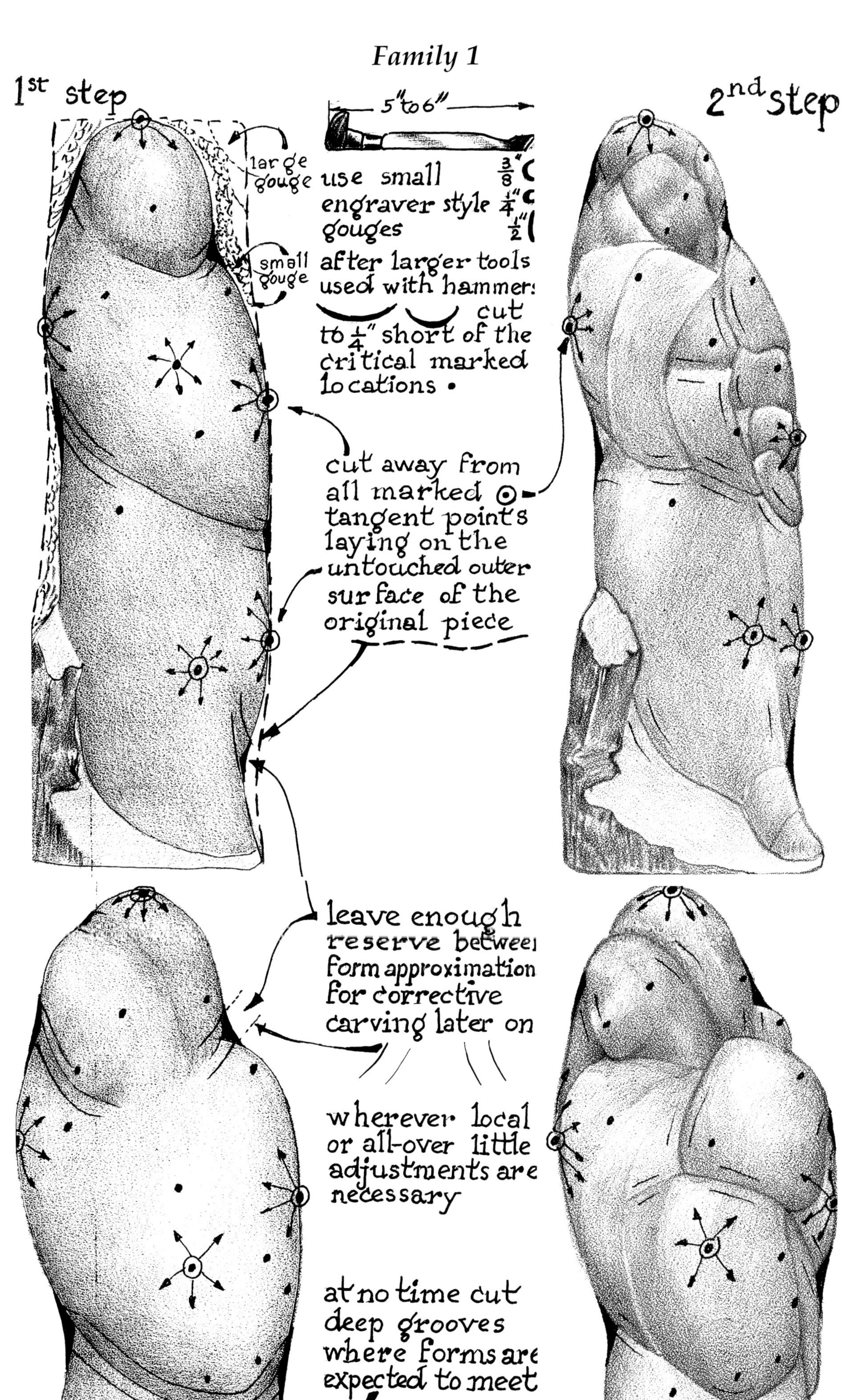

Family 1

1st step

2nd step

5" to 6"

large
gouge

small
gouge

use small
engraver style
gouges
after larger tools
used with hammers
cut
to 1/4" short of the
critical marked
locations .

3/8"
1/4"
1/2"

cut away from
all marked ⊙
tangent points
laying on the
untouched outer
surface of the
original piece

leave enough
reserve between
form approximation
for corrective
carving later on

wherever local
or all-over little
adjustments are
necessary

at no time cut
deep grooves
where forms are
expected to meet

details carved with shallow, flat and various widths engraver style gouges leave natural tool tracks for final textures **or** if smooth surfaces are wanted abrasive papers & polishing will bring out wood color

rough bark and texture of original piece left untouched for base

blend shallow relief carving of hands, feet, arms with full-round bodies, heads & avoid all under cuts

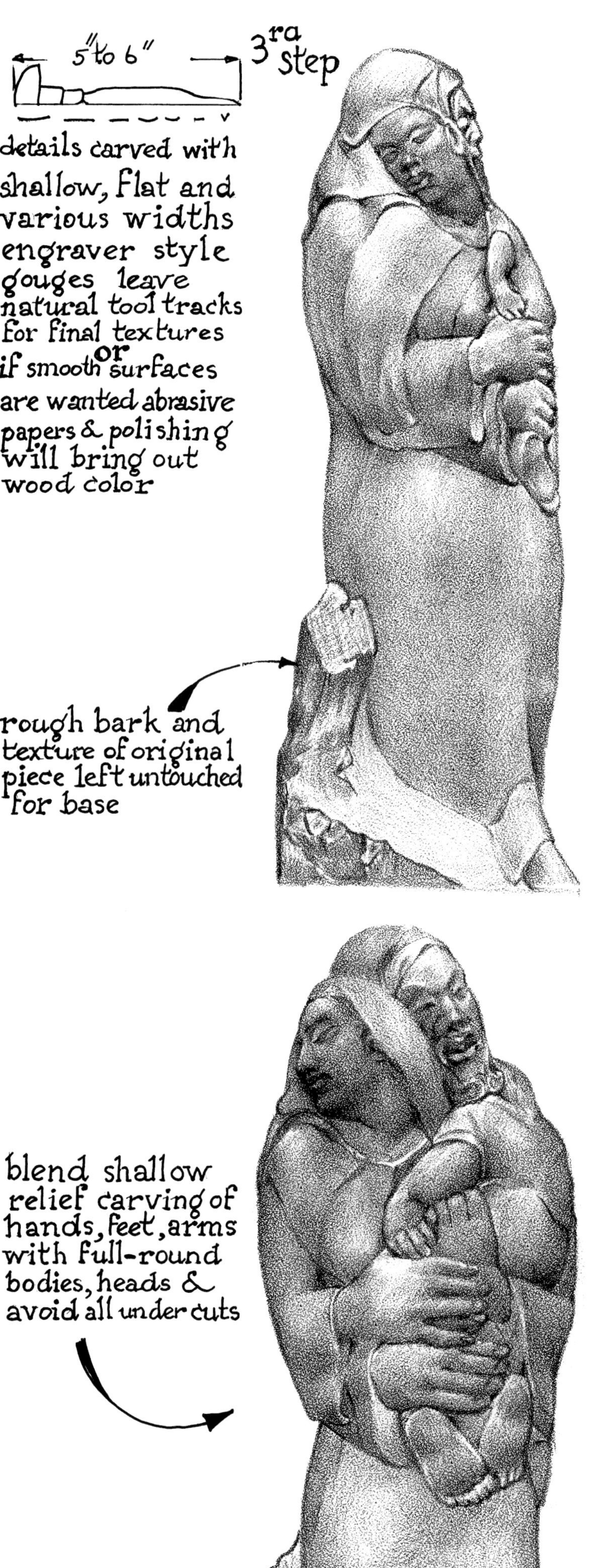

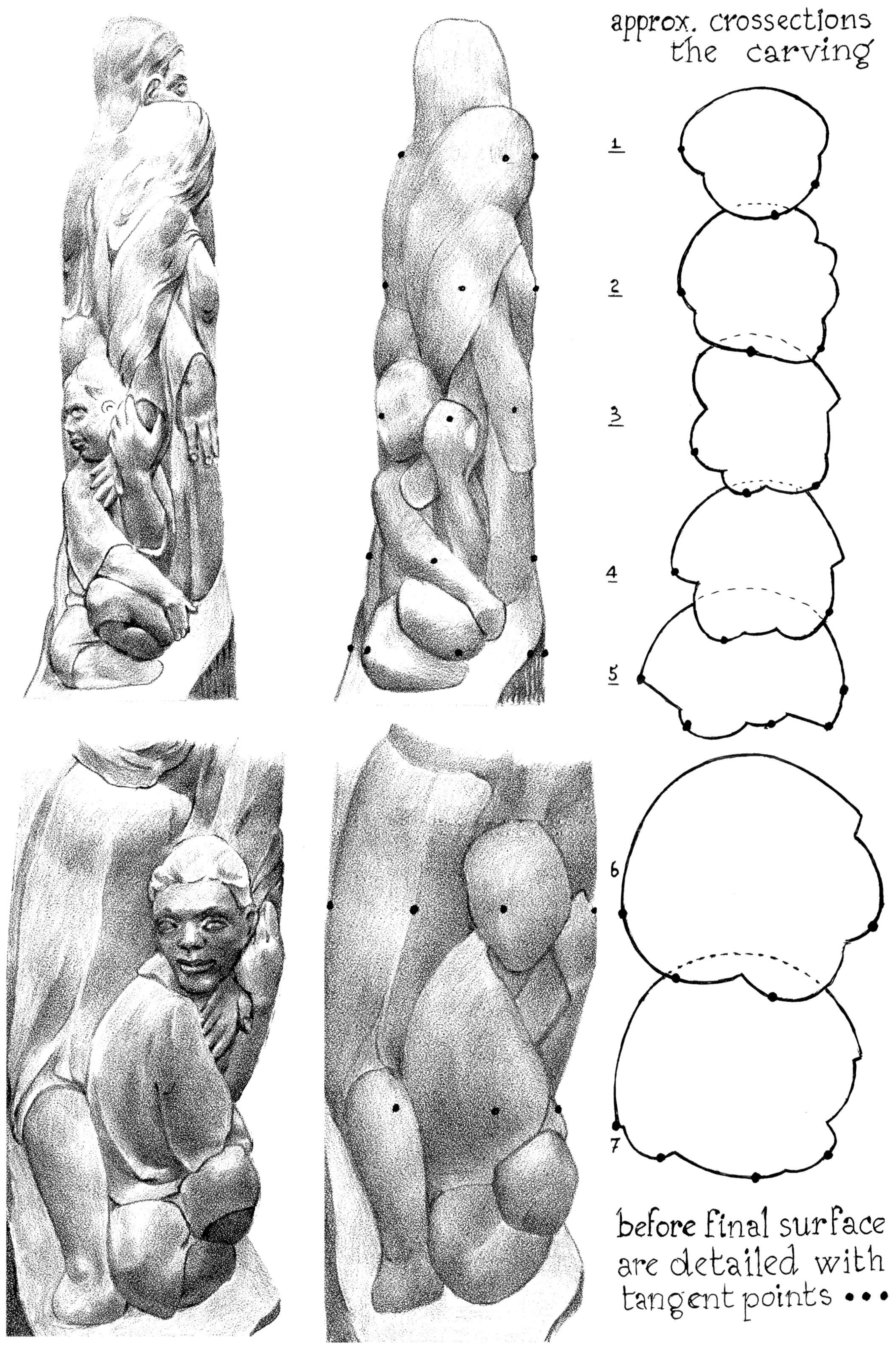
approx. crossections
the carving
1
2
3
4
5
6
7
before final surface
are detailed with
tangent points •••

Family 3

This composition also profits from having a large portion
of the available material remain as "atmosphere,"
a simple geometric-type portion out of which the subjects
seem to emerge. (See illustrations on next page.) Such
treatment has three advantages:

1. The realistic portrayal of the figures is favorably
offset by such an "abstract" form, as if by a base.

2. None of the logical extended parts of the subject
need be shown, and thus need not be carved.

3. The upward sweep of the abstract "atmosphere"
form meets the carved part of the figures sharply in
its frontal viewing as if revealing, instead of hiding,
body extensions beyond vision. "Showing by hiding"
is useful whenever we want to hold back that which
we wish the viewer to subconsciously visualize.
Thus,this effect allows the viewer to savor the
sculpture, as a "slow burn" occurs in his imagination
at the rate of his wanting it to.

The experience during prolonged or repeated viewing
makes the first reaction of "reading" grow as a product
of the viewer, over and above that of the sculptor. It is
thus that an art lover's "interpretations" while looking at
works of art become his spiritual participation, as he puts
himself into the other man's offering. Ultimately, what
the viewer sees, becomes his own, as a mirror image of
himself, albeit that the artist has made this translation
possible.

Family 3

approx. crossection
the carving

1
2
3
4
5
6
7

before final surfaces
are detailed within
tangent points • • •

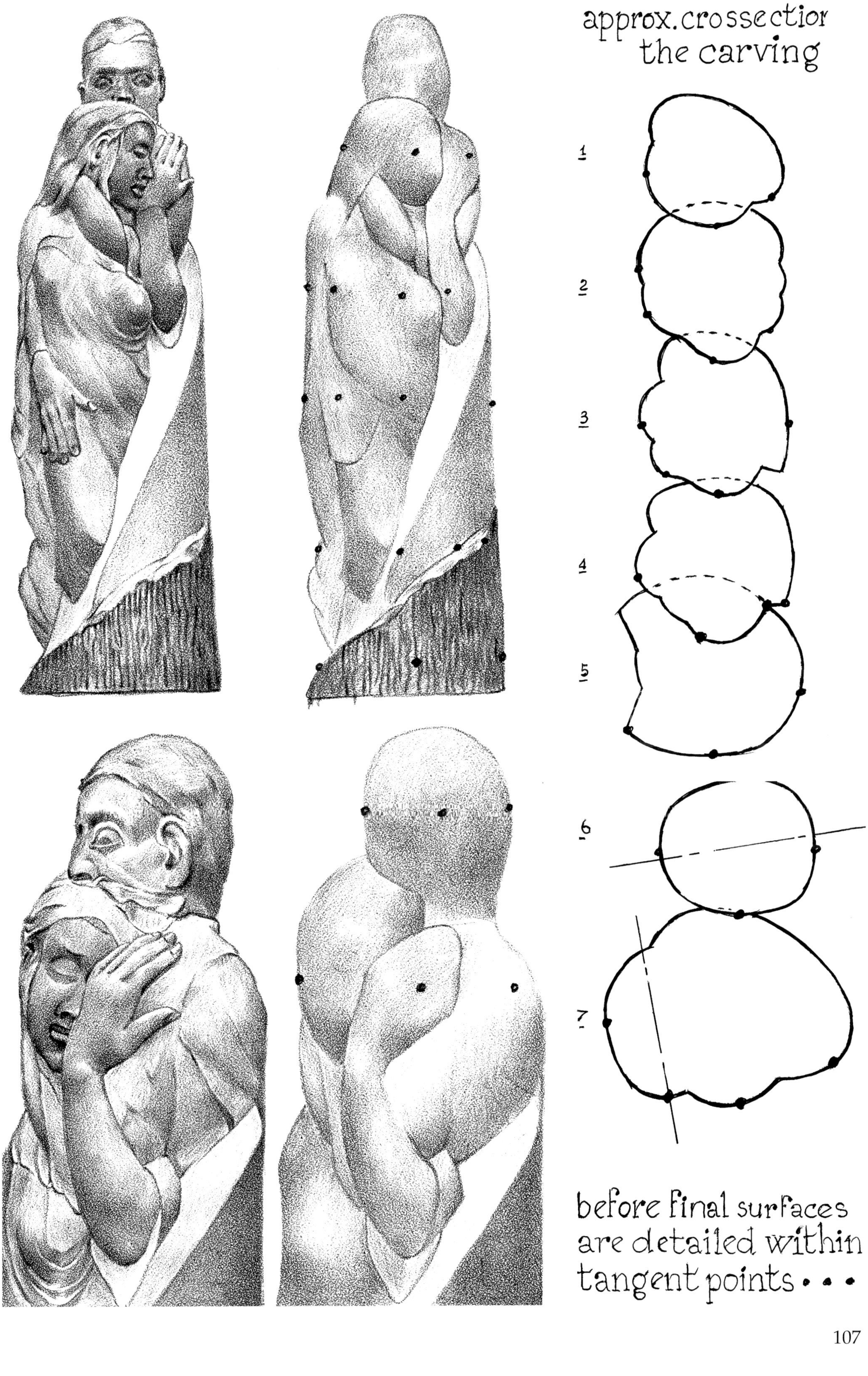

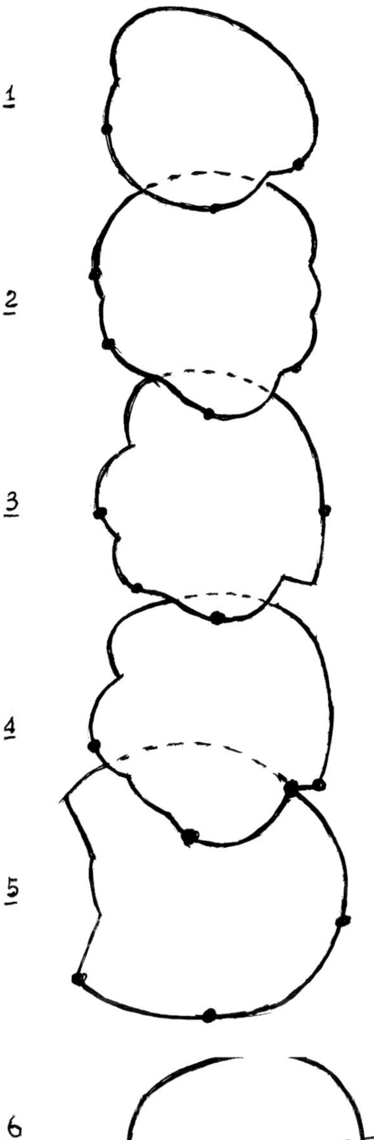

Cloud People

(See photo page 125)

I found this volcanic rock in a California quarry located in the foothills of the Sierra. Dynamite blasting had deposited all sizes of these rocks over an area where I could reach them with my little pickup. The foreman allowed me to choose one, from which I carved this piece.

I took a chance that the pieces would remain interlocked despite the cracks caused by the blast. After tapping the stone with a hammer, I concluded from the sound that it was safe to use. So far it has held up well, after fifteen years in the outdoors.

When I saw the stone in the quarry, I recognized its subject possibility. Once the grey-white stone was in the studio, my visualization of the sculpture forms sharpened, and I carved the life-size *Cloud People* fluently within about two weeks.

The blasting-cracks held perfectly under deliberate firm hammer blows. But toward the final carving I was careful not to crumble the surface at the exact meeting places of the cracks. All those locations were incorporated unnoticeably into the interweavings of the subject's form endings, so that the viewer's eye would find the three figures of the family group a relaxed and natural composition.

The frontal view of the piece demands that the viewer imagine the extended forms behind the group, and it was my challenge to encourage the viewer to accept it in this way. The woman's hand reaches from behind the man, where no material exists, to rest on his shoulder. This demonstrates what can be accomplished when one counts on the viewer's willingness to recognize the natural flow of body forms.

Note: The material, being only a little harder than hard chalk rock, was somewhat absorbent, and when later, during outdoor exposure, it showed a tendency to attract moss and lichen growth, I hosed it off and gave it a coating of Thompson's water seal to slow deterioration.

Why, then, work in fragile materials instead of more lasting and weatherproof ones? There is no satisfactory answer to those who find a personal need to have their work outlast them after death. An artworks durability has no bearing on artistic self-expression.

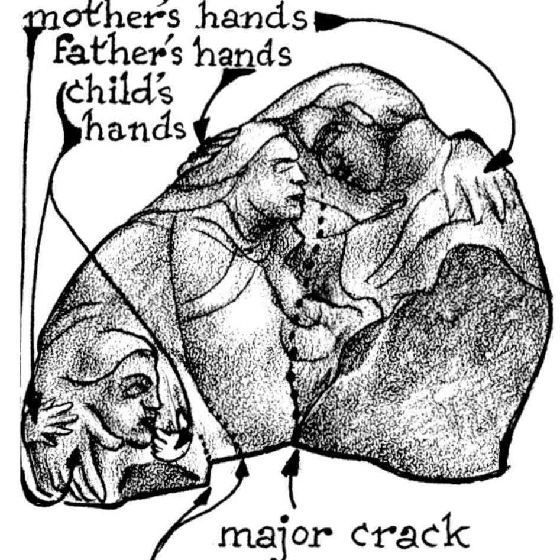

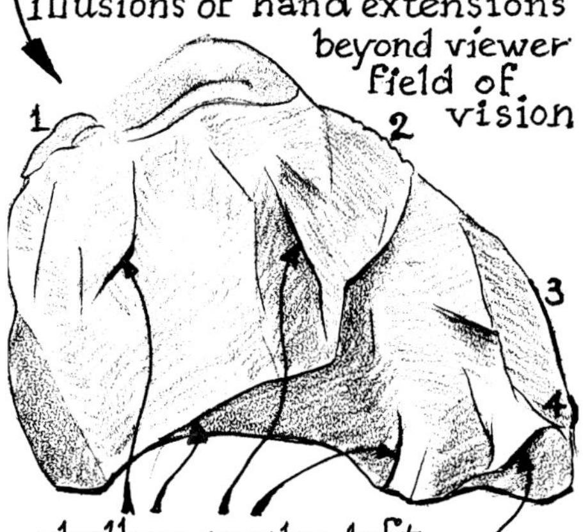

1 mother's left hand over father's left shoulder
2 father's right hand over mother's right shoulder
3 mother's right arm silhouette
4 child's right hand location

all hands visible from front viewing only

The Future

(See photo page 125)

Sometimes the material will be barely large enough to contain the desired form, or of a shape lacking in one dimension, as was the case in this composition, carved in marble.

The complication of compacting three life-size figures in this block of stone made me decide to do a small pre-study in wood to acquaint myself with the difficulties ahead. Two of the figures would be in almost full dimension and one much reduced to low relief.

Shown is the step-by-step progress in the carving of this large piece. Once the major roughing-out was done, it was no longer necessary to sight the little pre-study. With the discipline of continuous carving round and round over the whole piece, the correct locations of form approximations would fall in the right position, leaving the rest to be further detailed in perfect safety.

The remarkable thing in such projects is that the less material there is available for normal dimensions, the more the piece lends itself to the use of optical illusions to meet that lack. In this instance, where one of the three dimensions was insufficient, the use of low-relief treatment in combination with full-round enhanced the piece in the end. The more skillful the sculptor becomes in this type of blending of full round and low relief, the more he finds himself enjoying projects in odd-shaped material that others might consider unworkable. The illustrations on page (115) show several examples, with notes for the student to follow.

Students beware: Detailed treatment of every body part may detract from an overall mood. Much can be gained by subtle blending of correct forms, in which the sculptor gives just enough to extend the viewers own imagination. The lesson learned: *Overworked detail may detract from the whole.*

a nose of mother
b nose of child
c left elbow of father
d left shoulder of father
e top of head of father
f top of head of mother
g right shoulder of mother
h right hip of mother
k right knee of mother
m left knee of mother
n right hand of mother
o right elbow of mother
p left heel of fathers' foot

"the future"
back view of $\frac{1}{4}$ scale wood
carving for life size marble

tangent marks match those
on marble & remain untouched
by tools

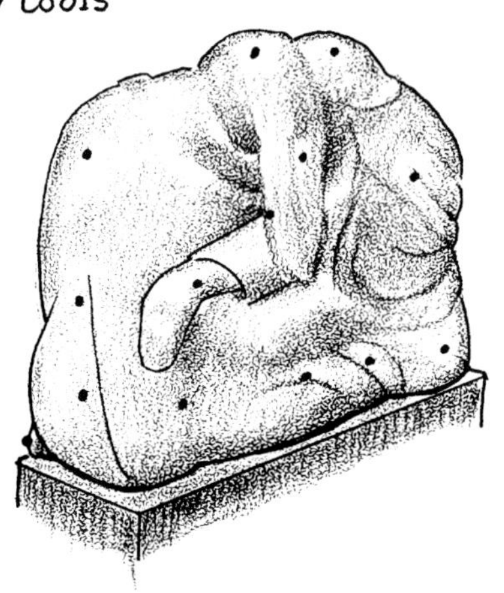

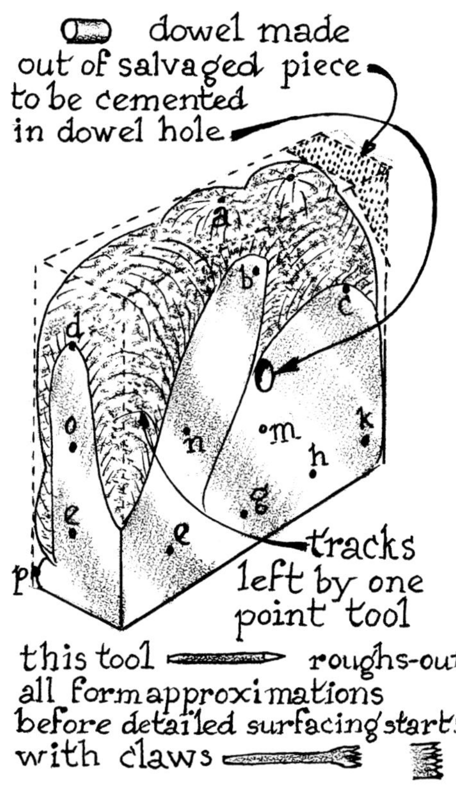

dowel made
out of salvaged piece
to be cemented
in dowel hole

tracks
left by one
point tool

this tool roughs-out
all form approximations
before detailed surfacing starts
with claws

a fathers' head
b hair mass of father
c back of mother
d left shoulder of father
e left hip of father
f right hip of father
g right thigh of father
h right knee of father
k right hip of mother
m right arm of father
n left hand of mother
o back of father
p left heel of father's foot

Ondine

(See photo, page122)

This life-size carving was done in a piece of local marble that I found on a prospecting trip along the California coast. I wanted Ondine's face to express a subtle emotion between happiness and sadness, a blend reflecting a peace of mind.

Blatancy vs. *subtlety*: These terms refer to instant recognition or afterthought, shallowness or depth . . . a shout or a whisper. Paradoxically, the spiritual aspects in art come through better the more subtly they are presented. The more gradual the unfolding, the stronger the message grows. It is therefore the wherewithal in the viewer's attitude and background that proves to what degree he senses true from false, finding in the more subdued presentations the depth of values he prizes.

The artist, with skill and insight, may portray an expression of uproarious laughter or a faint smile, or any emotion he sees fit to express. His pleasure is in arriving at the state of certainty that at last his hands have become the true servants of his mind, so that whatever he sets out to do remains clear no matter how much he restrains the message in subtlety. Thus, he exercises full control of his medium.

Triptych

I carved this low-relief piece in lemon wood. Shown are the preparatory steps. (See page 123)

Many carvers are inspired by sections of wood of promising shape: bent, arching, compound curves, etc.   In this instance the piece was cut in half lengthwise, each half with enough thickness so that the slightly curved, oval cross section had room for the assembly of body forms in low relief, in which the viewer can "see" the body in depth.

The optical illusions at the edge thickness of the piece suggest the full body, as if the forms "flow" into the piece and continue behind it. By careful examination the student can understand what takes place.

As in all relief carving of this kind, full control must prevail. It often becomes a sculptor's most enjoyable project when what he has to say is challenged by the techniques and skills he has mastered, and he can use his full range rather than only a portion of it. A confidence occurs that makes the seemingly impossible possible; this is particularly true when the sculptor uses optical three-dimensional illusions.

Correct and perfect lighting on low relief is necessary to bring out the total artistry that has been put into it. As with paintings, low reliefs hung on a wall should be lighted individually, not in combination with other adjacent works. The light can be arranged, by experimentation, to do the low relief the most justice, and this care should be insisted upon when one exhibits in galleries or museums. Often, sculpture is neglected more than painting in this regard.

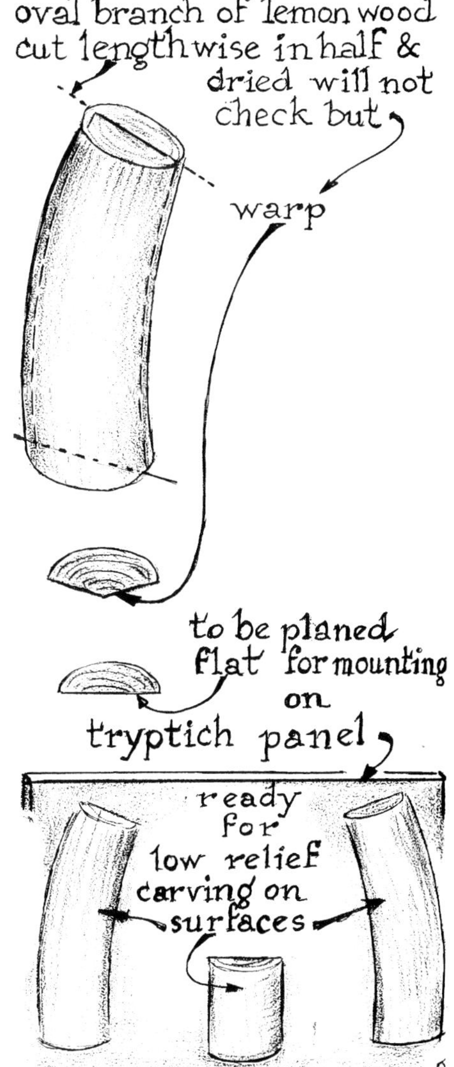

Self-Portrait from a Previous Life

The limestone rock was found as an outcropping on a coast range mountainside in California. After the eroded outer portions were scaled off, enough sound material remained for the carving of the satyr.

Satyrs, a blend between man and goat, must have filled the need of Greeks and Romans in their allegorical dramas and legends to make light of human folly. The appeal seems to be strengthened by a universal recognition that this type of imagery is based on mirth and not malice.

The grotesque subject matter lends itself ideally to caricaturization; it is as if all the forms were self-adjusting and made of push-and-pull rubber-like material. Once a sculptor gains a taste for the carving of caricatures, and experiences the extreme flexibility of accentuating local forms within their final assemblies, he may enjoy extending this approach to a wider range of subjects. The appeal of the satirical and humorous is irresistible to many artists.

Questioned in my studio about the "why" of this piece, my answer is simple: I love to pull the rug from underneath people who take themselves too seriously. Satyrs act as a catharsis. As a rule, a viewer's response to them is one of relief and laughter at himself and man's idiosyncrasies and self-importance.

No matter how serious an art product is meant to be or how well executed, viewers are better off, and so is the artist, when they keep their appreciation down-to-earth, without overrating or hero-worship. After seeing this piece in the studio, visitors who had been hushed as if in a museum, relax and identify with the artist.

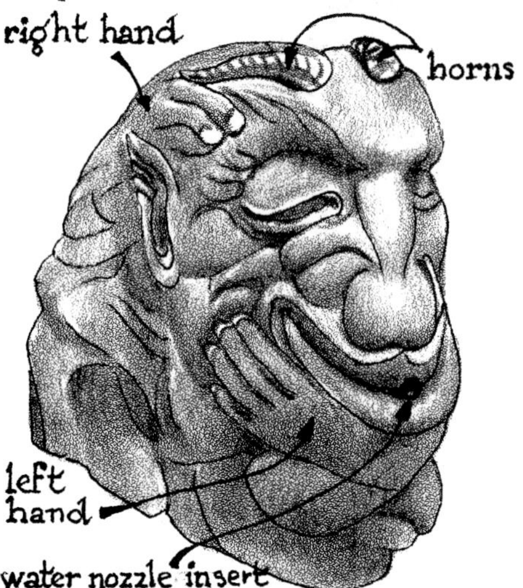

acting as a fountainhead, spout
is to hit humorously another
fountain sculpture

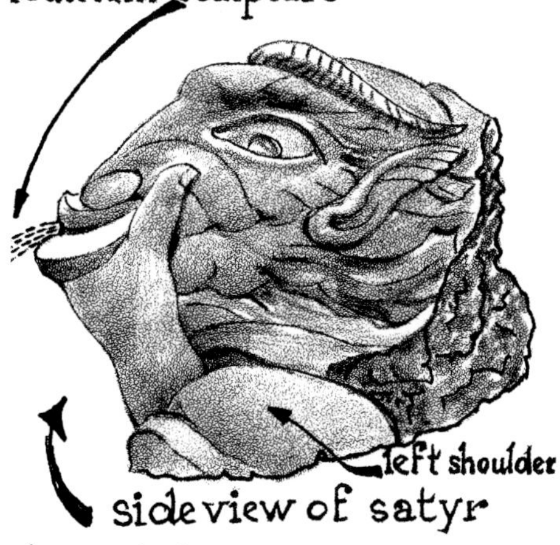

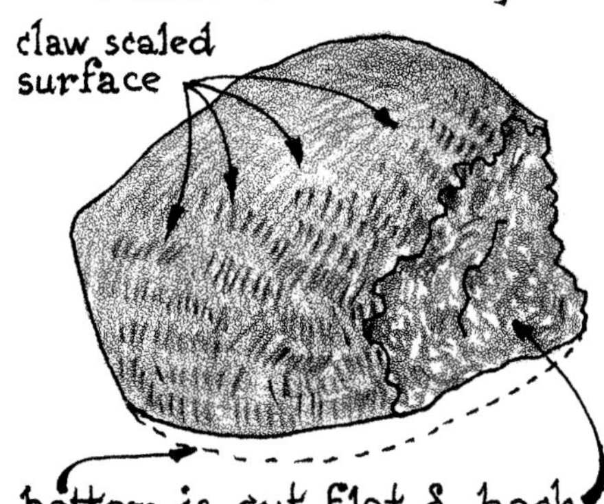

bottom is cut flat & back
part left uncut & rough
coarse 4 teeth claw scaled
vital surface first & next
4-6-8 fine teeth claws were
used to shape all finished forms

water spout hole is drilled with
carbon tipped drill & a copper
nozzle inserted
intake fitting at bottom has
standard threaded coupling
cemented in

Portrait of My Father

This piece was modeled in clay in 1933 and cast in
plaster. It shows my father looking somewhat
melancholy, but I wanted to express the man's sensitive
character. I knew him to have come closer and closer to
nature's language during his long years in the lush
tropics of Indonesia, and to being in harmony with all
living things: man, animal, insect, plant, as well as the
forces in wind, water and fire. In fact, I had the
impression that in death he fused with nature's truth,
from which springs all that "is." His life mirrored
this truth. (See page 124)

Mood. The heavy-lidded eyes express a melancholy
countenance, even when we do not see the rest of the face
in this photographic detail of the portrait. This detached
portion acts as an independent form-composition, an
abstraction in which form for the sake of form can stand
on its own.

In exploring the possibilities of *mood transfiguration,*
we can see that a pictorial blend of form assemblies can
produce surprising results. I used the portrait of my
father's eyes as subject, in combination with a wide
choice of photo transparencies. This gave me an
opportunity to mix two different moods to illustrate
such transfiguration.

> 1. A close-up photo transparency of a half-frozen
> mud puddle in the road superimposed over the
> eye portion of the face creates a mood of
> unworldly spiritual depth, as if an archaeologist
> had unearthed a sculpture portrait of a
> contemplative ancient philosopher.

> 2. In another combination, a close-up of an abalone
> shell and the sculptured portrait of my father's
> eyes shows two empty breathing holes of the shell,
> aligned with the human eyes. This creates the effect
> that, upon looking through the two holes, one
> receives back the penetrating look of the eyes of the
> man. This "in between" feeling of looking *out* and
> looking *in*, automatically activates a reversal factor,
> which in turn arouses that suspended feeling of
> watching while being watched . . . our zero
> (central) position in life. (See page 125)

Literally endless possibilities suggest themselves when
we work with *abstractions of forms* such as a detailed
portion of a well-shaped shoulder, limb or chest. When
a body detail is viewed as one would view a fine
painting, the rest of the body is not missed, even if the
detached portion is recognized as being only a part of
the whole human body. The *mood* of each form
abstraction uniquely emerges.

Thalidomides

When first the news of malformation at birth due to
Thalidomides reached me, I visualized this composition.
(See illustrations on following page.) The two distorted
victims seem to hold out hope that in *time, spiritual*
compensation may make living worthwhile. The man,
grown wise with years, holds the child protectively as if
reassuring that all may not be lost.

The carving. The body distortions are shaped within the
tight limits of the wood branch I chose. Each body zone,
when viewed separately, is anatomically plausible, but
all elements are distorted relative to the other zones.

How to Begin Carving a Rough Branch
or a Naturally Formed Stone

If a rock or a piece of wood resembles an approximately
recognizable subject, it is tempting to *draw* that subject
on it as if lines were to resemble the meeting places of
all forms. The drawn lines would invite use of a veining
gouge to cut deep grooves along those lines, to make it
appear that those "forms" are to meet there precisely.
The resulting image then becomes a bastardized
form/drawing mixture, neither fish nor foul. The rule
should be: *Never draw when sculpting.*

The illustrations (on next page) show where all expected
tangent points, which should remain untouched, are on
the wood branch. Even if lines should be drawn where
forms are expected to meet, one ought to mark *tangent
points* and use them instead as starting points when
actual carving begins.

Once one begins, carving little by little around the
tangent points, one overcomes all hesitancy. Soon,
sharpened visualization aids one's judgment in guiding
the tool unfailingly, and the temptation to draw
disappears.

Repeat: Even if all continues well in the location of
forms, my experience has convinced me that *a veining
tool should not be used at any time during sculpting.*
Instead, use flat-ended tool edges of different widths to
make forms meet sharply when needed, without loss of
continuity of surface. This preserves all form quality and
allows viewers to imagine the elements of such forms
beyond their field of vision.

As in all form-shaping, subtlety in appearance is
enhanced when most form intersections are kept
somewhat "atmospheric" where opposite forms meet.
"Atmospheric" indicates an imagery of locally foggy
or misty depressions between precise forms. Such
treatment leaves it to the viewer to follow his
imagination within the range of the artist's
communication.

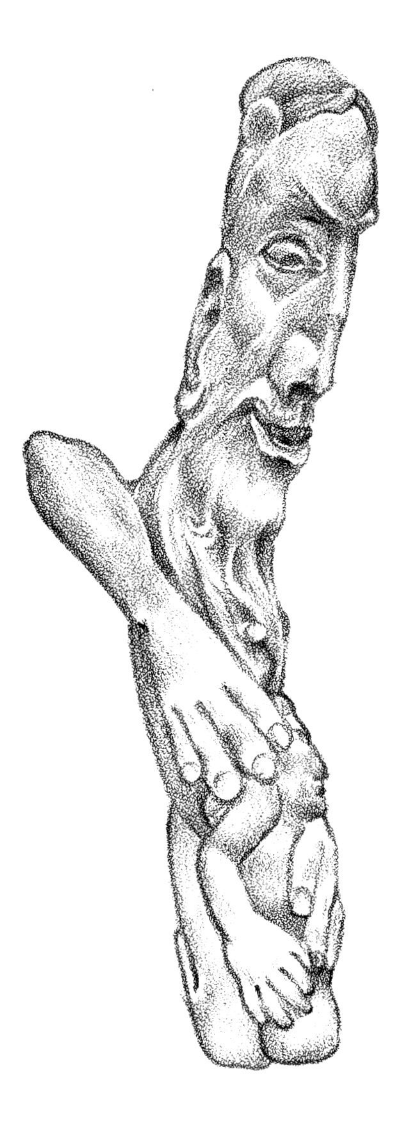

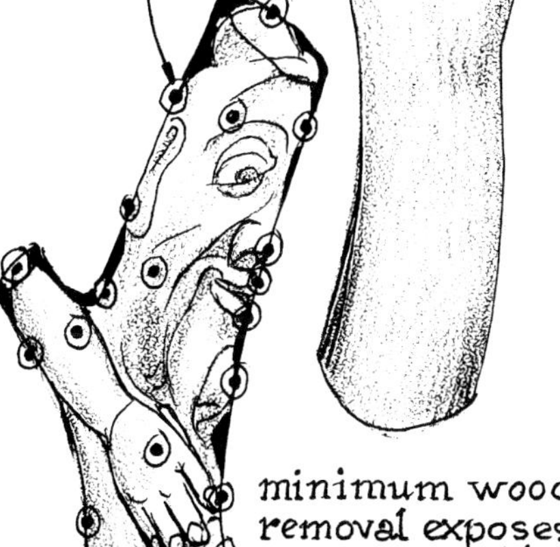

Thalidomides

carved in a branch of mountain cedar with engraver style gouges

tangent points show where approximations of forms touch branch surface

minimum wood removal exposes all forms in the final assembly in their finished state

mark all critical points before detail carving starts

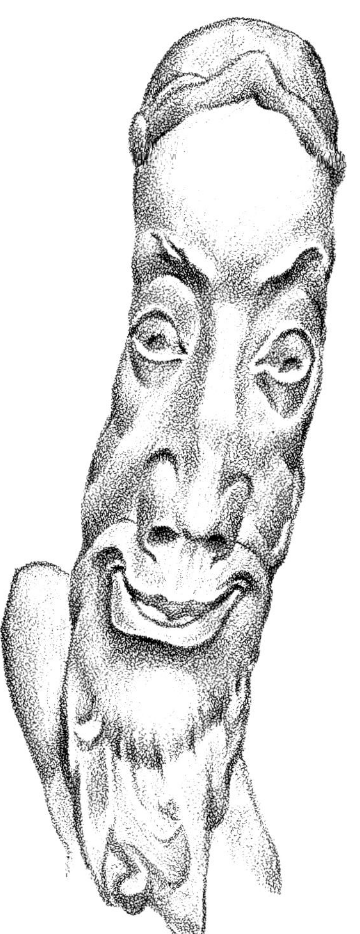

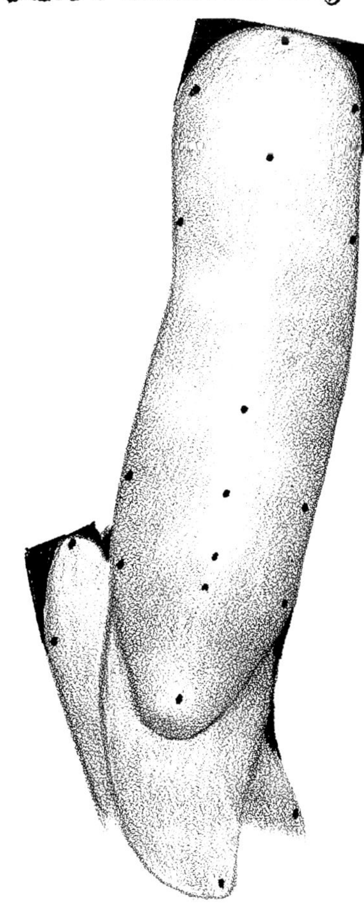

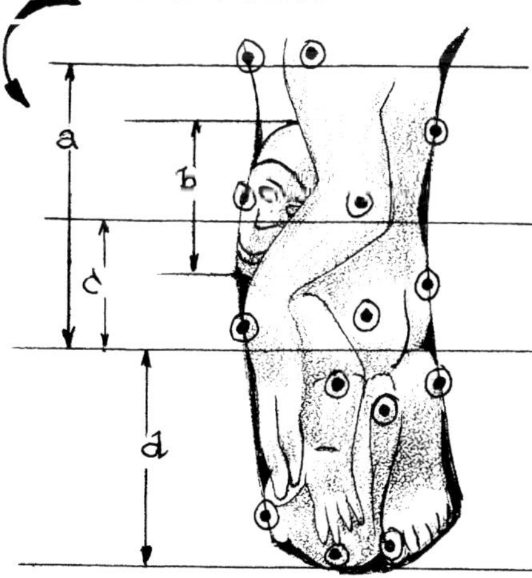

distortion zones

a mans torso shortened
b childs' face enlarged in relation to body
c pelvic region shortened to match thighs, legs
d mans feet larger to contrast with distorted childs body

within each zone anatomy is to appear normal, letting distortions spread step by step

The Prodigal Son

(See photo page 123)

Much in art derives inspiration from human experiences reflected through religion in books and records compiled in antiquity. The epic of *The Prodigal Son* (the rebellious youth returning to parents who saw him leave his origins to seek answers to life's problems elsewhere) is one of them. The poignancy lies in the son's return to the family fold, where he finds a bottomless well of love, devotion, forgiveness, hope, and resignation in despair . . . all springing from a single source: an underlying all-encompassing truth. Such intermingling and breadth of spiritual range is a wellspring for artistic work.

My interpretation of *The Prodigal Son* called for the emotion to be expressed in the son's body stance: kneeling with his face hidden. The father's face, as well as his body stance, expresses the depth of forgiveness and reassurance as it flows through his hands on the boy's sides. The mother's gesture completes the bond, with her embrace of the son's re-entry into this enigmatic mix of body and spirit.

Often the *body stance alone* is all that is needed to express three-dimensionally the "message" the artist wishes to convey. To add *more* does not necessarily increase the message's effectiveness. We see the actor, mime and dancer excel in this manner.

Some stones do not lend themselves to being carved in minute detail. Uneven color, stripes, spots, and large, flaky crystals interfere. *The Prodigal Son* was carved in a piece of large-crystal limestone that I found on one of my prospecting trips. The stone came so close to my visualization of the subject that I yielded to temptation, against my better judgment, and used it in spite of its suspect quality.

The viewing angles called for a composition limited to three-quarters of a circle, the back quarter to remain uncarved. I cut the final surface with fine-toothed claws. In the end, I decided to spray it with a dull white paint to hide the reflecting flaky crystals and spots, in order to show all form detail at its best.

Polishing the surface would have made matters worse, causing the crystalline facets to reflect like mirrors and resemble fish scales.

This experience taught me several lessons: to test all promising material first for unsuspected flaws, and to question whether, if the finished carving turns out to be in an unsuitable material, we should carve it over again in a better stone. However, a duplicate will lack the spark of verve and spontaneity of the original direct carving. Perhaps a plaster cast would be better, showing all of the sculptures forms at their best.

It is thus that we face the persistent controversy: *Can a perfect duplicate bring forth the same reaction in the artist and patron as the original?*

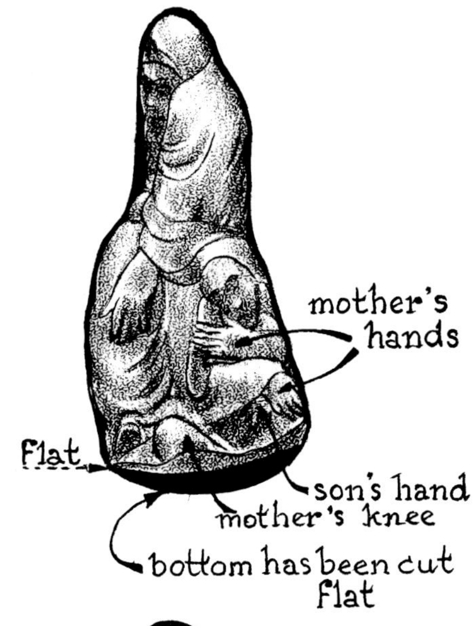

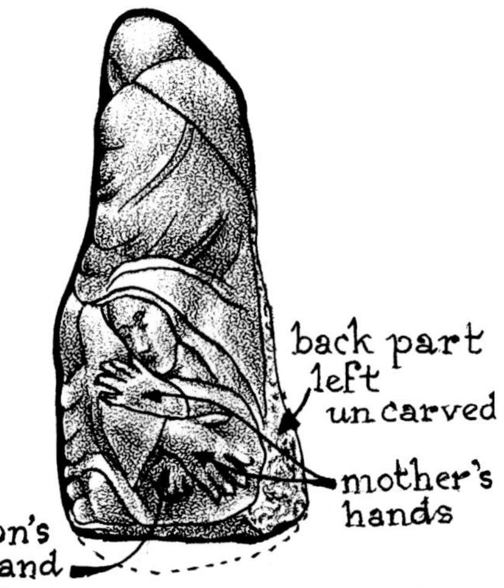

He can resort to making a mold and cast, using duplicating instruments and, if he can afford it, hiring a qualified artisan to relieve him of the dull "repeat" activity.

How Do Compositions "Unfold?"

The original shapes of wood and stone found in nature may trigger the artist's thoughts based on memories. In my opinion, this causes a reliving of past feelings, created by life's experiences and observations. There are too many to immediately remember them all. We can, as a rule, only retain the outstanding high points stored in our minds. I liken it to carrying a "memory bag" with us wherever we go.

We may come upon a stone or piece of wood of a particular shape that harmonizes with one of those stored memories, which then sets in motion a process of metamorphosis resulting in form transfigurations. Gradually the memory grows to fit the stone shape and ripens into a visualization of the sculptures final form assembly.

As a rule, I like to live with such a piece for a while as thoughts continue to clarify, until all has become so vivid that the time has come to have it off my chest. It is then that the artist removes with assurance and rapidity whatever is superfluous. This is the essence of direct carving coming into its own; all flows unrestrained because the necessary incubation time has been spent.

Carving then takes a minimum of time, rarely requiring more than a few days (or for larger pieces some weeks, due to the added physical effort and energy).

Individual Interpretations Regarding Subject Matter

The spiritual foundations upon which societies have built "workable" ways of life have created great diversity of customs, habits, behavior . . . making uniformity on a global scale seem impossible. It is therefore helpful, when searching for a common denominator, to trace our probings to man's "group" instincts. From them spring concepts of "right and wrong" and "trust and betrayal;" these form the backbone of family cohesion.

An anecdotal example regarding right, wrong and a test of faith: Two friends have sworn to protect one another against mortal danger in a tiger-infested jungle. They face the night sitting back-to-back. Each one has promised to protect the other in case a tiger should attack from his side. It is *wrong* if the one who is attacked jumps aside in order to save his own life, letting the tiger kill his friend. It is *right* if the one attacked takes the brunt in order to save his friend to whom he swore fidelity.

In human affairs, moralities based on values of right and wrong in this fashion seem shared among all societies; the traitor stands condemned. In matters of trust, the animal world also seems to react unforgivingly. Play with a puppy in good faith and if, after the animal begins to count on fair play, one should betray it with an unfair trick, that pup will grow up forever remembering deceit.

The poignancy of the prodigal son's return to the family fold emerges as a blend of sadness and happiness. Having escaped the poison of deceit that hangs as a sword of Damocles forever overhead, he has a restoration of faith which spells salvation.

Is it any wonder that artists throughout history chose this subject to depict goodness as man's hope that springs eternal?

Enid

This was carved in cascara wood, which is yellowish in color with gray bark. The tree grows profusely in Oregon, where its bark is stripped and sold to pharmaceutical companies who manufacture and market the laxative cascara.

The wood is close-grained and free of checking during drying, but if found dead and dry in nature, it is often beetle-infested.

The subject: The partial draping of the figure has a dual effect setting off the physical beauty of the body as well as keeping the base dimension sturdy. The tool texture around the base contrasts with the smooth sanded surfaces of the nude body.

Since cascara grows around my studio home, it was available for the carving of **Enid**. I noticed that wildlife (raccoons, birds, etc.) fed on its dark red berries. This prompted me to try some of the berries myself when a laxative was needed. Eating a dozen of them at one time, I soon found out that two of them would have been sufficient.

carving sideways around the marks along visualized forms, in time eases local adjustments in form relations well before errors in judgement could progress beyond repair

carving of final detail as lips mouth, fingers, toes, hair is best done after final surfaces of all forms have been reached while leaving enough reserve for such detail

use small engraver style gouges for carvings up to 20" high

momentarily 'steam' finished surfaces & smooth with fine grit abrasive papers, then seal with shellac & wax polish

Bookends

Whenever opposite sentiments are portrayed, as in the theater masks of Comedy and Tragedy, many sculptors reach for satire to underscore such contrasting facial expressions.

The satyr faces (3″ in height) make use of form detail within anatomically plausible derivation. The faces fit the confines of a right-angle sided piece of ordinary pine wood. The carving was actually begun as a "test" for a few small gouges I had made, and ended up as a pair of bookends. (See illustration)

Skewer Handles

I used sections of cascara wood where side branches were trimmed off, and the remaining little stub ends became chins and noses. The parting gouge left the contrast between light-colored wood and bark that remained attached which gave the carved handles a striking appearance.

The steel skewers were made of cold-hammered, galvanized, heavy gauge wire. The flattened cross section keeps the skewered foods from slipping when the skewer is rotated during barbecuing.

A Smoker's Pipe

This was carved in Algerian briar with small wood gouges (their design based on the engraver's tools). This tool technique ought to be studied seriously by the beginner so that he might benefit from this most valuable way of carving wood with the least waste of time and energy while maintaining full control of the tools.

Note the range of hand-turning movement in relation to the free downward-hanging elbow, as shown. This position gives maximum flexibility when working with, or without, the use of an engraver's glass.

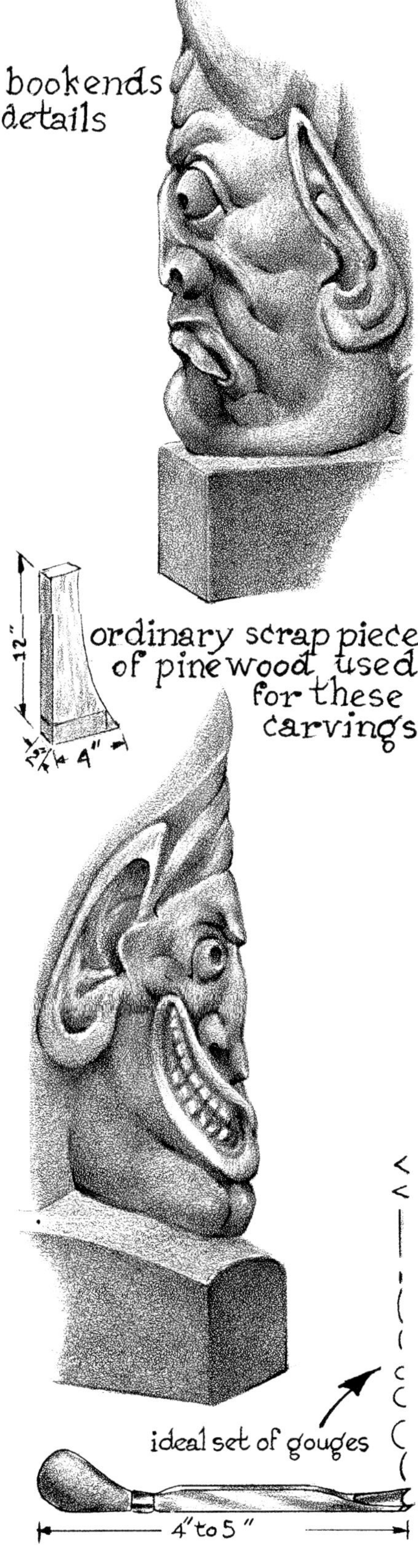

small wood sculptures carved with hand pushed small gouges designed on the principles of engravers' tool manipulation

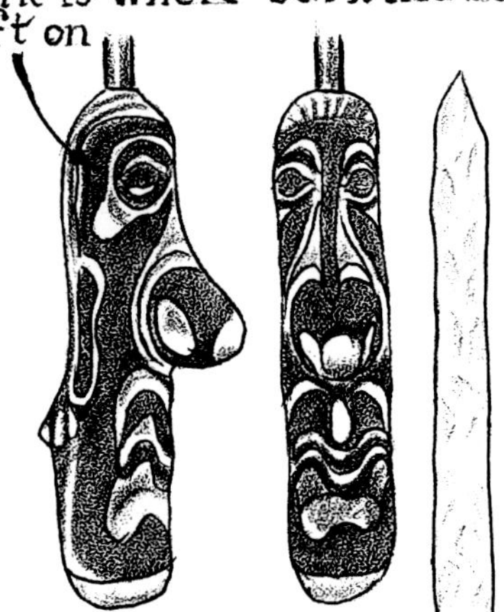

skewers carved from branch sections of the cascara segrada

dark is where bark has been left on

make use of knobs & side branches to become facial & hair detail

galvanized thick wire hammered cold on anvil until flat to secure meat etc when skewer rotates

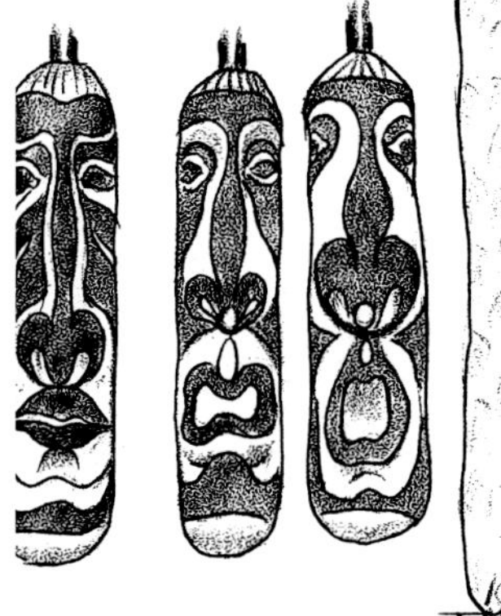

three inches or over to prevent scorching of wood handle during barbecueing

cold hammer square & burn in handle

predrill under size hole before burning in the squared wire end

small engraver style gouges are used

small & miniature wood sculptures are hand held while carved with engraver style gouges which are manipulated in the manner that engravers use their burins

standard hard rubber pipe stem fitted in wood with drill

use type & size gouge to suit all local forms

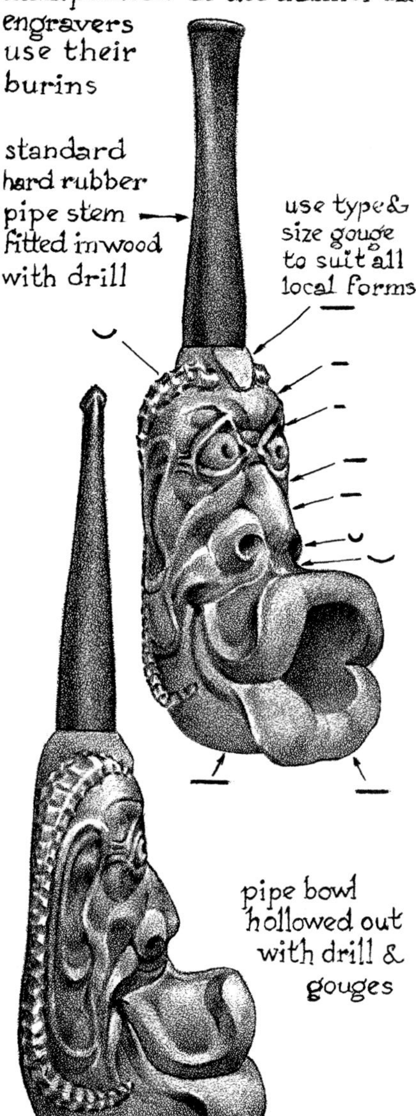

pipe bowl hollowed out with drill & gouges

pipe pressed on pillow placed on lap & thumbs held together

pillow

right way

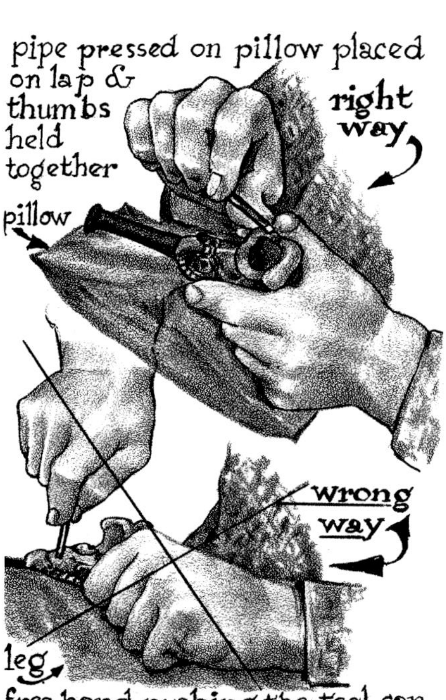

free hand pushing the tool can make it slip, causing injury

wood engraver's tools are manipulated by hand & finger movements while the arm hangs down loosly

manifying glass & stand

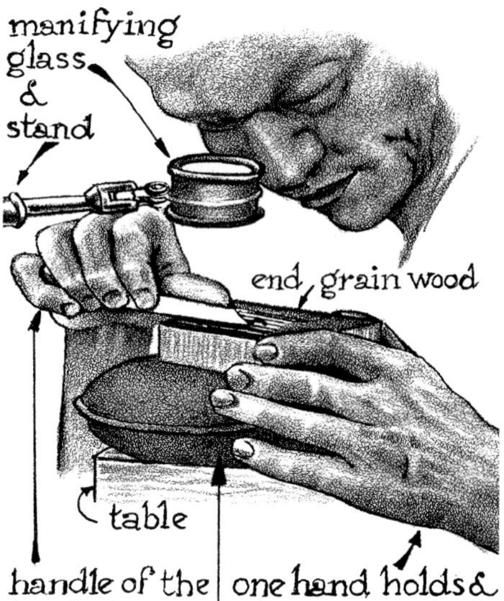

handle of the burin is cradled in crook of little finger & hand

one hand holds & slants the block to meet burin movements

leather pad is filled with sand

thumb remains pressed on the block while flat tool shank is made to slide back & forth along thumb pad

fingers line up flush with shank edge

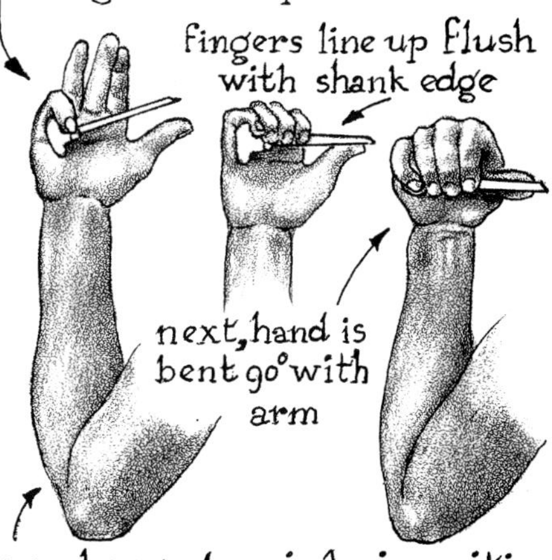

next, hand is bent 90° with arm

arm hangs down in basic position

with thumb pressed against shank while tool slides back & forth in cutting action

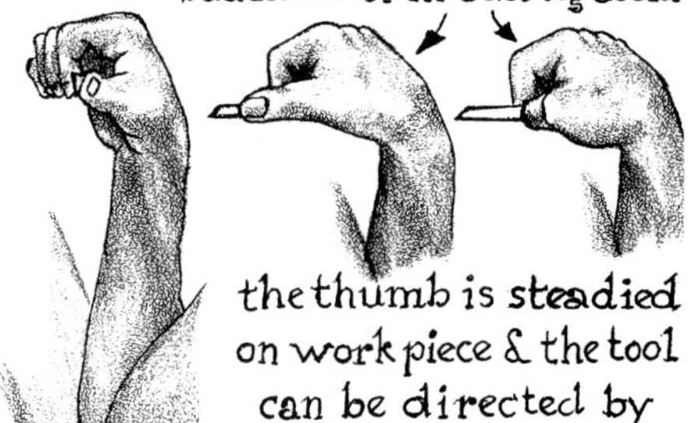

the thumb is steadied on work piece & the tool can be directed by turning the hand in any position within a range of 180°

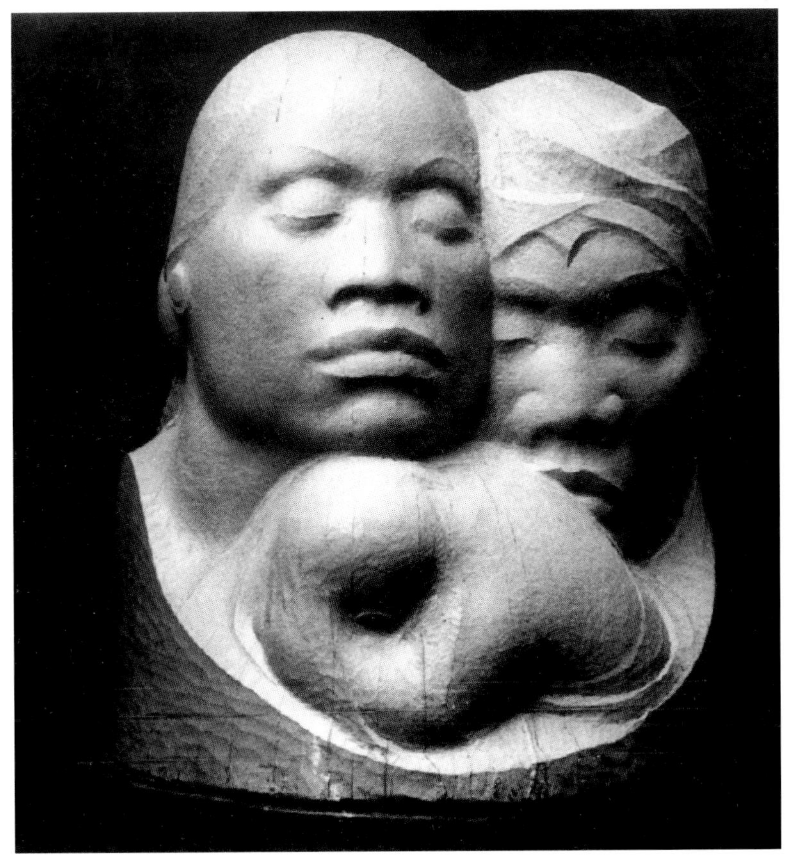

Malaya *Podocarpus Wood*

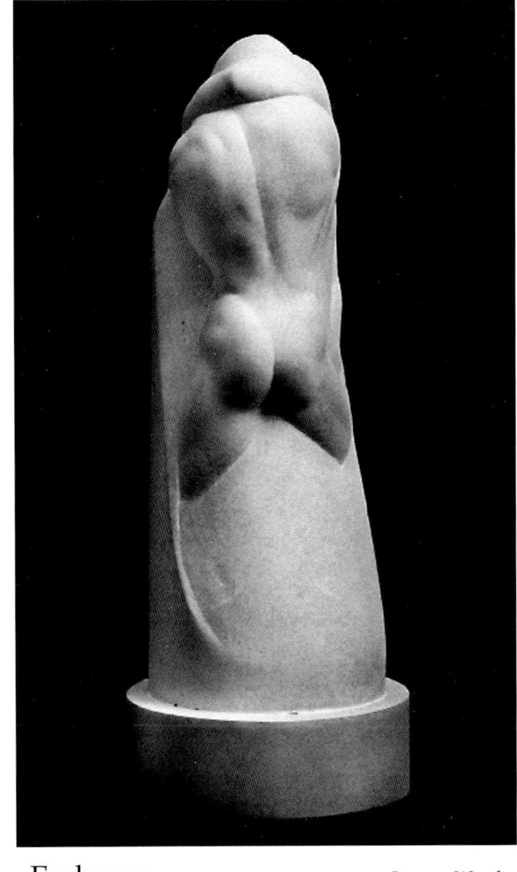

Embrace *Lemon Wood*

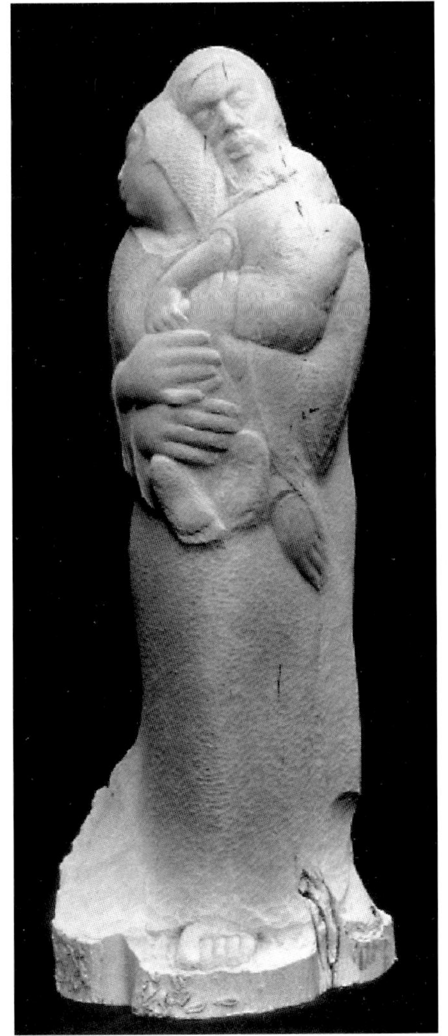

Family 1 *Olive Wood*

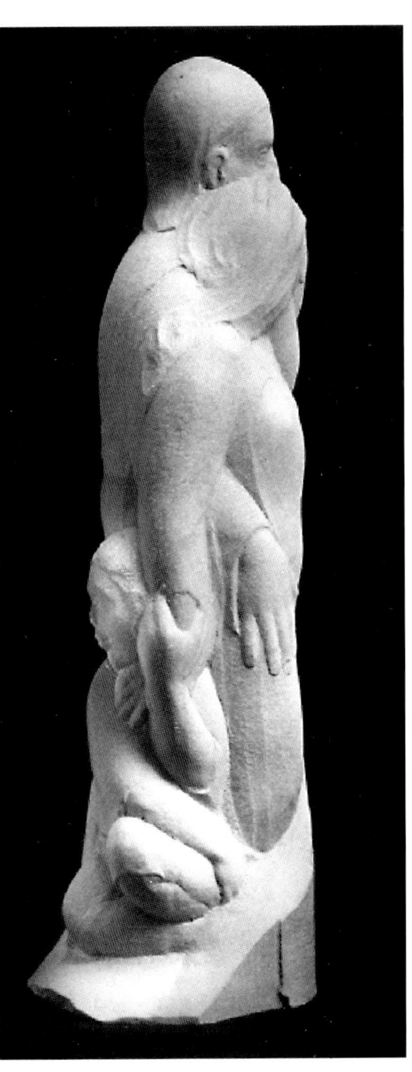

Family 2 *Toyon Wood*

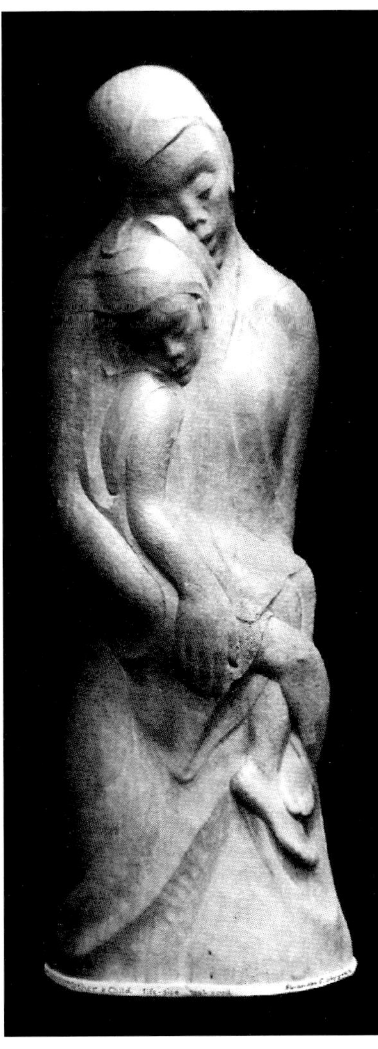

Mother and Child *Teak Wood*

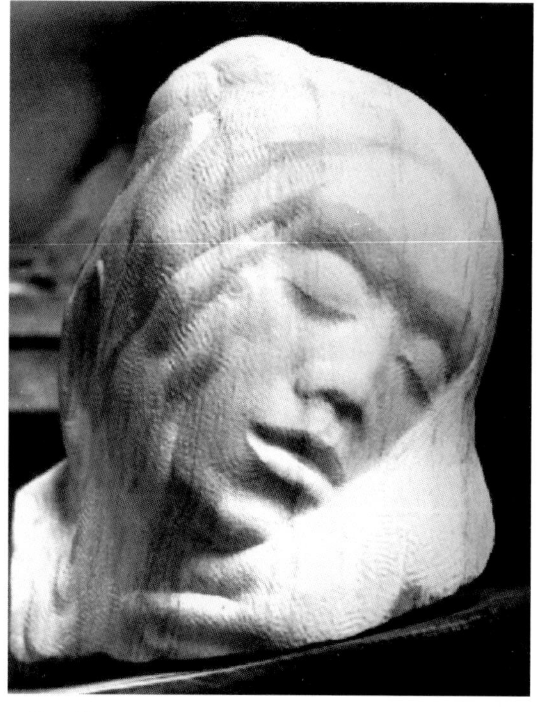

Ondine *California Marble*

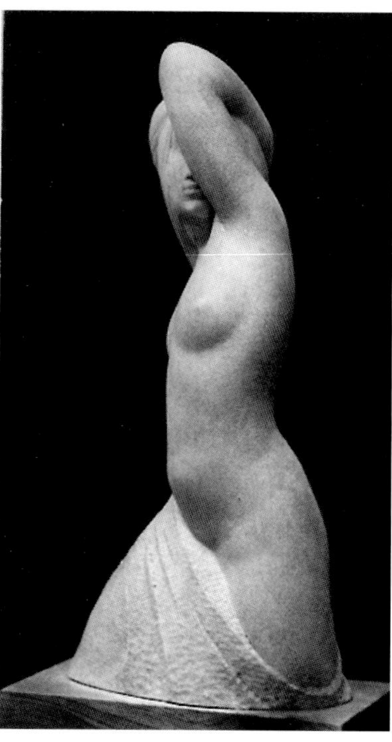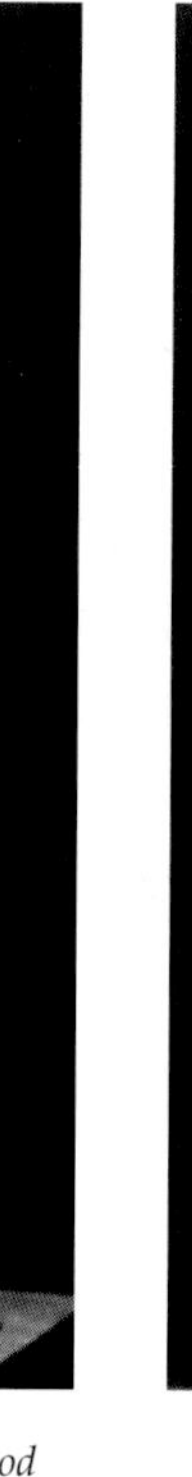

Nude Torso *Lemon Wood*

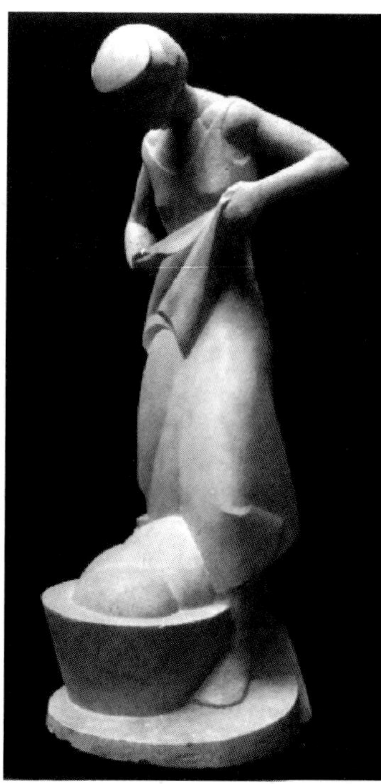

Monday Morning Wash

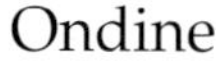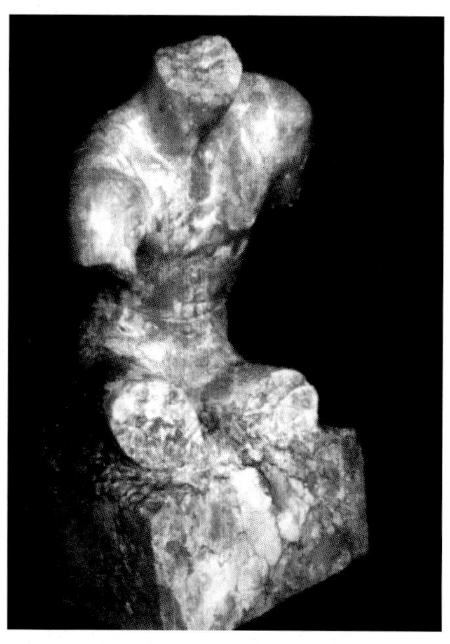

Red Marble Torso

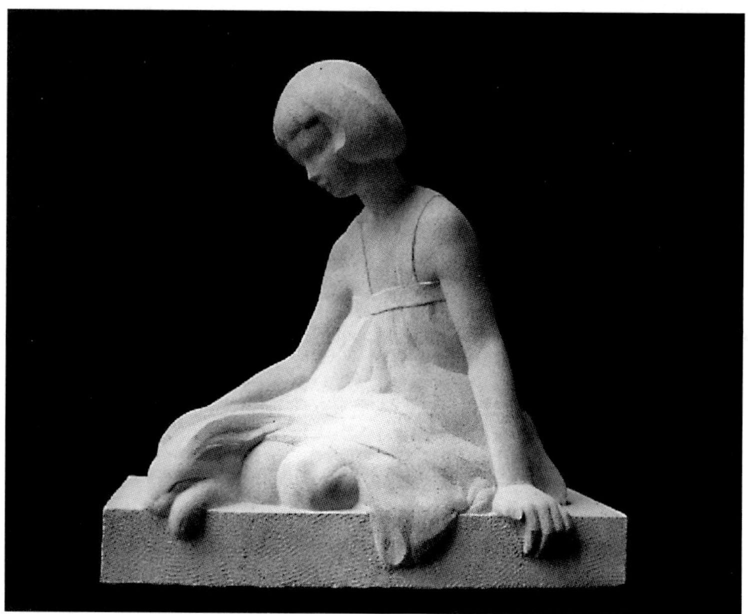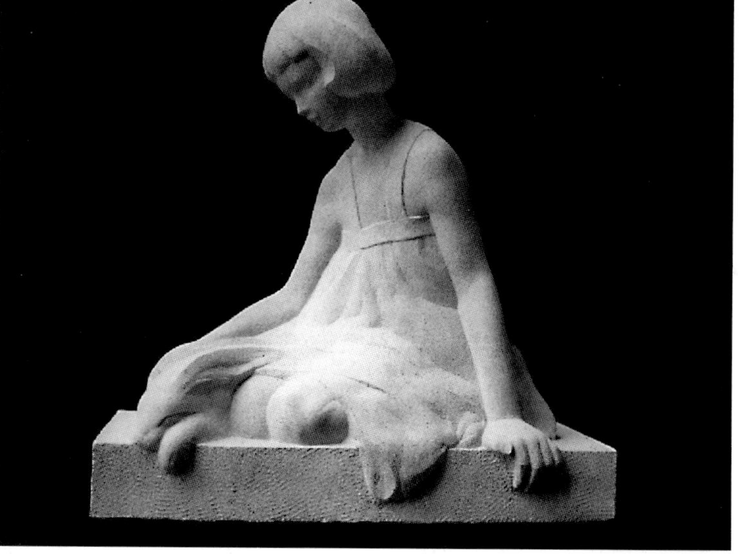

Girl and Rabitt *Limestone*

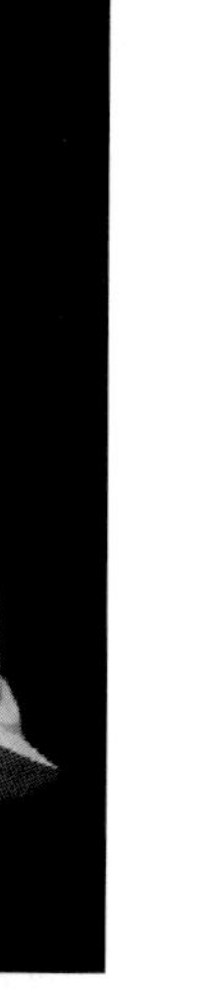

Meditation

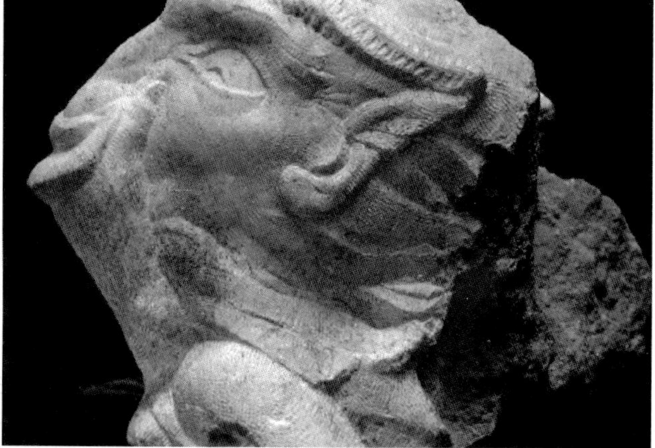

Self Portrait *Limestone*

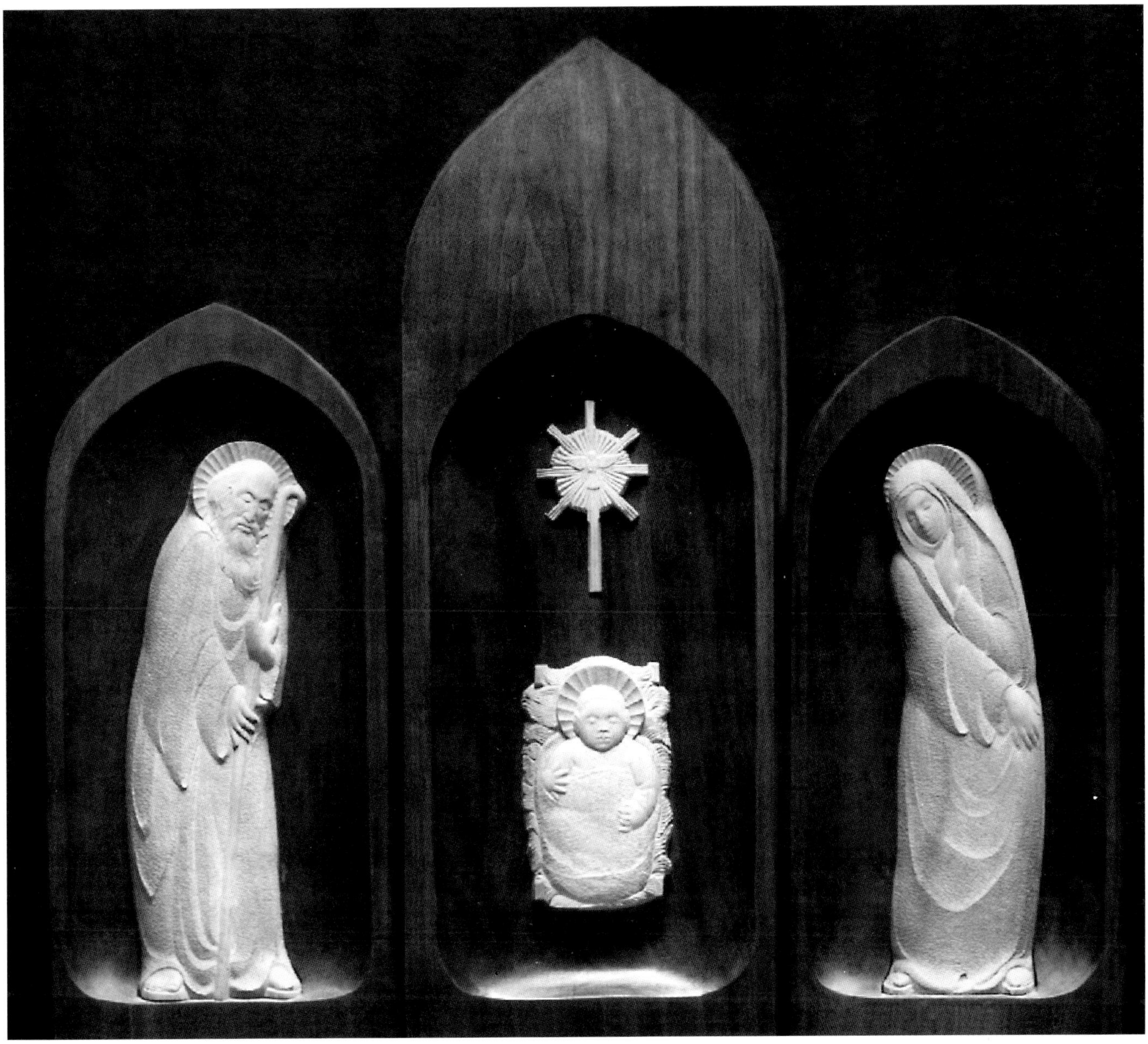

Triptych

Limon Wood on Walnut

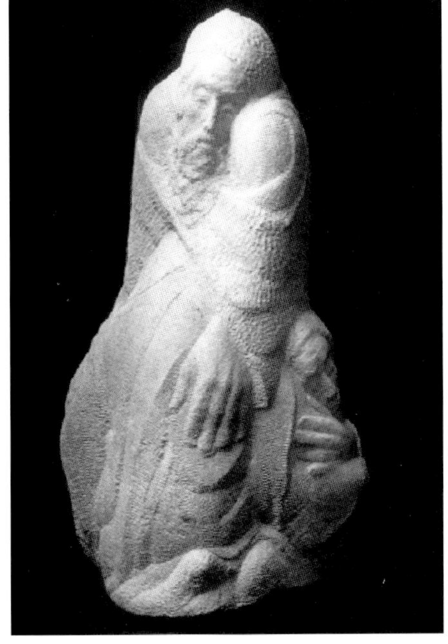

The Prodigal Son *Limestone*

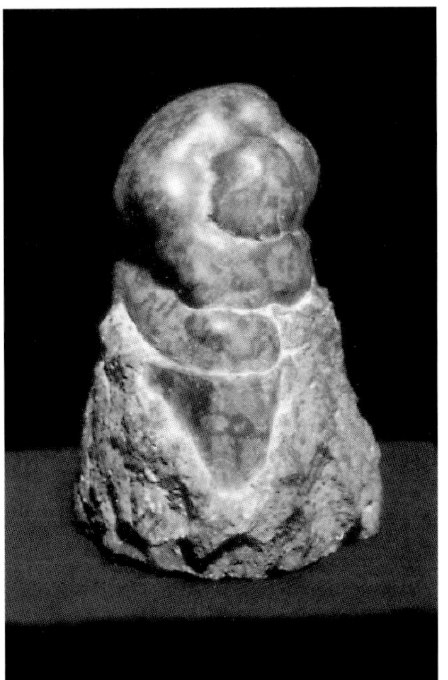

Cain *Marble*

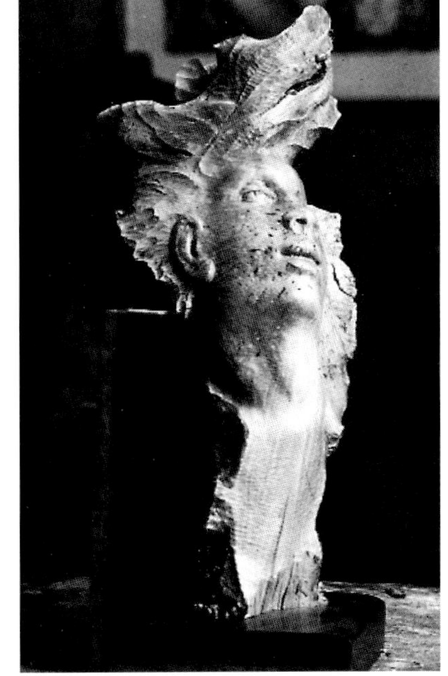

Windswept

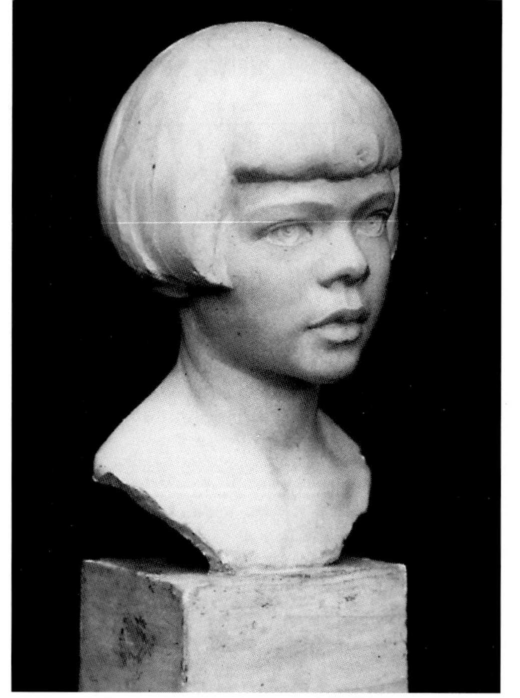

Barbara Scott

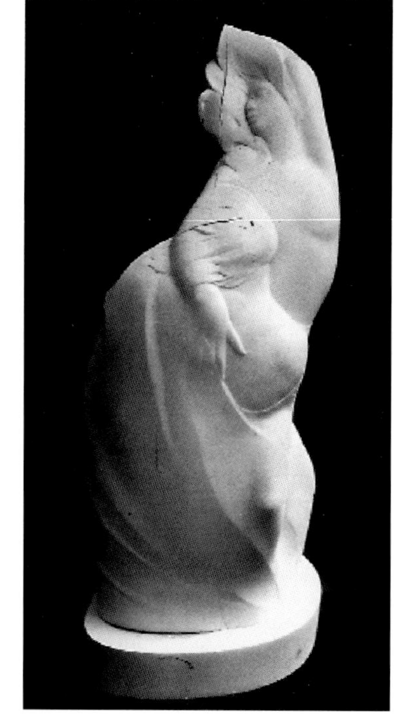

Zepher's Embrace *Lemon Wood*

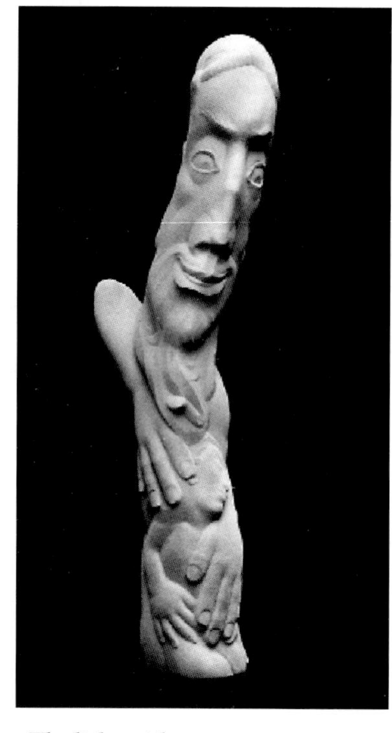

Thalidomides   *Mountain Cedar*

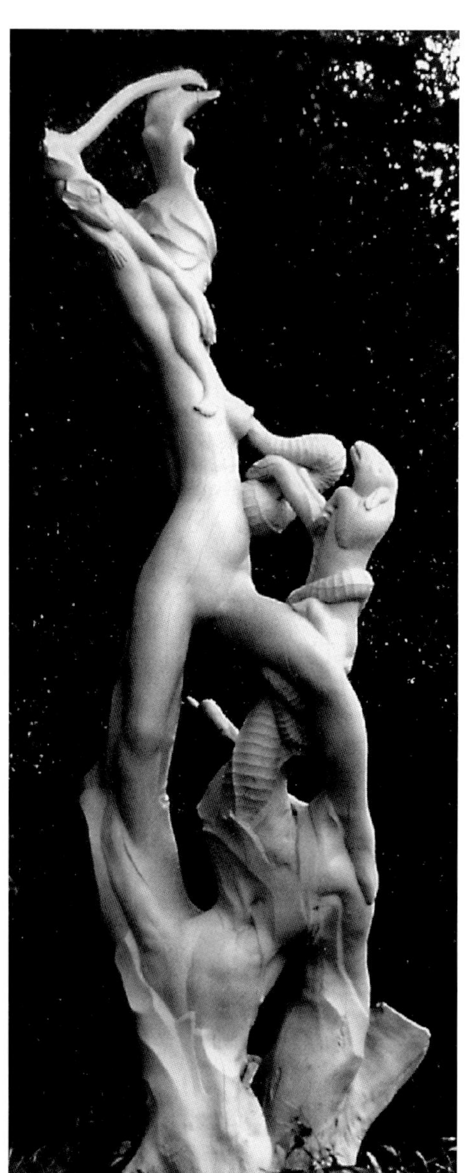

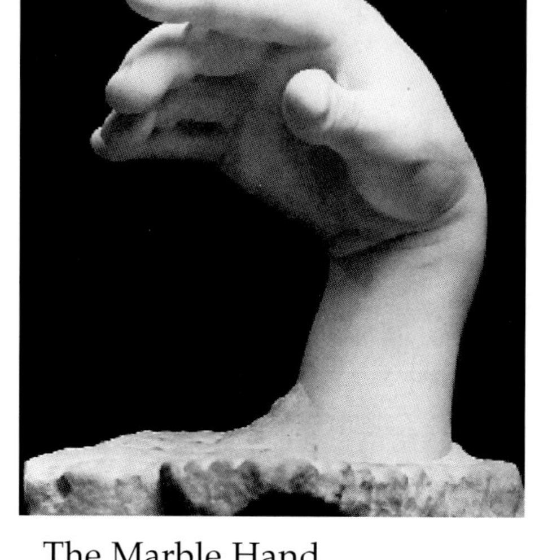

The Marble Hand

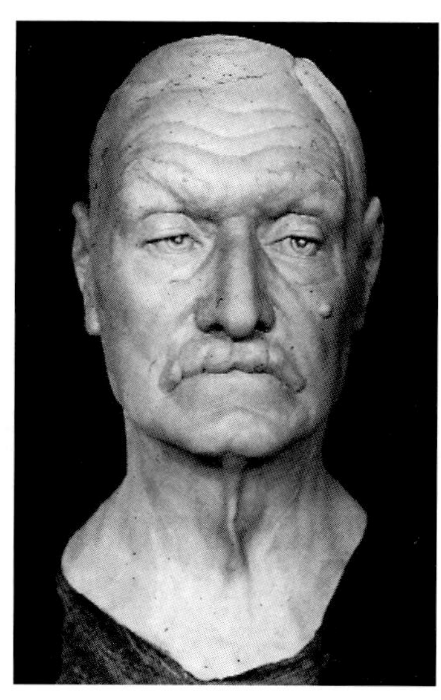

My Father

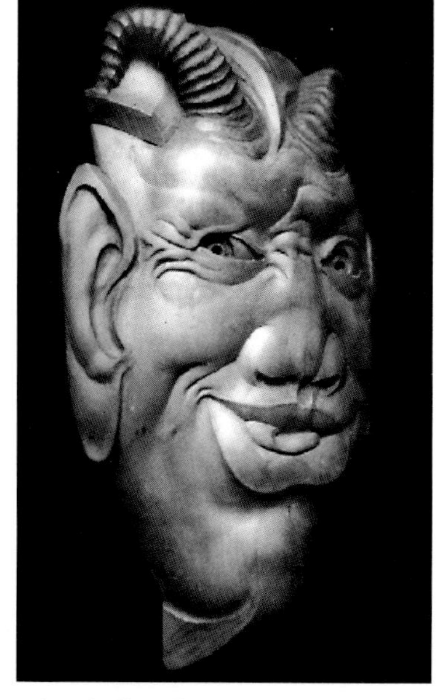

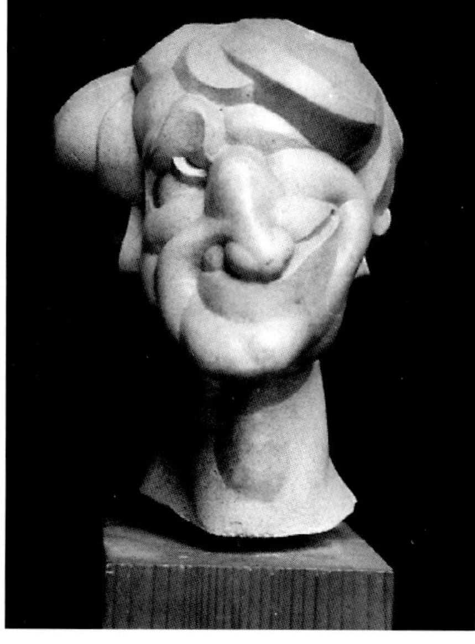

Deluge   *15′ Buckeye Tree*

Aw' Go On

Boccacio's Patron Saint

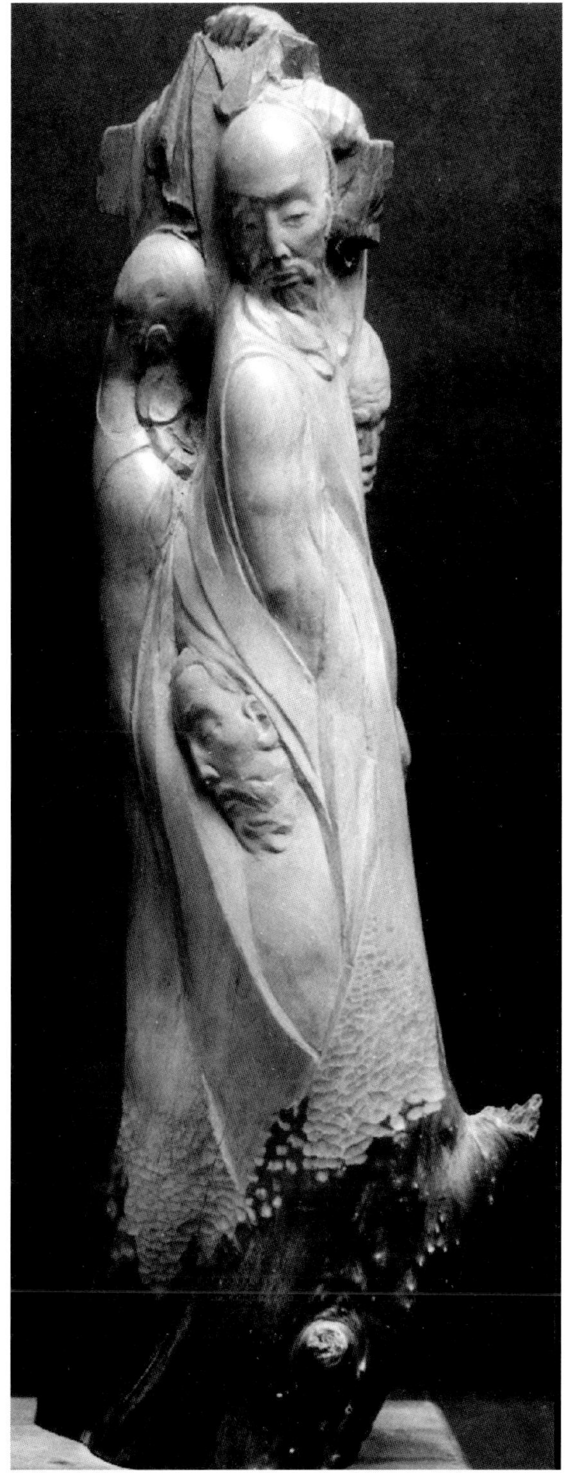

Descent from the Cross   *Manzanita Wood*

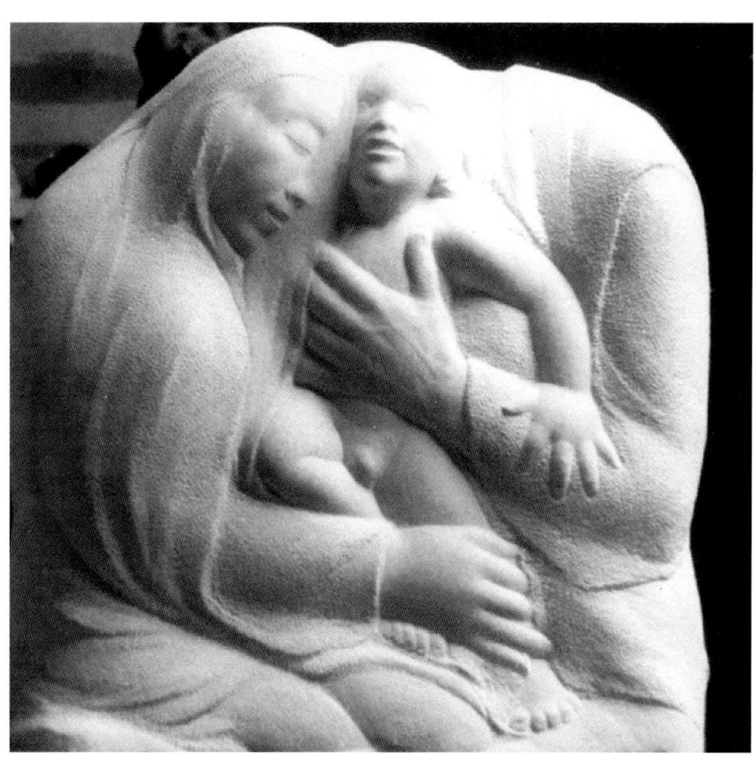

The Future   *Life-size, Marble*

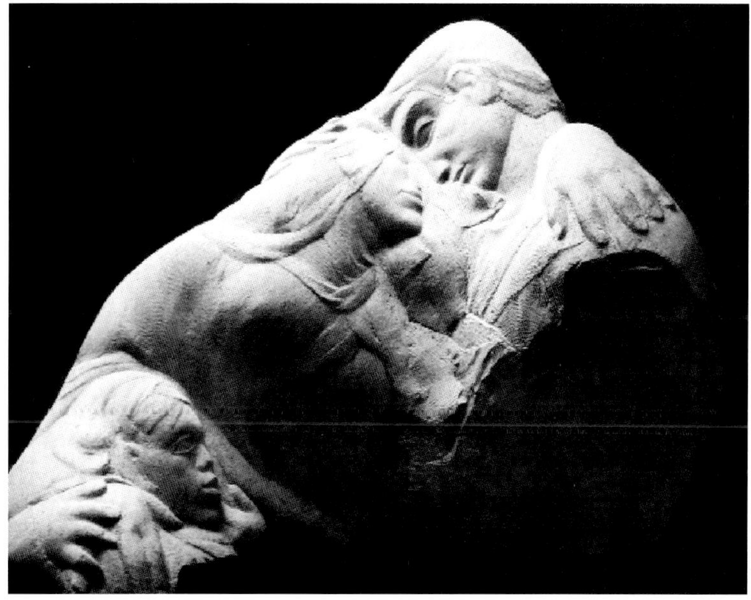

The Cloud People   *Life-size, Stone*

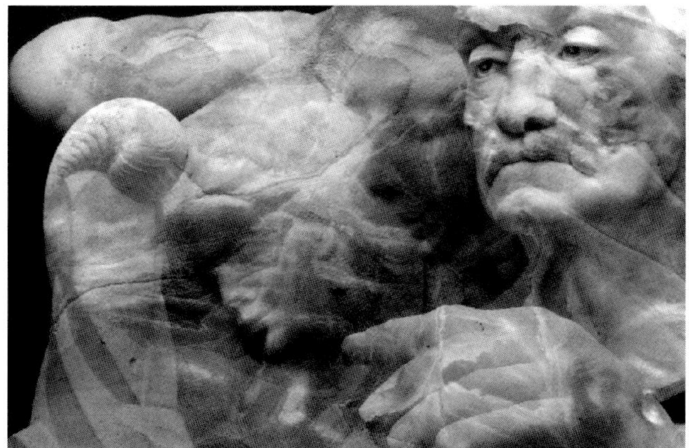

Composit Images. (See text on page113)

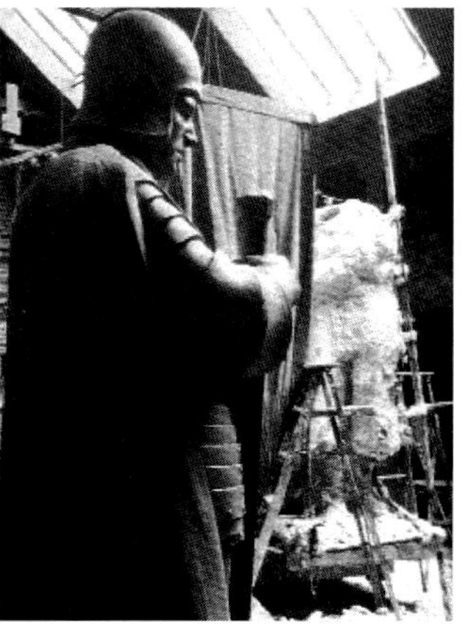

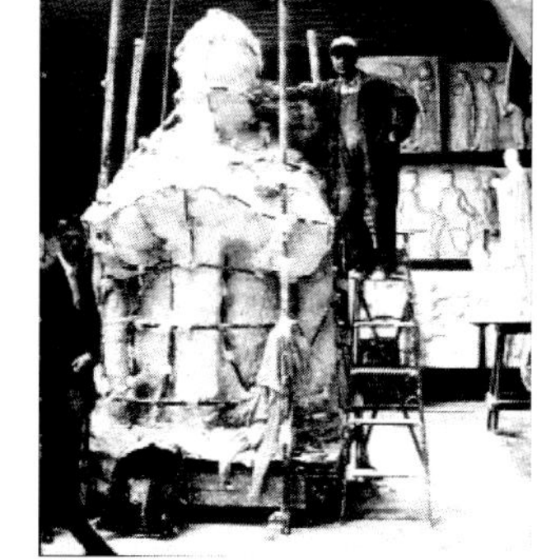

Plaster Molds in the studio of Lorado Taft used to cast his armored knights. (See page 1)

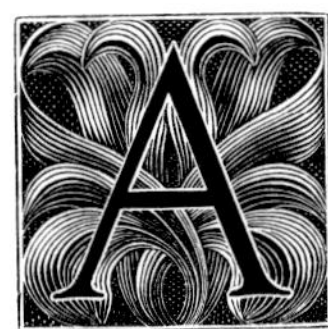# Anatomy For Artists

A simplified method for the study of anatomy *especially for artists* was taught by Professor de Hey, my teacher in The Hague, Holland, 1932-33. Although he was also teaching anatomy at the medical university in Leiden, he realized that artists had no need for the medical doctor's clinical know-how. In all my years of sculpting the human body as subject matter, I found his method filled my needs completely.

Forms of the Human Body

A working knowledge of *human anatomy* is useless to the art student unless he first can make his hand shape what his eye sees; that is why the study of anatomy comes *last,* following his earlier studies and training. Only when his hands can register, like a recording device, what he sees, can he easily and faithfully shape the forms of the human body when working from a live model. Remember that a physician, as well as an anatomist, can not necessarily become an adept sculptor or modeler of the human form, in spite of his technical knowledge of the body. Modeling skills are essential.

Clay Studies and Schematic Anatomical Drawings

The modeling of the hand, mouth, eye and face, allows for a range of improvisations in addition to a following of the more strict translations of anatomical realism. Photographic reality is replaced by schematic imagery to suit the artist's purposes. We therefore deliberately dismiss, as much as possible, the Latin names of bones and muscles in order to free the artist's mind of an unnecessary concern. All that matters is that he understands, and can visualize and retain in his memory, the body forms and their articulations (i.e., the limits of limb and torso movements).

Every human body distributes its *fat layer* differently between the muscles; sometimes that layer even envelopes them. Only without such fat deposits can one visualize anatomical forms as if the skin did not exist and the muscles were exposed. The sculptor is allowed ample artistic license in distributing those fat deposits to suit his purpose as long as every anatomical feature is in the right place. (See Giovanni Boccaccio's *Patron Saint*, page124)

The Teaching Method

The illustrations show how to superimpose the skeleton's bone positions over the drawings of the body. This exercise challenges the student's ability to visualize such bone and skeleton shapes from any viewing angle . . . to see all this as if he had X-ray eyes.

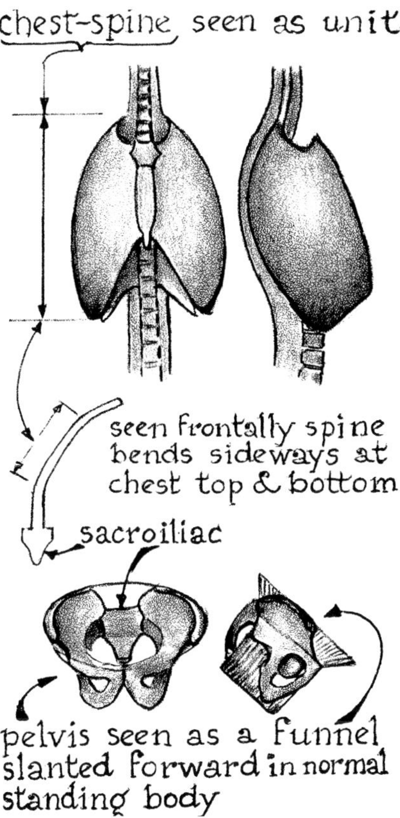

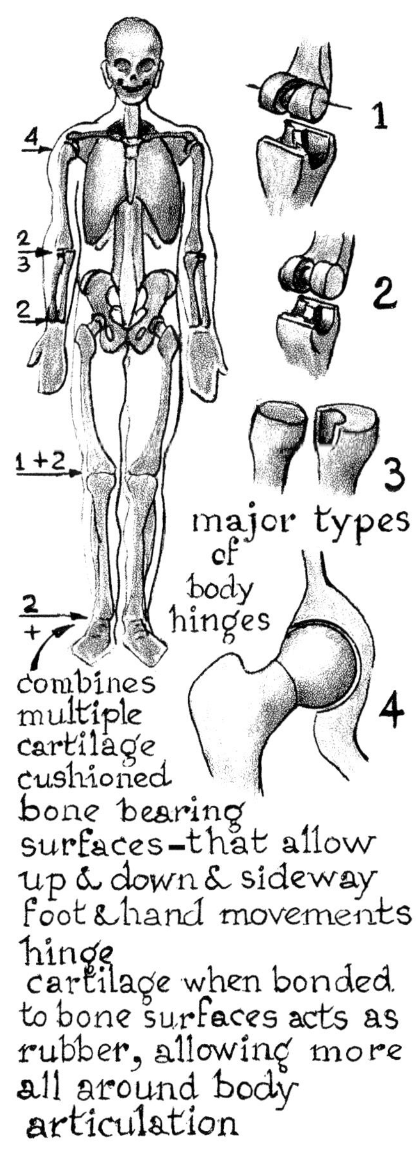

It should be the sculptor's aim to end up with an ease of thinking three-dimensionally, rather than in linear terms.

At the Academy of Fine Arts in Holland, a simple memory retention exercise was used. It begins with the studying of a single human bone. After examining it from all angles, place it behind your back and try to draw it from memory. Repeat this, looking at it and then sketching it from memory, again and again, until a true three-dimensional mental picture of it is acquired.

Next, every bone of the skeleton is memorized; each one is drawn from every angle. (You may have to locate a source of bone samples by consulting medical schools, doctors or their equipment suppliers.) Strange to say, most artists acquire this type of memory retention only after great effort and frustration.

Photo memory applies to those who are blessed with an inborn talent of visual memory retention. Gustave Dore, master illustrator in the 19th century, possessed it. Whenever his work called for gathering data in museums, he never needed to make sketches for reference. He simply registered in his memory, down to the smallest detail, all that he needed for his engraved illustrations. The wealth of the thousands of book illustrations he left us can be seen in all major libraries.

Modeling Anatomically Correct Human Figures

A practical armature is used that suggests the proportions, contour and silhouette of the human figure. Use aluminum sculpture wire, which bends easily to take on the recognizable stance of the figure.

Clay pellets are applied to fill out the required areas step-by-step. The size of the pellets are gradually reduced the closer one gets to the final surface. (See Chapter 3)

This procedure in modeling the human figure should be practiced extensively in life classes until the student overcomes the obstacles that may have held him back. Gradually his facility in clay modeling and his knowledge of the human figure will become acceptable. He will not make the mistake of anatomical blunders through lack of knowledge, which often cause viewers to wince.

Provided the student makes a serious attempt at acquiring the knowledge of anatomy geared to the sculptor's needs, he can rest assured that the residue of that know-how will be sufficient for all of his work with the human figure; he will have no need for a live model. In actual practice, my experience has been that any error during work will trigger some apprehension and will automatically prompt corrective action. As a rule, the sculptor recognizes anatomical misjudgments here and there, just in time to intercept irreparable damage as he works.

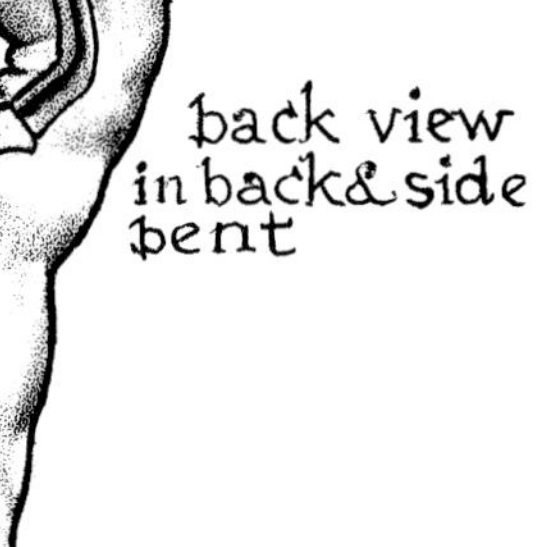

It seems strange but is true that "close calls" tend to draw out the best in the artist, bringing the end result still closer to the vision he aims to materialize.

One supplemental self-teaching possibility can be found in the wealth of material in good anatomy books, which are available in bookstores and libraries. The information they offer will round out details not shown in this book, should the student feel the need of it. Note: *Anatomie voor Kunstenaars*, Door Jac. Rijkse en B.Th. De Heij. H. Meulenhoff, Amsterdam. This is the book that has been most valuable to me. It is written in Dutch and profusely illustrated.

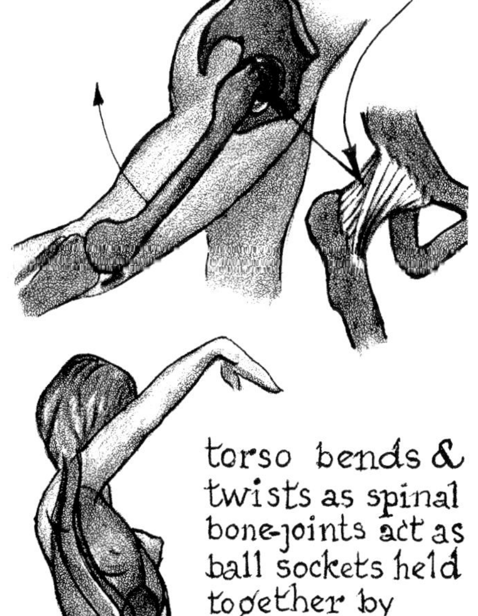

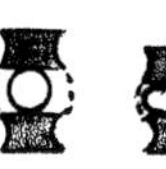
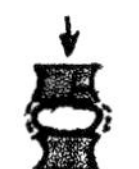
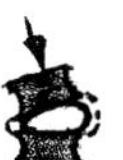

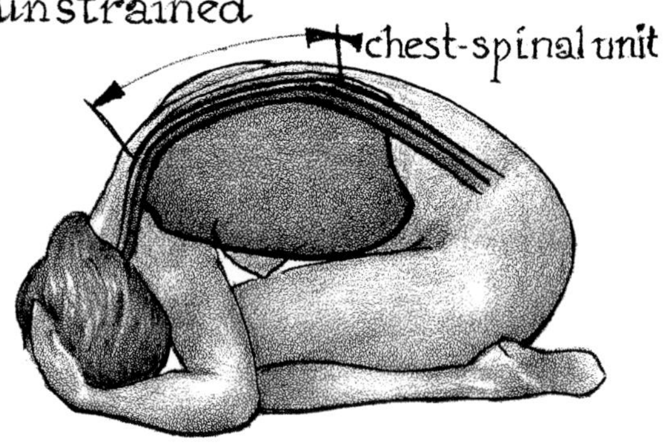

spinal column easily follows the
body's untwisted positions
unstrained
chest-spinal unit

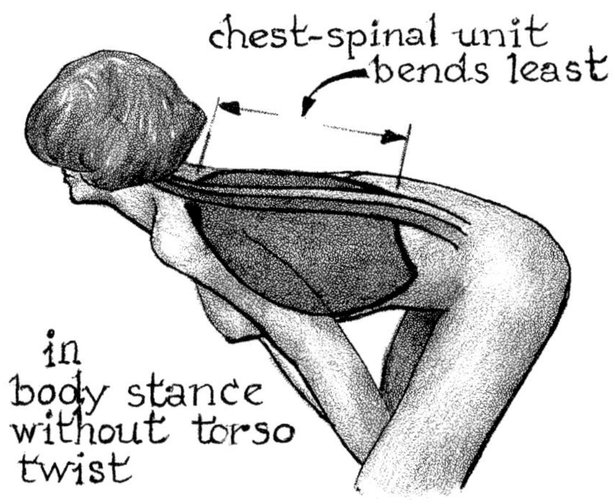

chest-spinal unit
bends least
in
body stance
without torso
twist

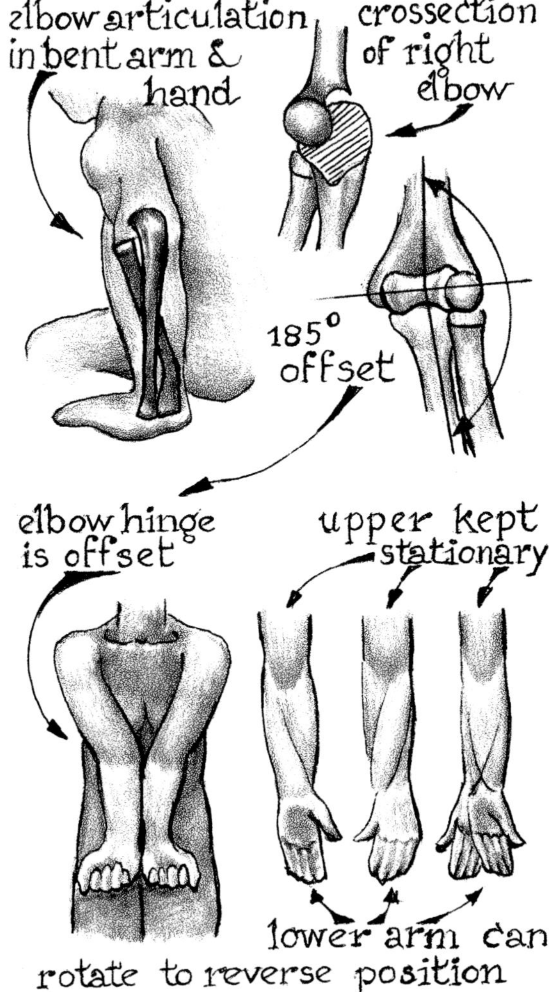

elbow articulation
in bent arm &
hand
crossection
of right
elbow
185°
offset
elbow hinge
is offset
upper kept
stationary
lower arm can
rotate to reverse position

bone structure location
in hand below skin
and muscles

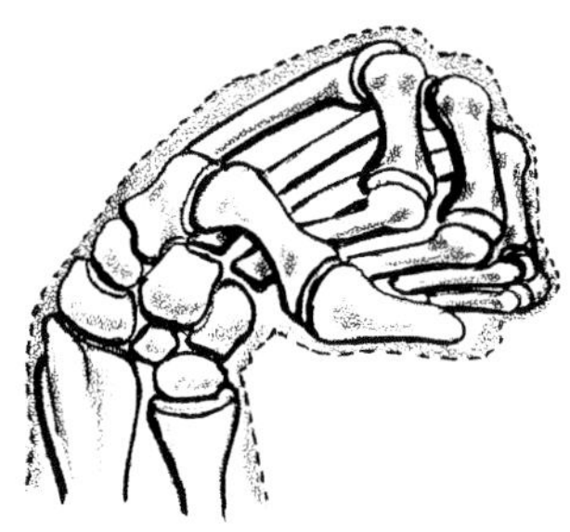

visualization of location
of hand bones

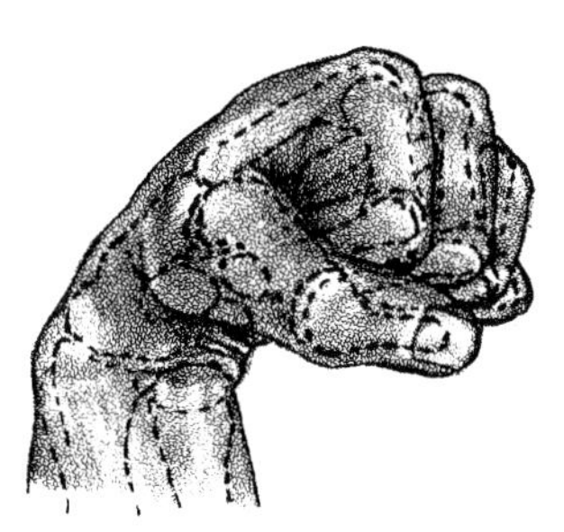

muscles & tendons over
bones in closed hand

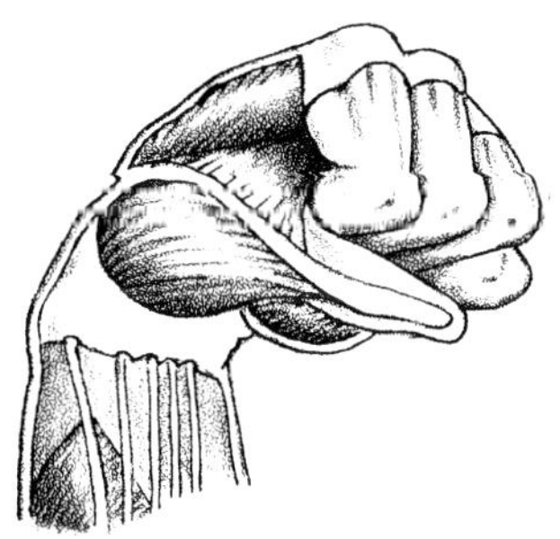

forms of bones & muscles
below skin determine final
forms of a
realistic
body part

relaxed standing leg
displays muscle assembly
as compound forms that
are pushed outward by
inner hidden muscles &
bones into final appearance
seen from

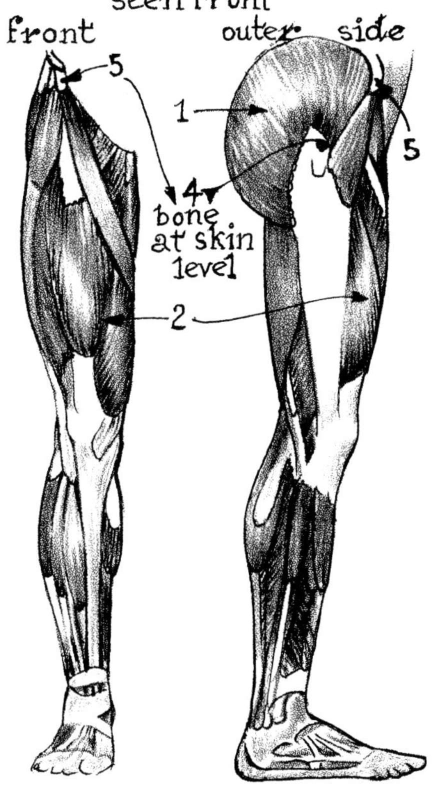

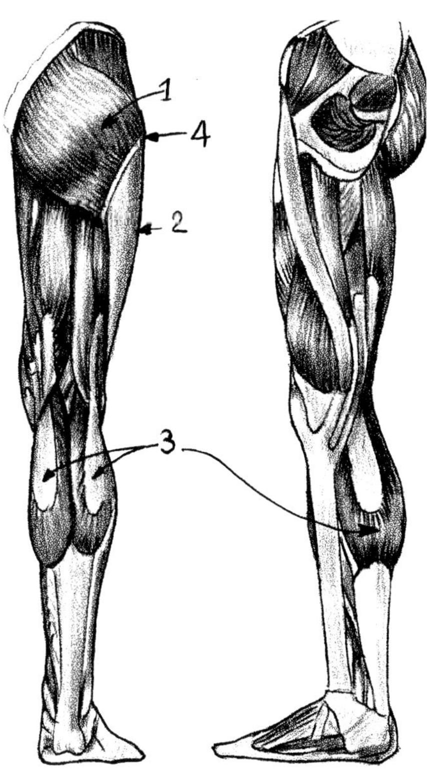

visual retention as a rule
hinges on outer surface
muscles (marked 1-2-3-4-5)
within silhouette outlines

neutral arm position
places all muscles around
arm bones as untwisted
rope

free hanging   arm seen
from

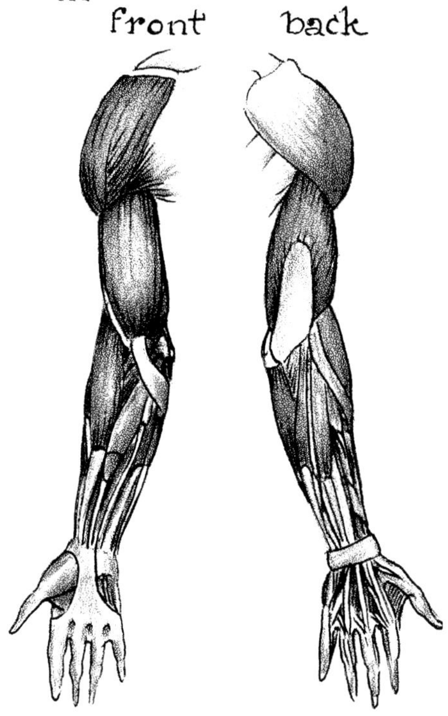

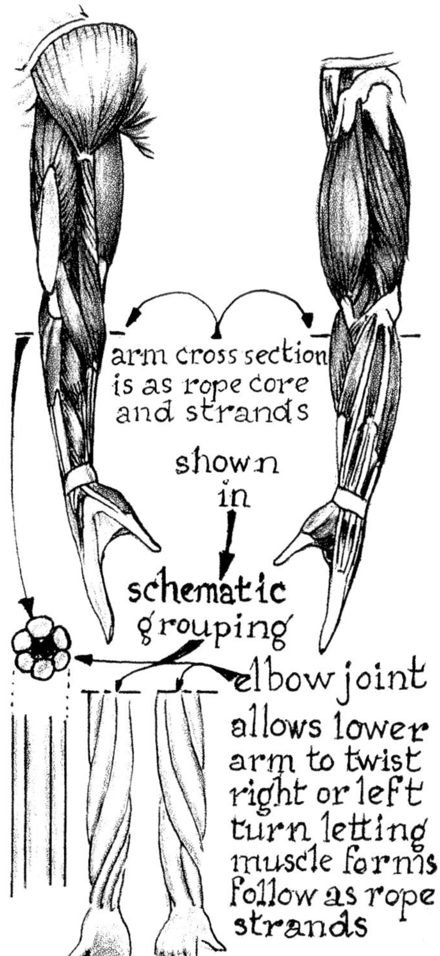

allows lower
arm to twist
right or left
turn letting
muscle forms
follow as rope
strands

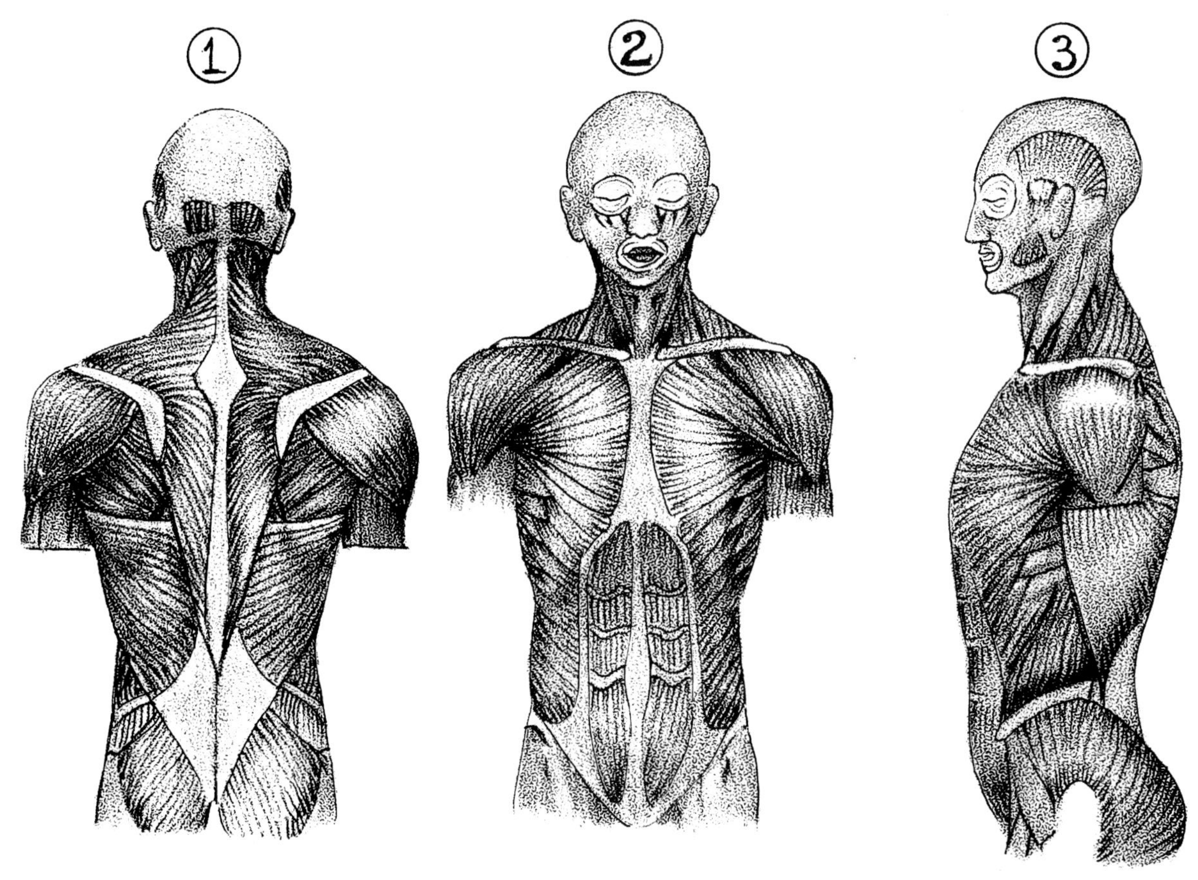

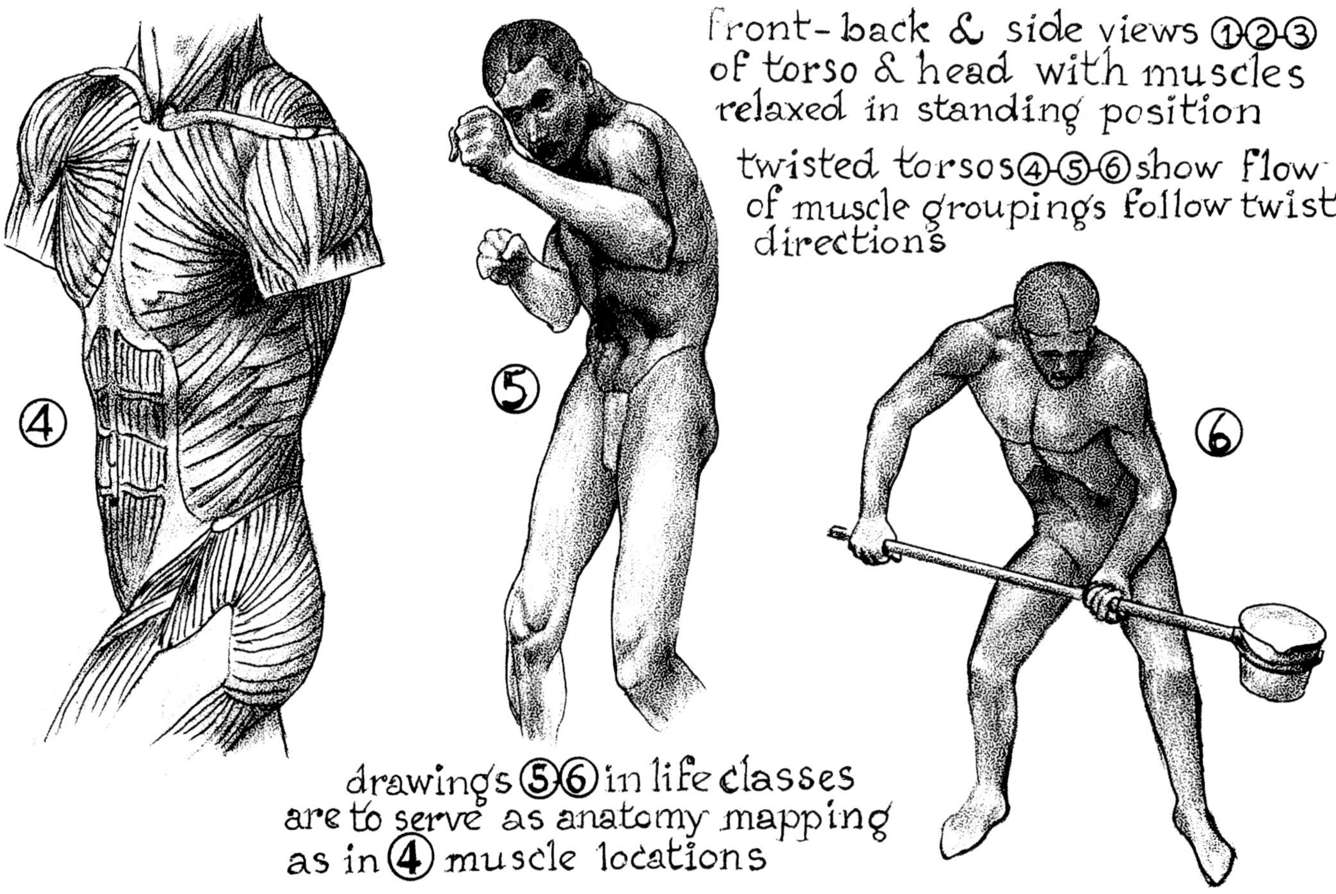

front-back & side views ①②③
of torso & head with muscles
relaxed in standing position

twisted torsos ④⑤⑥ show flow
of muscle groupings follow twist
directions

drawings ⑤⑥ in life classes
are to serve as anatomy mapping
as in ④ muscle locations

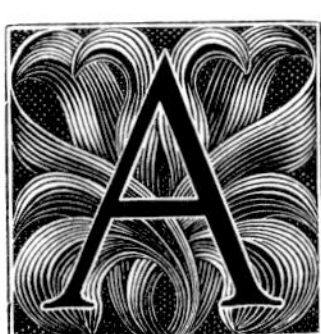rtistic Reflections

Originals and Duplicates

The art patron's demands often can be met through art merchandising based on reproductions made by people other than the artist.

Despite controversies over *originals versus duplicates,* the artist has a valid claim that the *form value* of a perfect duplicate remains identical in quality to that of the original. One difference rests on the patron's idea of the *value* of the material in which the original was carved.

Another consideration is the *durability* of the material. But, in all events, the artist should base his own judgment on art grounds only, insisting that it is *form per se* that has the final word in sculpture.

Puzzling implications:

> 1. The art patron favors an *original* over the most *perfect* duplicate. His sense of value is often based on the element of scarcity.

> 2. If an original or duplicate is made of a rare material, the value of the piece is supposed to increase that much more.

> 3. The lasting quality of a material often seems to influence the patron's evaluation, regardless of the intrinsic worth of the art for art's sake.

> 4. Regardless of the above factors, there is a fascination in seeing good art products mass-produced, similar to our feeling about mass printing, photography, and engraving output. This element may or may not affect the artist adversely. It is not lost on the merchant, who sees a most attractive opportunity to enhance his earnings from a receptive and fascinated public. Thus, swayed between an original and a vulgarized, albeit perfect, mass-produced duplicate, the art market thrives on elements that ought not to bear on art one way or another.

In review, the public evaluates artwork based on a logic that springs from the *merchandising* of art products rather than the appraisal of an object for its art qualities alone.

The Size of Things

We call things "small" or "large" in relation to our own size while standing in the middle of our yardstick at a position we call zero. We measure things in opposite directions from that position *zero,* things that grow bigger and bigger and things that shrink smaller and smaller until, in the end, the *reversal factor* makes the two directions meet in infinity.

For things too small to see with the naked eye, we use instruments to bring them within range of our vision. When things are too big, but far away, we again use instruments to bring them nearer for easy observation.

Small jewelry needs to be razor sharp and smooth in order for us to better see its form. Very large sculpture requires that we stand back far enough in order to see it at one glance.

It seems that artists, as well as art patrons, feel a sense of awe about extremes of size. This tends to throw off one's judgment, which I believe should not be influenced by size per se. Instead, our concern should be with the quality of form and tonal values in the third dimension.

Example: If we stand *close* to the Mt. Rushmore sculpture, awe of the gigantic size drowns out its esthetic value until we walk back far enough to see the whole project in one easy glance. But if we stand too far away, we then need binoculars to enjoy the same artwork. What Borglum, the sculptor, saw in his small plaster model placed in front of him on his desk was virtually the same as what we would see viewing his mountain sculpture from a few miles distant.

It is this strange thing of "awe" regarding size that causes many artists to believe that the bigger the piece the better and, supposedly, the more beautiful. It is unfortunate when an artist fails to realize that his work may be artistically mediocre and enlarges the work, creating a monstrosity.

I once saw a cartoon in which a father, holding his child by the hand at the rim of the Grand Canyon, exclaims in awe, "Johnny, look!" and Johnny's reaction is, "What do you want me to look at?"

If esthetics in art is to be our major concern, we must make certain that convenience to the eye brings out the quality of the product at its best.

Accidental Results

In the art world the question arises: Are *intended* results preferred over *accidental* ones?

Nature produces things that are aesthetically beautiful and comparable to an artist's deliberate best work. It is my belief that both are responding to nature's invisible forces of action and reaction. The potential differences of such forces are seemingly inexhaustible and regenerative. . ..

In nature, many dead, gnarled and convoluted trees in the high mountains, buffeted by storms and sandblasting in successive gales, become breathtakingly beautiful sculpture form assemblies created by nature's *blind* forces. Some surprisingly positive, abstract form-assemblies come about in animal and bird droppings, aesthetically quite acceptable.

In the kitchen, the cook might fling into a pan a dollop of batter, which then accidentally looks like a lion's head. Cast in plaster of Paris it could pass for a strikingly modeled artifact. If an untrained hand produces, by accident, an aesthetically beautiful result, should the result remain unsigned?

To sign accidental results can lead to self-deception, a false sense of accomplishment, or worse, the deliberate deception of the art market.

Fine Art and the Artisan Craftsman

It is an outgrowth of more modern tendencies to set the house painter apart from the pictorial painter, the stone carver apart from the sculptor, the engraver/plate maker apart from the graphic artist. "Art," as a word, became easily a subject of dispute between artist and artisan, the artist claiming to occupy a higher rung on the community ladder than the artisan. It remains a matter of semantics to know of what we speak when the word "art" is used by those introducing themselves as artists.

Just where do we stand in language communication? The term "fine arts" has become a fragile element in modern conversation ever since it found usage after the Renaissance period. It has been my impression that man's vanity and ego, in his wanting to be acclaimed in a world of "fame and glory" attached to the historic great, played a part in the definitions of art-related terms. Thus, word meanings became bastardized by motivations that have little or nothing to do with the original basic language.

Taste and Esthetics

These words launch anyone who is spoiling for controversy in art discussions into a never-ending attempt at determining what is supposed to be good or bad in art: Is it or is it not beautiful? Is it or is it not admirable?

The words *taste* and *esthetics* are bread and butter in the mouths of self-styled art critics and connoisseurs. In time these words awaken the serious art student to the fact that non-artist evaluations will prove worthless in his learning and that he is better off relying on his own judgment based on the gradual unfolding of his inborn talents and art insight.

The *Theory of Form* as presented in this book has offered the student a philosophical proposition that man's reaction to nature's unseen forces is one of harmony with those forces; be it in physical appearance or in the mind. *Taste* emerges as a strictly personal aspect of man's reaction to what appeals to him.

Esthetics, as defined in the dictionary, stresses the importance of "beauty" in art, thus opening a Pandora's box of what is to be considered beautiful or not; each claimant argues his case to satisfy his personal taste, offering examples of extreme beauty and extreme ugliness, things that attract and things that repel. I believe that all emotional reactions result from man's affinity to nature's unseen forces as they affect his built-in receiving instrument, his "nerve" system.

Since the strictly personal aspect of "taste" among artists and viewers will cause opinions to be as varied as their numbers, controversy about esthetics will be counterproductive in the end. Only the commercial art market stands to gain, by steering public opinion toward its own financial profit.

Creativeness, Inventiveness and Style

The final phases of the student's training bring him closer and closer to a *breakthrough* in his art studies. Creativeness at its best comes after such a breakthrough. Without it, an *invented* style will turn out to be simply one step in an evermore exciting process of learning.

The *breakthrough* is the artist's "moment of truth." After that, he easily reviews all his previous study pieces critically as being just "study pieces"—approximations of his intentions, certainly not to be exhibited without apology or explanation. Only his follow-up work will be worthy of public showing.

No longer does the artist self-consciously invent his style. All seems simplified, and what emerges is that the work automatically will carry a *style* all his own: an unwritten signature. From now on if he feels the irresistible urge to say what he *must* say, he can do so unhindered, simply expressing himself directly and fluently as the seasoned artist he has become.

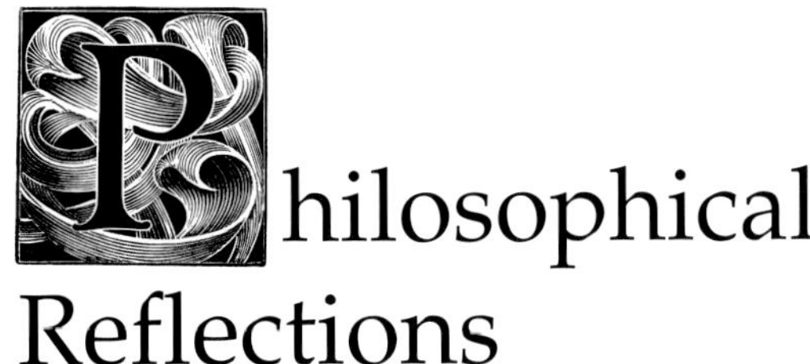

Chapter 18

Philosophical Reflections

Updating Word Meanings

Now that the word *form* has been defined (see page 17) and the *reversal factor* has been introduced as its midway point (see page 18), we can update many definitions, using meanings that were hidden before, of words all rooted in our three-dimensional world.

The *form visualizations* presented in this book may serve to facilitate the process of improving word meanings.

In many languages there are words that defy translation. Several related *feelings* are often blended in a single word, reflecting man's desire to grasp illusive concepts. We are expected to instinctively sense their meaning one way or another. Such ambiguous and multifaceted meanings give the poet leeway to expand beyond down-to-earth prose and explore symbolism, mysticism and allegory.

Modern scientific discoveries also dictate the redefining of words. New words are created to improve communication. Older words used by the early scientists who had to make do with them have become the layman's, rather than the scientist's, choice.

Concepts and Abstractions

Defining abstractions with words has kept philosophers busy throughout history. They used words such as *form* and *transfiguration* in their search for truth. Their writings admittedly leave stop-gap answers with baffling meanings.

Words may have numerous meanings. For instance: The sculptor *formed* a beautiful *form* while he himself was in good *form*. The word "form" then, is to mean the act of shaping, the shape itself, and the state of being while doing the shaping (or forming).

A thought on the word *transfiguration:* The figure of Christ in an act of transfiguration, ascending bodily to heaven, suggests an imagery needed by religionists to satisfy the faithful, without benefit of scientific commitment, as to the mystical meanings of such words. This approach allows free reign for fantasy.

Words such as *transfiguration* and *metamorphosis,* and many others bordering on the metaphysical, had to be used after the limits of reasoning ability had been reached. Next would follow instinct, intuition and "hunches" . . . a never-ending quest at the portals of the unknown.

The Workability of Thought

The mathematician, having to "make do" in the world of abstract thought, tantalizingly utilizes elusive concepts of the *infinite;* calculus formulas that lead to down-to-earth answers enable him to manufacture things precisely. He could not have done so, without such formulas born of abstract thought.

If, therefore, abstract thought can give workable results, no time will be wasted in daily life in the continued probing of the unknown, in spite of that eternal question mark delegated to the unknowable.

Search for the Truth

Modern enlightenment has placed us in the precarious position of the hypnotized person needing a hypnotizer to snap him *out* of his spell. His hypnotizer, the machine of his own making, may prove to be his worst enemy in the end, instead of a blessing. *Trying to control universal unseen and self-governing forces* resembles playing Russian roulette, or giving a child matches or a loaded gun.

Time and *space* await a more acceptable imagery in our comprehension of them. Modern scientists have offered several leads, but their answers have as yet remained inconclusive. So far, all seems to be based on peripheral conjecture, which fails as a perfect measuring tool.

Infinity is beyond measure, although we may indulge in word tasting. Our intimations of the unknowable lead our mind (with its limits) to combine reason with visualization through instrumentation. The illustrations here aim at some clarification, albeit schematically.

Light and Lens Illuminations

Drops of condensed water hanging from a section of plate glass, when exposed to bright sunlight, will reflect that light as if they were sparkling diamonds. A camera scanning over that subject while its lens is wide open, but out of focus, at a distance of about 12 to 6 inches away from the drops, behaves as a prism that refracts light. However, camera lenses, being ground round, or curvilinear, break up the light into *roundish* convolutions instead of the *straight* refracted light bands of a prism. My experience with this camera-induced light and refractory phenomenon exposed the results, as shown.

Should the reader see this type of camera recording of *light refractions* for the first time, he may well ask himself the following questions: "Where do the *extensions* of these flowing designs end or begin?" The picture frame of the illustrations limits the outward infinity-directed design patterns and extensions. If we detached a very small section of the design at any location of one's choice and enlarged it to fill our field of vision, it would bring forth hidden details that were documented during such inward-directed camera

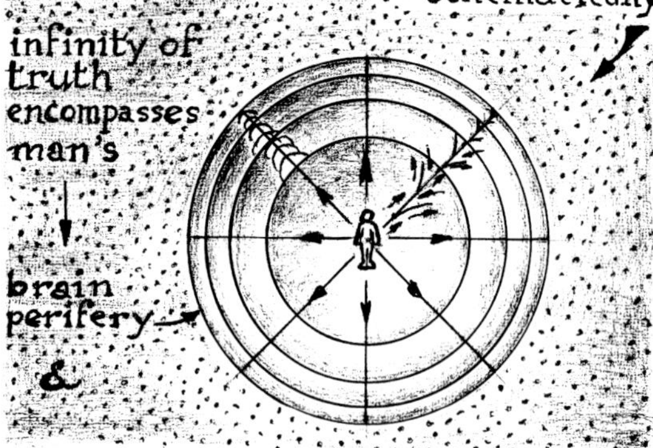

his thinking ability grows with diminishing speed comparable to the slowing rate of a bullet shot vertically upward

his world of thought grows as an expanding sphere with a final range beyond which the unknown has become the unknowable which dictates that only intuition through hunches & instinct (as built-in sensors) can create the break-through beyond pure reason; a man's "moment of truth" in life

the student's learning adds progressive gains in every direction of his search as shown schematically; each gain locally enlarging his thinking sphere until at last he reaches his limits

it is then that the imminent break-through may set him free of all confusion

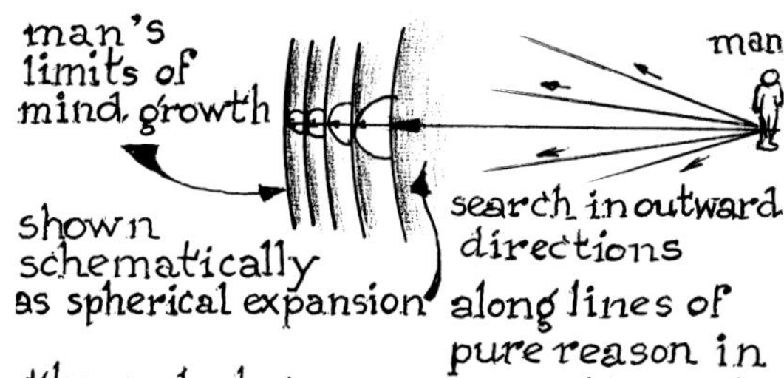

the end places man's position at form's inter-face akin to point zero where all values reach infinity in opposite directions subject to the reversal factor recording. This recording is similar to the action of an ever deeper penetrating electron microscope. Perhaps space convolution studies such as this can teach us something about infinity and truth. Does infinity beckon in opposite directions? Must all explorations from our position zero move outward and inward?

Space Convolutions

In a camera view-finder, such images can be observed *in movement as the lens travels.* We can witness a blend of the presumed *time-space-reversal* factor. Could this be an imagery of "existence" as we understand this word, its range being "is, was, and is to be?" At least our hunches and intuitions stem from seeing such space convolution images *in motion.*

Do these invisible forces made visible hold out future answers that may yet spring from the refinement of previously accepted premises? Thus, all visible aids lend themselves to flexing our thinking ability; consider *"infinity conceived"* (page 19), the *reversal factor* witnessed in viewing the mold and cast simultaneously (page 18), and the definition of form as the contact area or interface between one space convolution and its opposite (pudding and pudding mold, page 19).

Visualization Aids

Science and science fiction writers have offered imaginative visualizations in attempts to probe man's world of the mind. Logic and cautious rationalization lead us to ever more aspects of truth, so that we might tiptoe around it as if to "box it in." The book **Flatland, A Romance of Many Dimensions**, by Edwin A. Abbott, is one such science fiction exercise in mathematics. I believe that all such mental exercises can aid us as long as we recognize that the players are delighting in a game of mental gymnastics.

An example of Flatland rationalization: A flat world, as in a level plane, is inhabited by beings not able to think *three-dimensionally.* When that plane is intersected by a sphere, they first see a *point* appear in their midst; the tangent point of the sphere with a flat plane. Then after the growing circle has reached its maximum dimension (the largest diameter of the sphere), it shrinks successively to become a point once more and disappear. Flatlanders cannot help but be baffled by such a happening.

Perhaps man, as a three-dimensional being, fails to comprehend a visual *fourth, fifth, sixth, . . . nth* dimension. Maybe time/infinity/everlasting /space is a four-dimensional concept.

In any event, we must wait for science to progress and discover needed facts to pave the way for answers that are harmonious with previously accepted and workable premises and solutions.

progressive path finding in search for truth slows down at similar rate as the rising bullet, the closer one gets to its culmination point

when lost in confusion one must retrace his steps until the search direction has been corrected before proceeding albeit at an ever slower pace until once more one may get lost, prompting retracing wrong paths, etc.

at last man reaches the limits of his brain functions at which point intuition, hunches, instinct backed-up by pure reason will enable him to face the unknowable with resignation & peace of mind

Philosophical Implications

Admittedly, if *art* communicates well, commercial interests
are attracted. The artist can ignore them if he practices art
for the sheer love of it. He can work in any material, be it
granite or a bar of soap, whether it is long-lasting or subject
to early disintegration or being easily damaged. True, the
art patron has difficulty seeing in a soap carving an image
that is as desirable as its duplicate in lasting marble.
Artist and art patron therefore may clash in their opposing
attitudes, the one producing art, the other having or selling
it. This separation of motivation is an inherent part of the
art world. Is it spiritual or material value that is most prized?

I have used many vulnerable materials in the making of
sculptures. When prompted to "have it off my chest" in a
hurry, the less durable material could often give me a more
rapid and fluent way of carving. I would avoid all material
that would be too hard and resistant and therefore require
endless grinding or necessitate specialized machine tools.
The notion that the more labor spent, the more beautiful
it is bound to be, never had room in my thinking.

In Conclusion

The diagrammatic aids, as schematically illustrated,
present a degree of assurance as to how to conduct our
pathfinding in search of enlightenment. If we instinctively
feel ill at ease and sense that we have become sidetracked,
we should stop and, with self-discipline, retrace our steps
until we are reassured that we are on the right path.

In my opinion, we should respond to "hunches." The
diagrams intimate that hunches can aid us. Self-teaching
in areas that are new to us calls for inventiveness. Scientists
must inevitably play hunches, intuition and instinct in the
hope of discovering keys toward extended ranges of reason.

When we sidestep reason carelessly, we risk being thrown
off track and becoming bogged down in a mental morass.
Faulty paths set us back and threaten to doom us in the
end. A scientist's motto suggests itself: Let answers be
kept in abeyance pending factors that justify answers.

Man's search for truth throughout history has been directed
outwardly as well as *inwardly*, with tools that range from
the products of his brain (pure reason) to his natural
built-in sensors (seeing, hearing, smelling, tasting and
feeling).

Today, scientists and laymen alike are threatened to
drown in unprecedented outpourings of facts and figures.
Theirs has become a state of "machine hypnosis," the
machine's gear-works ready to do them in.

The imagery of man's climb into the tree and to the
furthest reach of branches, as he leaves his origins farther
and farther behind until the very end of the branch
threatens a fall to destruction, may well arouse our hope
that we will awaken in time to retrace our steps. We can
then resign ourselves to a philosophical peace of mind . . .
knowing that ours is a path toward fusion with the stuff
that is the universe itself and that made us to begin with.

Index